EVALUATING SUSTAINABLE DEVELOPMENT
in the Built Environment

This leading book is about one of the greatest challenges faced by human kind. Sustainable development impacts on everyone and all need to take ownership of, and get involved with, the concept. Universities are strongly engaged in this process, as recognised by both the Hokkaido and Turin G8 Summit Declarations. This book represents a reference point in the field, for both students and lecturers. It is clearly written and it illustrates evaluation approaches to, and frameworks for decision-making for, sustainable development. The book was selected to be circulated to the over 150 delegates who attended the G8 countries' Turin University Summit on this important subject.

Professor Francesco Profumo – Rector of Politecnico di Torino,
Italy, Chair of the 2009 G8 University Summit

This book addresses a key aspect of sustainable development. It asks what framework is required to answer the question 'have we made progress?' and it also suggests the mechanisms and methods which might be used in the assessment of such progress. The first edition of the book has been well received and this revision updates the reader and suggests in more detail how it might work in practice. It is an enormous issue and the authors have provided a very clear introduction to this complex subject. The book is fast becoming a standard text in the field and has an international readership. Practitioners, academics, students and universities will find it extremely useful in developing their thinking.

Professor Martin Hall – Vice Chancellor of
the University of Salford, UK.

EVALUATING SUSTAINABLE DEVELOPMENT in the Built Environment

SECOND EDITION

Peter S. Brandon
and
Patrizia Lombardi

A John Wiley & Sons, Ltd., Publication

Blackwell Publishing was acquired by John Wiley & Sons in February 2007. Blackwell's publishing programme has been merged with Wiley's global Scientific, Technical, and Medical business to form Wiley-Blackwell.

First edition published 2005
Second edition published 2011

Registered office
John Wiley & Sons Ltd, The Atrium, Southern Gate, Chichester, West Sussex, PO19 8SQ, United Kingdom

Editorial office
9600 Garsington Road, Oxford, OX4 2DQ, United Kingdom
2121 State Avenue, Ames, Iowa 50014-8300, USA

For details of our global editorial offices, for customer services and for information about how to apply for permission to reuse the copyright material in this book please see our website at www.wiley.com/wiley-blackwell.

Library of Congress Cataloging-in-Publication Data
Brandon, P. S. (Peter S.)
   Evaluating sustainable development in the built environment / Peter S. Brandon and Patrizia Lombardi. – 2nd ed.
      p.   cm.
   Includes bibliographical references and index.
   ISBN 978-1-4051-9258-3 (alk. paper)
1. Urban ecology (Sociology)   2. City planning–Environmental aspects.   3. Sustainable architecture.   4. Sustainable development.   I. Lombardi, P. L. (Patrizia L.)   II. Title.
   HT241.B73 2010
   307.76–dc22
                                                        2010029191
A catalogue record for this book is available from the British Library.

Set in 10/12pt Palatino by SPi Publisher Services, Pondicherry, India
Printed and bound in Malaysia by Vivar Printing Sdn Bhd

1   2011

Contents

About the Authors

Professor Peter S. Brandon OBE was a pro-vice chancellor for research and postgraduate studies at the University of Salford and the director of the University Think Lab and is now a professor emeritus in the School of the Built Environment. He has played a major role in the development of research in the UK and internationally, and when head of the present School of the Built Environment at Salford, he led the school to the highest ratings for research in the UK, a position they have held ever since. He has written widely on a number of topics, including building economics, construction management, construction information technology and sustainable development. He has over 30 books to his credit as author, co-author or editor, and has published over 150 papers in more than 30 countries.

Professor Patrizia Lombardi from the City and Housing Department at the Politecnico di Torino is a leading expert in the use of environmental assessment methods and an established figure in the field of evaluating sustainable development and has been active in the field for

over 20 years. She has coordinated or served as lead partner in several pan-European projects on topics related to sustainable urban development, including the BEQUEST network, the INTELCITY Roadmap, the INTELCITIES integrated project, the SURPrISE (Sustainable Urban Renewal Programs In Southern Europe) Interreg III C, the ISAAC (Integrated e-Services for Advanced Access to Heritage in Cultural Tourist Destinations) project and PERFECTION (Performance Indicators for Health, Comfort and Safety of the Indoor Environment). She is the editor or co-author of about 10 books on sustainability evaluation and is the author of over 100 papers in specialised textbooks and international scientific journals.

Preface

Five years is a long time in the development of an emerging subject, especially when it seems the whole world is now interested in its content. Since the first edition, the concept of sustainable development has risen in the human consciousness and is beginning to change behaviour around the globe. It is being driven by the concern about climate change and the impact this will have on human settlements. Individuals, governments, institutions and agencies are making their own contributions to change the rate of global warming or at least to mitigate its consequences. The situation is considered to be extremely serious and every 'foresight' type exercise has placed 'sustainable development' at the top of its agenda. In 2008, the US National Academy of Engineers identified 13 'grand challenges' for engineering and of these 5 were directly related to climate change and all of the remainder were related to human survival.

In fact, human survival is at the root of the whole debate on sustainable development. The planet will look after itself and, indeed, it has for millions of years. It is life forms, sustained by the planet, which suffer as the surface is altered and changed by the natural evolution of planets and cosmic systems. It is estimated that 97% of all species that have lived on earth are now extinct. However, the human species is a relative latecomer to life on earth and is the first to begin to exercise conscious mediation of the planet's subsystems. In previous millennia, 'nature' would have controlled human growth and its chance of survival. As Derickson (2006) suggests 'We are not dumb enough to survive, but are we clever enough?' In other words, if nature took its course then natural selection would take place and it is probable that the earth's population of humans might well diminish. The current massive interest in what is often described as 'the most important issue to ever have faced mankind' is largely concerned with the human race attempting to prove it can be sufficiently clever to adapt to a change in climate which threatens a very significant proportion of the population. The question is still whether we can do it.

However, climate is not the only feature of sustainable development, important though it is. Within the subject is also the quality of life enjoyed by current and future generations. Survival is the most important factor but even without this threat there appears to be a moral duty not to impair the life of future generations by the actions we take today. Once we move into the quality-of-life dimension, the subject becomes exceptionally complicated. It is one reason why there are so many definitions of sustainable development. All aspects of life are interrelated and a decision in one area has impacts elsewhere, often without our knowledge. It is one of the reasons why we face climatic problems. Our decisions, particularly with regard to technology supporting economic development have resulted in consequences which were not foreseen. The subject becomes so complicated that simple definitions always appear inadequate in time (see Chapter 1). Perceptions change, needs change, the technological infrastructure changes, our scientific knowledge changes and what future generations of humans will require is impossible to predict. However, we believe we can avoid creating an environment which destroys the capacity for future generations to respond positively to change; otherwise, the subject would be pointless.

The last 30 years have seen a plethora of measures, indicators and evaluations which attempt to make some assessment of what is happening to our planet and the actions of human beings upon it. The origins of this book lie in trying to get a grasp on what we mean by 'sustainable development'. The authors felt, in their research, that if they could measure it then they would be forced to define it, otherwise how would we know what to measure? In addition, the measure would allow us to discover whether we were making progress or not. However, the complexity of the problem makes an exhaustive measure impossible. Whatever we do, it will be partial. That is not to say it will not be useful and provide potentially new insights. It will and it does. It can only be part of a recognition that our tools and our 'cleverness' are often helpful but inadequate for the task as defined by most commentators.

So, how do we address this problem? At the heart of the issue is the interdependence between events, activities and processes. To address this, it is important to ask 'why' these events occur and where their behavioural relationship lies. This leads to a much more fundamental investigation of the problem and engages philosophy. Philosophy is 'the academic discipline concerned with the nature and significance or ordinary and scientific beliefs, investigating the intelligibility of concepts by means of rational argument concerning their presuppositions, implications and inter-relationships' (*Collins English Dictionary*, 2000).

It should shed light on the key issues and how they emerge and evolve over time. It recognises that its work is almost never complete but it guides and directs our thinking towards solutions which are appropriate for the time, including our response to future events.

Like all emerging subjects for study there is a period of transition from the original concept to an established structure upon which knowledge can build. This structure needs to be robust yet flexible enough to accommodate new thinking. In Chapter 6, we have put forward a secularised view of one philosopher, Herman Dooyeweerd, as a possible basis for this structure. The background material for Dooyeweerd's work is complex but rich and at an application level the authors and others have found it intuitive and enlightening particularly with regard to interrelationships between all the aspects of the cosmos which impinge on sustainable development.

This book will focus on two main issues. These are, firstly, how do we create a structure of knowledge and thinking which will allow us to develop a vocabulary which all participants in sustainable development can own and to which they will feel able to contribute and, secondly, how do we assess progress in sustainable development? The first is important because it enables a dialogue to take place between all the stakeholders in such a way that the complexity of the problem can be exposed, structured and communicated in order to gain confidence from all the parties. The second is important because unless we can evaluate what contributes to sustainability it will be very difficult to know whether a sustainable environment has been created.

These are fundamental and important issues. Implied in the structuring is not only a recognition that many people are engaged but also that they come from a variety of backgrounds, disciplines and levels of commitment which all provide a different 'filter' for the individual or group to view the problems or issue through. For them to come to agreement requires a structure which they can all understand and to which they can contribute their particular view. It also requires mutual respect and a desire to come to a solution that may involve compromise. It involves education because all need to understand the position of the others and it needs a language, which is not exclusive, but which includes all participants wherever possible. In terms of technique, it requires a confidence that the techniques for evaluation are fair and transparent so that the inputs and outputs are not favouring one particular view or, if they are, that all parties are aware of this limitation. There are very few, if any, techniques that are completely neutral in their advice.

This book is an explanation of some of these concepts and it attempts to provide an approach that can be built on and evolve over the ensuing years. There is a fast-developing subject known as 'sustainability science' which has been described by the Harvard University Centre for International Development as seeking to 'advance basic understanding of the dynamics of human–environment systems; to facilitate the design, implementation and evaluation of practical interventions that promote sustainability in particular places and contexts; and to improve link-ages between relevant research and innovation communities on the one hand and relevant policy and management communities on the other'. Others have focused more on the practical application and have defined it as 'use-inspired basic research that seeks to learn about the interac-tions among humans (including their cultural, political, economic, and demographic characteristics), their technologies and the environment' (Burns & Weaver, 2008). Note that it is the dynamics of the human/ technology interface which is central. One without the other will not result in a satisfactory understanding of the problem.

This subject is emerging and evolving as the subject matter becomes more of an established domain of study. Our understanding of what we mean by the term, and how it will be viewed, will change, but this book attempts to provide a contribution towards a structure and approach which will endure these evolving concepts and processes and provide a platform which allows the subject to grow and develop in a consistent and coherent way.

Peter S. Brandon and Patrizia Lombardi

Acknowledgements

The authors acknowledge the important contribution made to this book by a number of individuals, including:

❏ The members of the BEQUEST European Network (sponsored by the European Commission and led by Professor Steve Curwell of the University of Salford), who have debated many of these issues over the past 12 years. Their work has provided a useful source of information for many aspects of this book and we value the critique that they have provided of many of the ideas presented. In particular, we would like to thank Steve Curwell and Mark Deakin (of Napier University, Edinburgh) who have critically analysed and interpreted the results of the assessment methods survey reported in Chapter 5.

❏ Hanneke van Dijk, who has played a very important role in bringing this volume to print. Her patience, particularly in the later stages, was exemplary and we appreciate the task she undertook in conforming to the publisher's requirements.

❏ Dr Andrew Basden, who provided guidance on the work of Herman Dooyeweerd and enabled us to create the structure proposed in Chapter 6.

❏ Our respective families, who suffered from the time demands but provided support throughout.

The sections "Monetary (capital) approach" (part of), "The driving force–state–response model", "Issues or theme-based frameworks" (part of) and "Accounting frameworks" (part of) in Chapter 3 and "Aggregated indicators" (part of) in Chapter 4 are reproduced with permission from *Indicators of Sustainable Development: Guidelines and Methodologies* © United Nations, 2007.

Setting the Context for Evaluating Sustainable Development

The environmental perspective

The subject of sustainable development is one of the key research and policy issues as we enter the early years of the twenty-first century. This book takes the broad view, but the world focus at the time of writing appears to be the concerns on climate change and on pollution levels threatening the survival of the human species. The importance of this focus can be seen by the high regard that the global community places on these problems. At the Rio conference in 1992, 100 heads of states attended, representing 179 governments that committed themselves to an agenda for addressing the perceived problem. In 2002, 109 governments were represented at the Rio + 10 conference in Johannesburg and vowed to continue the focus on what they considered to be an important area. More recently, the Kyoto Protocol regarding carbon emissions has been ratified by most of the countries of the world and the Copenhagen World Summit on climate change has committed itself to an accord to prevent the rise in global temperature going beyond a further 2°C (although this was not made legally binding). This is the maximum that experts feel the world can accommodate without major catastrophe, although many will still suffer. Over the past 5 years the European Union has committed a substantial proportion of its research and development monies to sustainability issues and the majority of governments that have a national research programme have also committed funds to the cause. So why the interest and why is it at, or near, the top of global policy for research and development?

Evaluating Sustainable Development in the Built Environment, Second Edition
By Peter S. Brandon and Patrizia Lombardi © 2011 Peter S. Brandon and Patrizia Lombardi

With all new ideas, there is a long gestation period before they are taken up as policy or identified as a key issue for researchers to address. There is little doubt that the current interest in sustainable development has come from the pressure groups and particularly those associated with the green movement who saw the depletion of non-renewable resources (and particularly energy stocks), the pollution of the air and water and the breakdown of social conscience through globalisation as leading to the demise of mankind and the balance of nature (the ecosystem), which presently sustains living creatures. They considered that there was a moral imperative to take the long-term view and to consider the impact of decisions taken now on generations that would follow. It is true to say that within this general thrust there was, and probably will be, a variety of opinions on such matters as the extent of the damage being done to the environment, the responsibility for the current situation and the manner in which it can be remedied.

There is, however, a growing consensus that something is wrong and that mankind has a duty to do something about it. There has been a crescendo of concern from almost every quarter of human society led by some very significant figures in government, academe and pressure organisations. These are the new prophets, forecasting a calamity and demanding that the world turn from its fallen ways! In nearly all cases, their forecasts have been on the conservative side in recent years, particularly with regard to global warming. It appears that the world is getting warmer at a faster rate than was expected, that it appears to be accentuated by the behaviour of mankind and that humankind is facing a losing battle to remedy the situation. Hence, the focus on resilience (i.e. the ability to retain function through adversity) to assist in containing the problem. Leading thinkers and politicians such as Gore (2006), Lovelock (2009), Rees (2004), Jackson (2009) and many others have brought to the attention of the world the potential plight which faces life on earth.

Knowing what to do is of course another matter and there is a spectrum of views (see Fig. 1.1). At one end of the spectrum are those who suggest that we should conserve at all costs, change the way we live and seek a reduction in economic growth as a means of reducing consumption. At the other end are those who believe that necessity is the mother of invention and that a 'technical fix' will be found which will remove the need for such drastic measures to be taken. They believe that the markets will drive up the price of non-renewable resources and that this in turn will encourage innovators to provide sensible alternatives. Against this argument others would say that in the time it takes for the markets to realise what is happening, irreparable damage may have been done to the planet for which future generations may have to pay the full price.

These two extremes can also be viewed through the themes which arose from the Johannesburg Summit. There were two major schools of thought. One appeared to be arguing that man could exercise control and dominion over the earth, mainly by technological advancement. The other thought that humans must review their position as part of nature

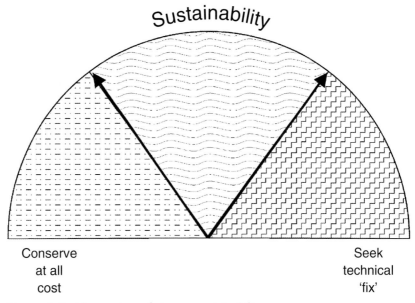

Figure 1.1   The spectrum of views on sustainability.

and seek to work in harmony and in empathy with the cycles of nature and the planet. This polarisation of view is often seen as detrimental to advancement and that much can be achieved by developing the technology whilst appreciating, respecting and recognising the second. There is a paradox in this dialogue because if we were not able to intervene then nature would probably have found ways to limit population growth (as it has with so many species) and avoid the excessive use of non-renewable resources. Population growth is at the heart of the problem – we cannot sustain this number of people with the resources available.

Despite this, much of this debate is at the level of the planet. Saving spaceship earth is the clarion call and we must all be engaged in the earth's preservation and its delicate ecological systems. This attitude may also be debated, for many would point out that the earth has been in turmoil ever since its formation and species have come and gone, climatic changes far outweigh the actions of mankind in terms of their devastation and in the very long term the earth itself will disappear and will probably be engulfed in a black hole or other stellar catastrophe. The response to this would be that we are the first species able to create its own downfall and the first to be able to at least extend its sojourn on earth, so why should we not rise to the challenge and try to extend the life of the species? The focus is on the environment and it is through this filter that human activity will be judged. This does not seem unreasonable as future generations will probably judge the activities of the current generation in the same way that we often judge the misdemeanours of the past: by the way they affect us now.

The question of time is a key one and the text will return to this in due course. Over what period should we view sustainable development? It is a critical issue for the systems and techniques we employ to measure progress. If we take the very long term, the planet is probably doomed anyway. If we take the short term, we can probably muddle through and overcome or manoeuvre around the problems that we have created. How far ahead can we look? Is it one, two, several or hundreds of generations? Most commentators would suggest that our ability to make interventions that would aid future populations is limited to two or three generations. Beyond this, we would probably need to be prophets or exercise witchcraft to know what to do. Predictions made 200 years ago, extrapolating the knowledge of the time, seem naive and stupid with the benefit of hindsight. For example, it was thought that London would be waist-deep in horse manure at the turn of the nineteenth/twentieth century because of the growth of horse-drawn transport! Would it have been sensible to ask the people of Europe 300 years ago to sacrifice their gruel in order that our generation would benefit from having the asset of computer technology? Of course not.

There is perhaps one area where we can predict a potential problem and that is with the demise of non-renewable resources. Who knows of what value these resources will be to those who will follow? We do not know what benefits to health, to quality of life and to the supply of useful products these resources will bring, because our knowledge of their potential is still limited. We do not understand how they may be used in different, complex combinations linked to other knowledge, for example of the nature of genes, to the benefit of our children and beyond. If some of these resources disappear, what legacy are we leaving? We tend to view these resources in terms of what they can provide *now* and not what their potential benefit could be in the *future*. Our outlooks are determined by their impact on us and the horizons that science and technology have set for us at this point in time. Often these are limited to the human lifespan.

Since the mid-1970s, these debates have grown in intensity and have risen up the international agenda to the point where it is heads of government who find themselves gathered together to address the problem. Partly this is a recognition that it is a global problem. Most of the environmental problems are not confined within national boundaries. (A hole in the ozone layer or a leak from a nuclear energy plant does not respect the arbitrary limits of territory designated by human beings.) Partly it is because this subject is recognised as being an issue of morality in which all must cooperate if action is to be taken that will change the course of environmental well-being. No one wants to be seen to show a lack of commitment to such a key issue. Partly it is because in each country there is a political imperative to address these issues because the nature of the problem has permeated the public conscience. It is unlikely that the subject will go away and indeed for some time to come it is likely to be a major item on the international agenda despite the fact that there are differences of opinion on how the matter should be tackled. For example, President George W. Bush of the USA refused to sign the Kyoto Agreement on greenhouse gas (GHG) emissions in his first term of office because of the vested interests of industry in the USA. It was not until President Obama came into office that a new narrative was created and the USA joined in the debate to limit the speed of climate change. Sometimes the rapidly developing countries such as China and India are criticised for following the development path of the developed nations but the signs are that they are more sensitive to this problem and are addressing the issue whilst still encouraging economic development. They face a dilemma in improving the economic prosperity of their people whilst avoiding the pitfalls of the past. The developed nations such as Europe and the USA face the dilemma of maintaining what they perceive to be a high standard of living whilst at the same time addressing the kind of world they wish to leave for their grandchildren. They may have to decide to make sacrifices now in order to protect the future. This may not be easy.

The international policy debates

Table 1.1 shows some of the key events in the development of the world approach to addressing the problems of sustainable development. All have made their contribution since the 1970s and it is this groundswell of views at the very highest levels of global governance that has begun to change the actions of government and the investment in research into sustainable development. Many of the world conferences and the publications were about the context within which the discussion should take place. This context included the debates on the reduction in non-renewable resources and the apparent pollution of land, water and air. However, at the Rio Earth Summit in 1992 (UNCED, 1992) a significant change took place. An agenda for change (Agenda 21) was agreed upon and signed up to by 179 world governments. Not only did they sign up, but they also defined sustainability in a new way, extending its boundaries beyond just environmental issues.

The full implementation of Agenda 21, the Programme for Further Implementation of Agenda 21 and the Commitments to the Rio principles, were strongly reaffirmed at the World Summit on Sustainable Development (WSSD) held in Johannesburg, South Africa, from 26 August to 4 September 2002. The Summit confirmed that significant progress has been made towards achieving a global consensus and partnership among all the people of our planet. The Johannesburg Declaration on Sustainable Development highlighted the important role placed by governance at all levels for the effective implementation of

Agenda 21, the Millennium development goals and the Plan of Implementation of the Summit. The leadership of the United Nations was also reaffirmed as the most universal and representative organisation in the world which is best placed to promote sustainable development, and a commitment to monitor progress at regular intervals towards the achievement of the sustainable development goals and objectives was undertaken under the slogan 'Making it happen!' (http://www.un.org/). Finally, it also acknowledged the key role played by education as the primary agent of transformation towards sustainable development, increasing people's capacities to transform their visions for society into reality. In recognition of the importance of education for sustainable and responsible development, the United Nations General Assembly declared 2005–2014 the UN Decade of Education for Sustainable Development while UNESCO was requested to lead and to develop an International Implementation Scheme for the Decade.

The signatories of these various agreements embraced the notion that environmental issues often had their origins in the behaviour of the human race. When humans dump toxic chemicals or do not seek to conserve energy, or create social unrest leading to misuse or damage to existing resources, their behaviour has an impact on the environment. When the legal systems and regulations employed by governments make it difficult or even impossible to act in an environmentally friendly way, this aspect of human organisation has a detrimental impact on environmental issues. When the striving for economic growth results in poor use of the earth's resources, this human action and policy lead to more degradation of the environment. When there are big differentials between those who have and those who have not, unrest can follow and the damage can be substantial. The threat of terrorists gaining access to nuclear bombs is now spoken of quite openly and the terrorists gain much of their support from those who are economically or politically disadvantaged.

A tangled web of issues leads to actions that eventually have an impact on the environment. The way we live affects the world on a global scale when we piece the whole of the jigsaw together. In the words of John Donne, 'no man is an island entire of itself' (Donne, 1623). The environment at one level is fairly robust, taking care of the events that occur over time in a very practical way which is often not apparent to a single generation. At another level, it can be presented as a very sensitive entity in which it is easy, through the interactions of man, to destabilise the whole superstructure and the interrelationships which provide the balance and allow the life forms that exist today to survive and prosper. It is the survival of what we have today, the biodiversity, the climatic conditions, the level of water supply and so forth that provides the basis for the argument for sustainability. No one seems to be arguing for natural evolution which could see the demise of the human race in favour of some other life form.

Table 1.1 Significant international conferences showing the growing importance of sustainable development.

Date	Action	Output
1972: 6–16 June	UN Conference on the Human Environment, Stockholm	Need for a common output to inspire and guide the people of the world in the preservation of the human environment: (a) Action plan for the human environment. (b) Educational, informational, social and cultural aspects of environmental issues have to be faced. (c) Construction of a framework for environmental action. (d) Recommendation for action at the international level. (e) Identification and control of pollution of broad international significance. (f) Declaration of the UN.
1992: 3–14 June	United Nations Rio de Janeiro Conference The Convention on Climate Change was adopted on 9 May 1992 and opened for signature a month later at the UN Conference on Environment and Development in Rio de Janeiro (Brazil)	Agenda 21, the Rio Declaration on Environment and Development, the Statement of Forest Principles, the United Nations Framework Convention on Climate Change and the United Nations Convention on Biological Diversity. As an output the subsequent follow-up mechanisms were created: (a) Commission on Sustainable Development (b) Inter-agency Committee on Sustainable Development (c) High-level Advisory Board on Sustainable Development
1994: 27 May	The First European Conference on Sustainable Cities & Towns, Aalborg (Denmark)	A Charter was signed by European Cities & Towns 'Towards Sustainability' which provides a framework for the delivery of local sustainable development, and calls on local authorities to engage in Local Agenda 21 processes (http://ec.europa.eu/environment/urban/pdf/aalborg_charter.pdf).
1995: 7 April	Conference of the Parties to the UN Framework Convention on Climate Change 1 (COP 1), Berlin	The Berlin Mandate was adopted at the first Conference of the Parties (COP) on 7 April 1995. It acknowledged that the commitment of developed countries to take measures aimed at reducing their GHG emissions to 1990 levels by the year 2000 was not adequate to achieve the Convention's objective. The main objective of the Mandate was to strengthen the commitments for the developed-country Parties after the year 2000 without introducing any new commitments for developing countries, while reaffirming existing commitments of all Parties contained in Article 4.1 and continuing to advance their implementation.

Continues

Table 1.1 *Contd.*

Date	Action	Output
1996: 3–14 June	United Nations International Conference on Human Settlements – Habitat II, Istanbul	This was the second conference organised for discussing the issue of habitation (Habitat I Conference was held in Vancouver in 1976). It specifically focused on current built environmental problems in relation to major global changes (e.g. population growth, migration towards urban areas, tourism, urban regeneration).
1997: 8–19 July	Conference of the Parties to the UN Framework Convention on Climate Change 2 (COP 2), Geneva	At the second COP, a large number of ministers agreed on the Geneva Ministerial Declaration, which provided political impetus to the Berlin Mandate process.
1997: 1–10 December	Conference of the Parties to the UN Framework Convention on Climate Change 3 (COP 3), Kyoto Protocol (Japan)	The Kyoto Protocol sets up targets to reduce GHG emissions. The Protocol was initially adopted on 11 December 1997 in Kyoto, Japan, and came into force on 16 February 2005. Since the UNFCCC came into force, the parties have been meeting annually in Conferences of the Parties (COP) to assess progress in dealing with climate change, and beginning in the mid-1990s, to negotiate the Kyoto Protocol to establish legally binding obligations for developed countries to reduce their GHG emissions. From 2005, the Conferences have met in conjunction with Meetings of Parties of the Kyoto Protocol (MOP), and parties to the Convention that are not parties to the Protocol can participate in Protocol-related meetings as observers. Under the Protocol, 37 industrialised countries (called 'Annex I countries') commit themselves to a reduction of four greenhouse gases, in the hydrofluorocarbons and perfluorocarbons produced by them, and all member countries give general commitments. Countries agreed to reduce their collective GHG emissions by 5.2% from the 1990 level. The protocol left several issues open to be decided later by future Conferences of the Parties (COP).
1998: 2–14 November	Conference of the Parties to the UN Framework Convention on Climate Change 4 (COP 4), Buenos Aires	At COP 4 (Buenos Aires, November 1998), Parties adopted the so-called 'Buenos Aires Plan of Action', www.unfccc.int/resource/docs/cop4/16a01.pdf, setting out a programme of work both to advance the implementation of the Convention and to flesh out the operational details of the Kyoto Protocol. This programme of work was conducted in the subsidiary bodies and at COP 5 (Bonn, October/November 1999), with a deadline of COP 6 (The Hague, November 2000). However, Parties were unable to reach agreement on a package of decisions on all issues under the Buenos Aires Plan of Action at that session. Nevertheless, they decided to meet again in a resumed session of COP 6 to try once more to resolve their differences.

Date	Event	Description
1999: 25 October–5 November	Conference of the Parties to the UN Framework Convention on Climate Change 5 (COP 5), Bonn	Ministers and officials from 166 governments agreed on a timetable for completing the outstanding details of the 1997 Kyoto Protocol by November 2000 in order to intensify the negotiating process on all issues before the sixth COP.
2000: 13–24 November, The Hague; 16–27 July 2001, Bonn	Conference of the Parties to the UN Framework Convention on Climate Change 6 (COP 6), The Hague and Bonn	Pledge to contribute €450 million per year by 2005 to help developing countries manage emissions and adapt to climate change. The Convention on Climate Change has been ratified by 37 countries.
2001: 29 October–9 November	Conference of the Parties to the UN Framework Convention on Climate Change 7 (COP 7), Marrakesh	Parties finally succeeded in adopting the Bonn Agreements on the Implementation of the Buenos Aires Plan of Action, www.unfccc.int/resource/docs/cop6secpart//05.pdf, registering political agreement on key issues under the Buenos Aires Plan of Action. The final Kyoto rulebook was set. Countries must cut 80% emissions. The Marrakesh Ministerial Declaration emphasises the contribution that action on climate change can make to sustainable development, calling for capacity building, technology, innovation and cooperation with the biodiversity and desertification conventions. Up to Marrakesh, 40 countries had ratified the Kyoto Protocol.
2002: 26 August–4 September	United Nations World Summit on Sustainable Development, Johannesburg	Key objectives to reach: (a) A revitalised and integrated UN system for sustainable development. (b) A new deal on finance – enabling a deal on sustainable development. (c) An integration of trade and sustainable development. (d) A clearer understanding of how governments should move forward nationally in implementing Agenda 21. (e) A new charter which could lay the foundations for countries to frame their sustainable development policies. (f) A review of the work of the present set of Rio conventions – looking at the overlaps, gaps and obstacles. (g) A set of new regional or even global conventions. (h) A set of policy recommendations for the environmental security issues that face the world. (i) A clear set of commitments to implement agreed action by the UN, governments and major groups.

Continues

Table 1.1 *Contd.*

Date	Action	Output
2002: 23 October–1 November	Conference of the Parties to the UN Framework Convention on Climate Change 8 (COP 8), New Delhi	The usual division between developed and developing country positions on many issues was in evidence at COP 8. Parties convened in negotiating groups on a number of issues previously left off the agenda due to the pressing negotiations under the Buenos Aires Plan of Action. The Delhi Declaration reaffirms development and poverty eradication as overriding priorities in developing countries and implementation of UNFCCC commitments according to Parties' common but differentiated responsibilities, development priorities and circumstances, but it does not call for a dialogue on broadening commitments.
2003: 1–12 December	Conference of the Parties to the UN Framework Convention on Climate Change 9 (COP 9), Milan	According to the way the Kyoto Protocol (KP) was written, it will go into effect only if 55 of the signatories ratify. These signatories must account for 55% of the CO_2 emissions at the then specified date – 1990. There is no problem with the first condition, as 121 countries have ratified the KP but the USA (the country at the forefront of GHG emissions) stated that it was not going to represent the required minimum of 55% of emissions without a Russian ratification of the KP.
2004: 8–11 June	The Aalborg +10 conference, Aalborg (Denmark)	One objective of the Aalborg + 10 conference was to assess the 10 years of experiences since the establishment of the Aalborg Charter and the European Sustainable Cities & Towns Campaign. Nine hundred participants shared their experiences and met in open discussions and dialogues. Currently the Charter is signed by 2764 cities (see: http://www.aalborgplus10.dk/media/short_list_18-02-2009_1_.pdf).
2005: 28 November–9 December	The first Meeting of the Parties to the Kyoto Protocol (MOP 1) along with the Conference of the Parties to the UN Framework convention on climate change 11 (COP 11), Montreal	It was one of the largest intergovernmental conferences on climate change. The event marked the entry into force of the Kyoto Protocol. Hosting more than 10'000 delegates, it was one of Canada's largest international events ever and the largest gathering in Montreal since Expo 67. The Montreal Action Plan is an agreement hammered out at the end of the conference to 'extend the life of the Kyoto Protocol beyond its 2012 expiration date and negotiate deeper cuts in greenhouse-gas emissions' (Wikipedia).

Date	Event	Description
2005: 6–7 December	The EU Ministers on 'Creating Sustainable Communities in Europe', Bristol Accord (UK)	The 2005 Bristol Accord says that: Sustainable communities are a big idea for a bigger Europe. It offers a chance to create thriving and successful places in which the people of Europe will have a more secure and prosperous future. The Accord builds on the work of preceding initiatives in the area, such as the Rotterdam urban acquis 2004 (principles of common successful urban policies), the revised Lisbon cgenda for jobs, competitiveness and growth, the goals of environmental sustainability agreed at Gothenburg 2001, the Lille Programme (2000) (long-term cooperation on urban sustainability within the EU) and the effective democratic governance agreed at the Warsaw Summit in May 2005 (see: http://www.eukn.org/binaries/eukn/eukn/policy/2006/5/bristol-accord.pdf).
2007: 24–25 May	Informal Ministerial meeting on urban development and territorial cohesion, Leipzig (Germany)	The 'Leipzig Charter on Sustainable European Cities' says that strengthening European cities and their regions – promoting competitiveness, social and territorial cohesion in Europe and in its cities and regions are key policy issues that impact on the European Council decisions on sustainable development that need to be applied in concrete terms to the spatial development of urban neighbourhoods, cities and regions (see: http://www.energie-cities.eu/IMG/pdf/leipzig_charter.pdf).
2007: 15 December	UN Conference on Climate Change (COP 13), Bali (Indonesia)	Agreement on a timeline and structured negotiation on the post-2012 framework (a successor to the Kyoto Protocol) was achieved with the adoption of the Bcli Action Plan (Decision 1/CP.13). The Ad Hoc Working Group on Long-term Cooperative Action under the Convention (AWG-LCA) was established as a new subsidiary body to conduct the negotiations aimed at urgently enhancing the implementation of the Convention, up to and beyond 2012. These negotiations took place during 2008 (leading to COP 14/MOP 4 in Poznan, Poland) and 2009 (leading to COP 15/MOP 5 in Copenhagen, Denmark).
2009: 7–18 December	UN Conference on Climate Change (COP 15/MOP 5), Copenhagen (Denmark)	The overall goal was to establish an ambitious global climate agreement for the period from 2012 when the first commitment period under the Kyoto Protocol expires. Ministers and officials from 192 countries took part in the Copenhagen meeting and, in addition, participants attended from a large number of non-governmental organisations. A large part of the diplomatic work that laid the foundation for a post-Kyoto Agreement was undertaken by the COP 15. At the end of the conference an accord was agreed but this was not to be legally binding at this stage. However, it was signalled that this would be the longer term objective.

Therefore, there is an element of conservation that features strongly in much of the above debates – the maintenance of the *status quo*. Few developing countries want to disturb or reduce their economic competitiveness. However, a recognition that the world is constantly changing and must be accommodated is also there. Evolution is thought to underpin much of this change but it is of course enhanced or aggravated by the activities of humans, not only in science and technology but also in the culture that they adopt and the growth of populations. It is the pace of change that has altered and our impact grows greater by the day. The obligation to the needs of future generations weighs heavily within the argument.

The report of the Rio Summit (UNCED, 1992) recognised these issues and identified some major themes. Mitchell *et al.* (1995) have distilled from the literature of Rio and other reports four principles which underlie the guidance and advice that is given and take us beyond the pure environmental agenda, or at least to a better understanding of *why* environmental conditions change.

These principles are:

❑ *Equity*: The concern for today's poor and disadvantaged.
❑ *Futurity*: The concern for future generations.
❑ *Environment*: The concern for the integrity of ecosystems.
❑ *Public participation*: The concern that individuals should have the opportunity to participate in decisions that affect them.

Only one of these themes is directly concerned with the environment. The others are moral imperatives or cultural endorsements or mechanisms by which change can be effected through common ownership of the problem. However, they all impinge on sustainable development and their selection as major themes has come from the environment debate. They arise from a collective view of 'what is best' for the world both now and in the future. They represent our current stance on these issues but it is not necessarily true that these principles will hold in the future even though most of us would subscribe to them today.

Extension of the debate

The scope or focus of the debate has therefore been extended into new realms concerned with social, legal, economic, political and technical aspects of how we live (commonly known under the acronym SLEPT). The shift has introduced a much wider debate about the values we place on various aspects of our lives, how we treat others and what level of intervention it is appropriate for a state or organisation to adopt to address these issues. Hence the move to an agenda with a different focus, known as sustainability. Since the word 'sustainability' has come into frequent use, many commentators have queried whether it has any meaning – even though they acknowledge that the term has created an important agenda. It is rather strange that a term which has favourable connotations and is used as the basis of some major research funding and government and industry initiatives is still considered rather vague by many individuals. Sometimes the concepts underlying the term get dismissed because the term itself is not sufficiently defined for these people to 'buy' into it. For some, the term 'sustainable development' is more meaningful as it suggests that it is concerned with interventions by humankind into the environment that can be analysed to see whether they have a positive or negative impact on the environmental issues of concern.

It may be helpful to look at the root words in sustainable development. To *sustain* means to continue without lessening, to nourish, to allow to flourish. To *develop* means to improve or bring to a more advanced state. Sustainable development is therefore about facilitating improvement without jeopardising what exists already. Sustainable does not mean that nothing ever changes, nor does it mean Utopia where nothing bad happens. It is not about maintaining the *status quo* or reaching perfection. Development does not mean continually getting bigger but is about qualitative improvement. In addition, sustainability does not mean sustained growth. At some point a community stops getting larger but it continues to improve the quality of life of its inhabitants.

This book has used sustainable development in its title for the above reasons. The book is largely concerned with the built environment which by definition is concerned with humankind's activity in creating shelter and accommodation for itself, an act which inevitably changes the environment in some way. In particular the development of cities, and the underlying social cohesion and culture which is created through cities, has a big impact on the use of resources, the way people behave, their interaction with nature and the waste products that ensue from this type of living.

The impact of the built environment

Unfortunately, most of the interventions created by building accommodation in which to reside or to work have a negative effect on the environment. For example, the UK government has suggested (DETR, 1998) that consumption associated with the built environment is as follows:

❑ Consumption of each person in the UK averages 6 tonnes of material per year broken down into 1.5 tonnes for new infrastructure (roads, railways, etc.), 1.5 tonnes for new buildings and 3 tonnes for repair and maintenance.
❑ Of the 300 million tonnes of quarried aggregates per annum only 10%–15% is recycled.

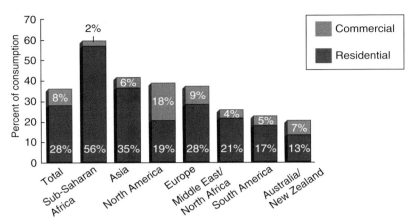

Source: McGraw-Hill Construction, 2008

Figure 1.2 Building sector share of total energy use around the world. (By Permission of Earth Trends. Taken from *Global Green Building Trends*, SmartMarket Report, McGraw-Hill Construction, 2008. Used with permission.)

❏ Over 70 million tonnes of construction waste is created per annum which represents 17% of the total UK waste.
❏ Around 70% of energy use can be directly or indirectly attributed to buildings and infrastructure.

These are frightening statistics and reveal how important the built environment is to any policy and evaluation of environmental sustainability.

It is even more bleak when the contribution of the building sector to total energy use around the world is considered. Just in commercial and residential building the amount of total energy use varies from 20% to 56% of total energy use (see Fig. 1.2).

So where does the built environment fit into the big picture? As Fig. 1.3 shows, there is a growing complexity as we move away from the actions of individuals towards the actions of groups and nations and their interaction with the global environment. The more people involved, the more the interactions and the more decisions become driven by policy. These policies may not be coordinated and therefore may conflict with each other. If this is coupled with the normal vagaries of nature, a very complex set of interacting systems emerges. This is what makes the holistic study of the environment and sustainability such a difficult research issue.

The built environment is just one strand of development found in this complexity and there are many more. Nevertheless, the construction and use of buildings is an important factor in the overall game. Buildings and structures use raw materials, some of which are non-renewable. They use energy to extract these materials and to manufacture components and, once in the structure, these affect the heating and cooling

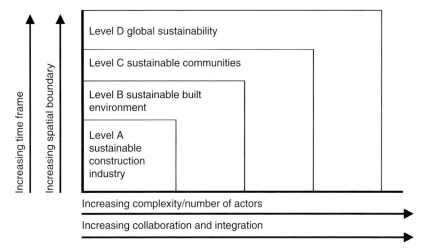

Figure 1.3 Levels of response to sustainable development. (Source: Construction Research and Innovation Panel Report, *Sustainable Construction: Future R & I Requirements: Analysis of Current Position*, 23 March 1999.)

requirements of the accommodation space. The manner in which people use the space could well affect the energy requirements too; for example, if a family has a pet dog in the house it is likely that they will open the back door more frequently to let the dog out. This in turn will increase the energy loss, creating demands for the use of more fuel which may come from a non-renewable source. These are factors affecting environmental sustainability but as we shall see later this is only a part of the problem even though it is the biggest driving force at the present time.

Figure 1.3 attempts to show the relationship between different parts of the built environment, including the communities that exist within it and the global environmental agenda. It starts with the construction industry and its suppliers, moves on to the built environment and the infrastructure required to sustain human activity, and then moves up to the communities themselves. This structure is quite useful for classifying the broad areas that need to be addressed for sustainability when viewed from the built environment perspective. It shows a continuum between the elements but gives focus for particular groups of decision-makers. Broadly, level 'A' would be addressed by building contractors, consultants and clients of individual structures, level 'B' would be primarily the decision-making area for the planners and local government and level 'C' would be the province of central government.

This series of statements is, of course, too simplistic. For example, as public participation is increased, so the representatives of citizens will need to be engaged. Ideally, we would want a common structure that allowed information to flow freely from one level to another and a

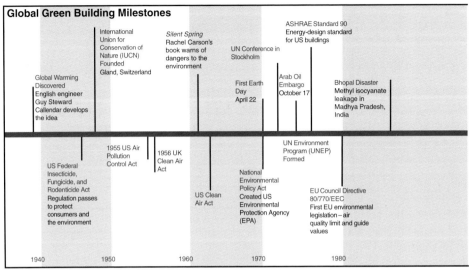

Global Green Building Milestones

Source: McGraw-Hill Construction, 2008

Figure 1.4 Global green building milestones. (Taken from *Global Green Building Trends*, SmartMarket Report, McGraw-Hill Construction, 2008. Used with permission.)

common language to allow full communication both across disciplines and between different levels.

This book attempts to provide the starting point for such a language and structure and there will be more on this later in this chapter and beyond. There is of course an interdependence between all the issues. The environment determines our need for a certain type of accommodation, the built environment is largely determined by the communities that dwell there and the buildings reflect the needs of the individuals and groups, the culture and the location of the structures. So what are the driving forces in the built environment which encourage a change of practice towards 'green' buildings?

The current response of the built environment community

In a complex market such as the built environment it is sometimes difficult to discover the key milestones which are identifying a response to the issues of sustainable development. There is no doubt that the 'green' agenda is permeating much of the developing policy for new building. This provides a basis for future development but does not deal with the immediate problem. Governments seem to be moving towards a reduction in carbon emissions which could be as much as 50% by the year 2050. If this is true then the contribution of the built environment could

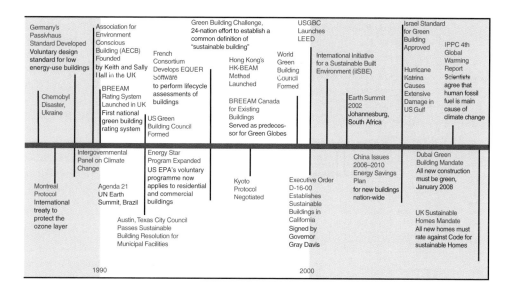

be a problem. Professor Mike Kelly, Chief Scientific Adviser to the Department of Communities and Local Government in the UK, has suggested that 87% of the existing building stock will still be standing by 2050 which means that major renovations and refurbishments of existing buildings are needed to make the required targets.

Nevertheless, governments in consultation with industry are endeavouring to create the legislative framework and the tools to address the issues involved. Figure 1.4 is taken from an excellent 'Smart Market' report entitled *Global Green Building Trends* (Bernstein & Bowerbank, 2008), one of several by the same publishers. It shows the global responses to the green agenda against the significant broader agenda of international agreements and actions.

There is a wealth of information in these reports but the following provides a particular insight. Figure 1.5 shows the importance of green building to stakeholders when viewed across the globe. It is interesting to note that it is government followed by designers who are leading the way.

However, it is when the client bodies demand this service that real change will occur and there are signs that this is happening. The business reasons for green building (global) are shown in Fig. 1.6 and market demand and transformation together with client demand occupy three of the top four positions. However, the moral driver of doing what is perceived to be right takes top spot. The market is following public opinion. It does vary from continent to continent but nevertheless this ranking would not have been identified even a decade ago.

Many clients, however, are not business orientated and have social objectives. Their reasons are slightly different and they are firmly concerned with what is right for the world and their community.

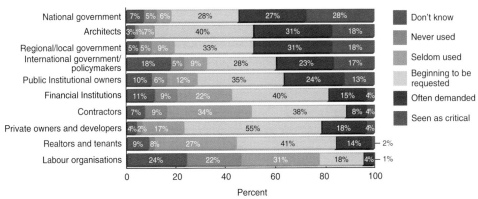

Source: McGraw-Hill Construction, 2008

Figure 1.5   Importance of green building to stakeholders – global. (Taken from *Global Green Building Trends*, SmartMarket Report, McGraw-Hill Construction, 2008. Used with permission.)

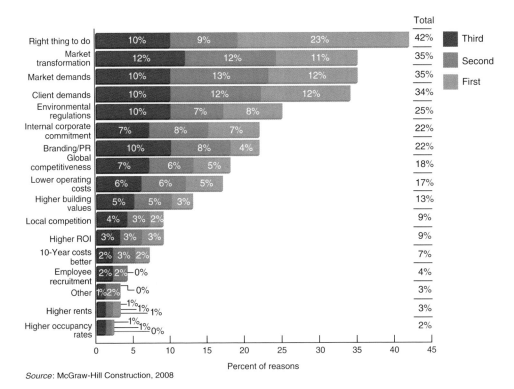

Source: McGraw-Hill Construction, 2008

Figure 1.6   Business reasons for green building – global. (Taken from *Global Green Building Trends*, SmartMarket Report, McGraw-Hill Construction, 2008. Used with permission.)

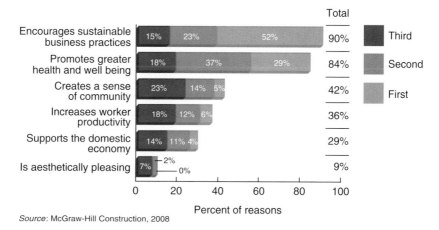

Source: McGraw-Hill Construction, 2008

Figure 1.7   Top global social reasons for green building. (Taken from *Global Green Building Trends*, SmartMarket Report, McGraw-Hill Construction, 2008. Used with permission.)

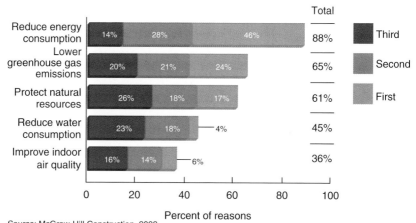

Source: McGraw-Hill Construction, 2008

Figure 1.8   Top environmental reasons for green building. (Taken from *Global Green Building Trends*, SmartMarket Report, McGraw-Hill Construction, 2008. Used with permission.)

Figure 1.7 shows the top global *social* reasons for green building. It is clear that the encouragement of sustainable building practices is agreed by virtually all but perhaps the second most important factor *provides greater health and well-being* is something of a surprise. However, this factor appears to be assuming more importance as time goes by as people recognise the health benefit of the technology.

Finally, the top environmental reasons for green building are shown in Fig. 1.8 and these follow the pattern of public debate with regard to climate change and environmental sustainable development.

Sustainability: a definition

The discussion to date has centred around the transition from the general environmental debate to the wider discourse which includes those factors that influence the environment and therefore contribute to sustainability and to the role that the built environment has to play in these matters.

It was the 1992 Earth Summit in Rio that provided a fresh understanding of the intimate link between the earth's environmental problems and such issues as economic conditions and social justice. It showed that the social, environmental and economic needs must be met in a balance with each other for sustainable outcomes in the long term. It showed that if people are poor, and national economies are weak, the environment suffers; if the environment is abused and resources are over-consumed, people suffer and economies decline. The conference also pointed out that the smallest local actions or decisions, good or bad, have potential worldwide repercussions. The Rio conference outlined the way that various social, economic and environmental factors are interdependent and change together. It identified the critical elements of change, showing that success in one area requires action in others in order to be sustainable over time.

A major achievement of the Rio conference was the development of what became known as *Agenda 21* – a thorough and broad-ranging programme of actions demanding new ways of investing in our future to reach global sustainable development in the twenty-first century. Its recommendations ranged from new ways to educate to new ways to care for natural resources and new ways to participate in designing a sustainable economy. The ambition of Agenda 21 was extraordinary, for its goal was to make a safe and just world in which all life has dignity and is celebrated (see http://www.johannesburgsummit.org).

As the basis for the programme, the conference took the definition of sustainable development provided by the World Commission on Environment and Development (WCED) and its 1987 report entitled *Our Common Future* (WCED, 1987). The Commission was chaired by Gro Harlem Brundtland from Norway and the report is sometimes referred to as the *Brundtland Report*. The Rio conference took much of the argument in this report as the basis for its own recommendations. It is one of the most important documents in the field of sustainable development.

The definition is as follows:

'Sustainable development is development that meets the needs of the present without compromising the ability of future generations to meet their own needs'.

(WCED, Brundtland Commission, 1987)

This simple statement has provided the basis for most of the debate and actions those engaged with sustainability have chosen to follow.

However Brundtland went on to say:

> 'In essence sustainable development is a *process of change* in which exploitation of resources, the direction of investments, the orientation of technological developments and institutional change are all *in harmony* and enhance current and future potential to meet human needs and aspirations'. (Note: author's italics.)

There are a number of points to be made from these statements for what follows in this book. Firstly, the definition itself has been criticised because it is argued that it is difficult, even today, to determine people's needs. To try to forecast what they might be in the future is an impossible task. It is too difficult – let's all go home!

However, the further statement above does give a better picture of what can be done. It refers to sustainable development as a *process* and not an end goal or destination. It is therefore open to further learning and adaptation, and to evolution as knowledge progresses. It is about creating a learning environment in which all participants strive to improve the situation that exists for the needs of today and tomorrow. It acknowledges aspirations as well as needs and therefore engages the drive for improvement that is seen in all societies. It is not necessarily conservative and conservationist but it does recognise that a change of approach is needed in which the wider sustainable objectives are part of the agenda for change. In addition, it recognises that it is about *harmony* and balance between often conflicting aspirations and needs. It therefore requires, on occasions, compromise and negotiation rather than imposition. No doubt there are times when imposition is essential, for example, when irreparable damage might be done to the environment if action is not taken quickly. However, on the softer issues related to social issues a local democratic approach, where consensus is sought, might provide an appropriate solution.

If we can add to the list of definitions it might therefore look like this:

Sustainable development is a process which aims to provide a physical, social and psychological environment in which the behaviour of human beings is harmoniously adjusted to address the integration with, and dependence upon, nature in order to improve, and not to impact adversely, on present or future generations.

Again this definition has limitations because it may require an adverse decision on the quality of life by humans now in order to provide the security required for future generations. The approach of the rest of this book could be included to further qualify this definition but it has been left at this generic level for further evolution as the debate continues.

(Please note: There is a site dedicated to definitions of sustainable development, see: http://www.gdrc.org/sustdev/definitions.html)

Seeking a shared set of values

If we are to engage in democracy, both in the imposition of laws regulating behaviour and in local debate and negotiation, there needs to be a set of shared values which allows discussion to take place. At one level it could be argued that the preservation of the human race and the planet to which we belong is a motivation we have in common. This is probably true, but there are some Eastern philosophies that might not consider the preservation of the human species as the pre-eminent driver for sustainable development. Nevertheless, most human societies by implication would place it high on their agenda. Even if some would place a different emphasis on the balance between species, all would agree that the preservation of the planet and its ecosystems are of considerable importance.

The establishment of a set of values is important if we are to strive for harmony. Indeed one definition of a philosophy can be 'the system of values by which one lives'. The system is supported by logic and reasoning but underpinning the conclusions is this concept of value. The problem is, of course, that there are many shared value systems. Figure 1.9 is a typical landscape of a city and it can be seen that there are many systems at work.

The photograph identifies many systems of which the following are just a few:

❑ *Religious system* centred around the church. In days gone by this might well have been the dominant set of values in the locality.
❑ *Community system* based on the interdependence between the activities taking place and the community that demands and/or uses them.
❑ *Transport system* which uses vehicles and cars and taxis to ferry people and products around the locality and beyond.
❑ *Biological system* which sustains human life but also maintains the landscape environment that people and other life forms enjoy.
❑ *Residential system* which allows people to have accommodation to meet their needs.
❑ *Business system* which provides wealth and economic activity in the region to support the local community and others.
❑ *Retail system* which allows the local community and those working in the area to purchase new items to develop their standard of living and sustain themselves.

It is not difficult to see that behind this list of systems there are also a multitude of different stakeholders. Stakeholders are those people who have an interest in the area either political, social, economic or legal. They will have different stakes but all contribute to the area's well-being and most will have an effect on its advancement or decline. They will

Figure 1.9   Value systems at work in the city environment.

include citizens, lawyers, developers, shop owners, priests, bus drivers, taxi owners, local authorities, politicians and many more. It is also not difficult to see that there is potential conflict between the systems identified as represented by their stakeholders. For example, the demand for business may squeeze out the residents from the area or create transport systems which are different from those desired by the citizens who live there or which have a detrimental effect on the health of both humans and plants. The noise level may increase to the point where the quality of life of the citizens is damaged and it may affect their ability to worship in the church. However, without the business centre it may be impossible to create the jobs people need to sustain themselves and the wealth which supports their life improvement. If the area is successful, the land costs rise and it may be that new forms of development take place which destroy the sense of community enjoyed by those living in the area and attract a different kind of person or activity which is hostile to the current environment.

There is a very complex interdependency between all these systems. Is it pie in the sky to expect that we can have harmony in such an environment? Many would say that it is, and yet our legal systems and governance attempt to create the framework in which, at the very least, minimal protection is given to many of these demands. In some cases, the legal systems can work against each other and set in motion plans and activities which are not conducive to sustainable development. Another important factor is the timescale over which the decision will be considered. What seems right and appropriate now may well seem entirely inappropriate in a generation or even less. Sometimes, and sometimes quite often, the changes that affect an area may come from adjacent areas over which the decision-makers in the locality have little control. Indeed, sometimes they may be dictated by policy decisions at national or international level. The harmony we aspire to may be difficult to achieve and yet it is something for which we strive. What is clear is that, whatever we do, it is likely to be imperfect and whatever systems we set up to address these issues must have within them a high degree of flexibility and be able to be altered and adapted within a variety of time frames.

Striving for a common framework and classification system

If we can accept that some degree of stakeholder engagement with decision-making relating to the built environment is desirable, it is also important to consider within what framework or structure we need to have the dialogue. If the dialogue is to be helpful it needs to be at various levels, depending on the participants. For example, it is unlikely to be helpful to have a highly technical discussion with a citizen who may be unaware of the techniques being employed in the assessment. However, it is also the case that every contribution should be able to be pulled together within an understandable structure which identifies where the comment or report is targeted and how it helps the elements of sustainability. The field is littered with models and reports and opinions which are partial and unstructured. It is difficult for anyone to piece these together in a structured way in order to derive coherence from the diverse contributions and also to allow comparison with other assessments. It is rather like a group of people who are getting together and are trying to communicate when each only knows part of a language and each language is different. Confusion will reign and in the end it will be the dominant participant who knows slightly more than the rest who may get his or her own way either because this person is seen to be superior or because his or her ability to communicate is just a little better. 'In the country of the blind the one-eyed man is king!'

A major part of this book is the attempt to deal with this issue of structure and it will be returned to in Chapters 3 and 6. However, it is worth noting at this early stage that the following are required from such a classification:

❏ The framework should be common to whatever form of sustainable development is being considered.
❏ The framework should allow for the evolution of knowledge about sustainability as time progresses.

❏ The framework should not impose solutions but should facilitate thought and debate on the issue.
❏ The framework should be understood by all participants.
❏ The framework should allow different levels of knowledge to be brought together for common understanding.
❏ The framework should contribute to the wider question of global sustainability.
❏ The framework should have a theoretical base from which practical decision-making can be implemented.
❏ The framework should encourage a vocabulary and thought process that aids communication.
❏ The framework should allow the complex interrelationships within sustainable development to be made explicit when required, together with their interdependency.
❏ The framework should provide a mechanism by which knowledge gained can be transferred in a clear and understandable way, assisting in the overall education process of society and of the participants in particular.
❏ The framework should be holistic and encompass all issues likely to impact on sustainable development.

This is not a trivial list. Many of these issues are fundamental and can apply to a variety of complex problem-solving issues. Although the structure itself is likely to require refinement in the light of new knowledge, it should be sufficiently robust for its own underlying principles to be kept intact.

The characteristics of assessment and measurement for sustainable development

Once a structure is agreed it should be possible to develop a method to establish whether progress has been made in sustainable development. This is difficult but is nevertheless vital to the field of study. If it is not possible to establish whether we have improved our performance in our move towards sustainable development it is difficult to justify any decision that might be made now or in the future. How do we monitor progress without some assessment? In addition, it is important to know whether this assessment, if it takes place, is confined by the techniques employed to assess. There is a danger that it might be restricted to those aspects that are easy to measure. This is not unlike the drunk being asked at night why he is searching under a lamp post for a coin he has lost and replying 'This is where the light is!' Measures that are easy may not produce the right results.

It may be useful at this stage to distinguish between *measurement* and *assessment*. Measurement involves the identification of variables related to sustainable development and the utilisation of technically appropriate data collection and data analysis methods. Assessment involves the evaluation of performance against a criterion or a number of criteria. Both performance and criteria can only be defined by a value-based judgement; they are not empirically verifiable. Indeed the term *performance* must refer to a goal-orientated behaviour, that is, a behaviour rendered meaningful by the existence of a criterion that specifies when a goal has been attained. So a publicly meaningful assessment can only be achieved if the value system underlying performance and criteria is shared by both experts and public (Francescato, 1991). This latter statement reinforces the discussion in the previous section – there must be common language and structure to make it intelligible.

The methods employed in assessment are dealt with in Chapter 5, together with the appropriate application areas. There are considerable limitations to all evaluation methods (see Bentivegna, 1997), but these should be made as explicit as possible in order for all participants to engage properly within the process, otherwise the techniques can be misused to exact power.

Certain principles should underlie all assessments in sustainability if they are to be used for maximum benefit. They should be:

❏ *Holistic*: They should encompass all the key aspects needed to establish sustainable development.
❏ *Harmonious*: They should endeavour to balance or be used to balance the criteria upon which sustainable development should be judged.
❏ *Habit-forming*: They should be a natural tool to all concerned and encourage good habits.
❏ *Helpful*: They should assist in the process of evaluation and not confuse matters by further complexity or conflict.
❏ *Hassle-free*: They should be easy to use by a wide range of people and not require extensive training unless they are to be used by experts, and even then the results and their limitations should be simple to explain.
❏ *Hopeful*: They should point towards a possible solution and not leave the users in a state where there appears to be no answer.
❏ *Humane*: They should seek solutions which by their nature assist the development of human beings without pain, suffering or undue anxiety.

Again, this is a daunting list which may at this stage of our knowledge be impossible to achieve in its entirety. Nevertheless, it provides an aspiration which should be in the back of our minds as we develop systems for evaluation. It is a sounding board for our development of such techniques.

A review of the literature on assessment techniques will reveal a number of what are called *indicators* for sustainable development. In some ways, this is a recognition that the subject does not always have absolute values which we can measure and present as fact. It may be possible to provide hard measures for physical entities such as carbon emissions and levels of radiation in the soil, but it is not possible to be so precise with issues relating to social questions or human behaviour. In these areas, we can use measures to indicate what is happening but we cannot necessarily measure the direct impact on the environment or sustainability. For example, the downward spiral of economic activity leading to inner city decay might suddenly change when an inner city area suddenly becomes fashionable as people move into it from the centre of a city because the centre has become too expensive. It is not possible to be sure that this will happen but it may be possible to plot trends that suggest the probability that it might. This could then be an indicator of the regeneration of an urban environment and subsequent sustainability. On the other hand, if the city were to have no water supply, this would be measurable and would lead to an unsustainable future, as has occurred in several cities around the world. These issues will be explored later in the book.

Another issue that is also relevant to this discussion is the categorisation of users or stakeholders of such information. There are bound to be different levels of knowledge among them and the techniques will have to be used where they are most appropriate. It would be easy to establish a very complex list of such people and this in turn would add to the complexity of addressing sustainable development. In fact, the French (ATEQUE, 1994) have suggested a comprehensive classification of participants in the built environment. The following list has been developed by the *Intelcity Roadmap* (EU-IST 2001-37373) from the ATEQUE classification of actors influencing the built environment (*Intelcity Roadmap* – version 4, June 2003).

Civic service providers: the pole of collective interest (ten actors):
- ❏ elected representatives
- ❏ city administrators
- ❏ government agencies
- ❏ regional authorities
- ❏ local authorities
- ❏ research institutions and technical centres
- ❏ vocational training institutions
- ❏ consumer associations
- ❏ non-government agencies for environmental protection and other relevant interests
- ❏ information and communication technology (ICT) standards organisations

Private service providers 1: the pole of operational decision-making (seven actors):
- ❏ property development companies
- ❏ non-managing building and infrastructure owners
- ❏ managing building and infrastructure owners
- ❏ banks and other financial backers

❏ ICT development companies
❏ non-managing ICT infrastructure, broadcasting and content owners
❏ managing ICT infrastructure, broadcasting and content owners

Private service providers 2: the pole of design (ten actors):
❏ designers – architects, engineers, etc.
❏ property and construction technical consultants
❏ town planners
❏ landscape architects
❏ construction economists
❏ designers – software engineers
❏ ICT technical consultants
❏ ICT systems designers
❏ network developers
❏ information and society technology (IST)/ICT economists

Private service providers 3: the pole of production (six actors):
❏ construction material producers and distributors
❏ construction contractors and managers

❏ development control officers
❏ ICT component producers and distributors
❏ network and ICT equipment manufacturers and managers
❏ network development control officers

Mixed public/private service providers: the pole of use (five actors):
❏ transport and utility service providers
❏ facilities managers
❏ insurers
❏ network and network service providers
❏ network and ICT facilities managers

Citizens: the pole of use (six actors):
❏ users of buildings
❏ users of public open space
❏ users of transport and utility services
❏ users of city ICT services
❏ users of ICTs
❏ users of network and network services

However, a much simpler grouping which might also define the nature of the techniques that might be employed could be as follows:

❏ *Citizens*: This general group would include all laypeople engaged in the process who have no formal training in evaluation but nevertheless should be engaged with the decision-making process.
❏ *Clients*: This group would be largely the people who directly commission development within the built environment. They are interested in the impact on their own or corporate objectives. In private development, this can either be for the client's own

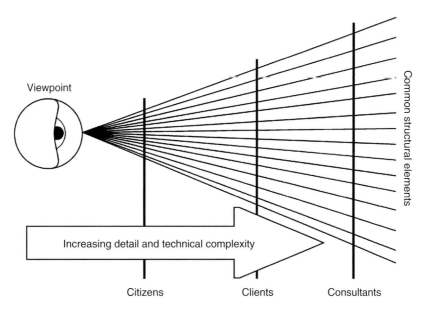

Figure 1.10   A consistent and integrated view for all parties to the sustainable development process.

accommodation or speculatively for tenants and users. In the public sector, their interest will be to establish value for the community.
❏ *Consultants*: This group would include the specialists and experts employed to create change and see through the procurement process. Their main objective will be to provide for a reasonable fee a service that satisfies the demands of their client base, as defined by themselves or the people who pay them.

Each may require a different set of techniques but within a standard structure and with consistency in the messages that derive from the techniques (see Fig. 1.10). This approach is still in its infancy but will be addressed further in Chapter 5. The key issue is whether the techniques employed encourage debate within the stakeholder group and whether they direct the decision-makers to a more sustainable development and/or one that has the flexibility to adapt to new circumstances relating to sustainability over time.

A helpful further approach might be that defined by LUDA – *Large Urban Distressed Areas* (http://www.luda-project.net/) in their Regeneration Process Framework which is shown in Fig. 1.11. This brings together many of the issues and participants which are critical to an understanding of evaluating sustainable development and echoes of this structure can be found in the chapters which follow.

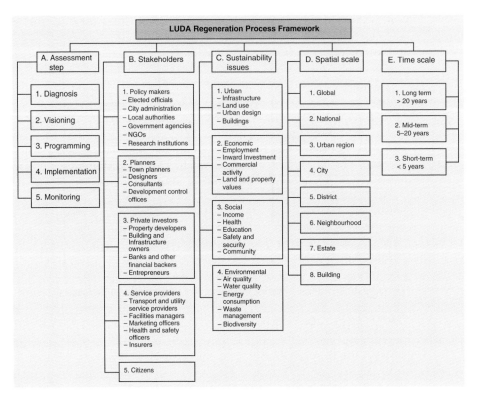

Figure 1.11   LUDA – 'Large Urban Distressed Areas' – Regeneration Process Framework. (Taken from http://www.luda-europe.net/hb5/evaluation.php. Used with Permission.)

Management and intervention for sustainable development

The discussion so far has focused on the underlying issues related to sustainability and our understanding of the term itself. The concept of evaluation has been brought in and some of the issues related to measurement and assessment have been addressed. But for what purpose are these structures and measures? They are of little value on their own unless we can use them to do something which will alter events. To do this, it is implied that human beings must intervene to ensure that something positive results. There is an irony here because it is often human intervention in the past that has created the severe problems we have today. Now we have a different set of assumptions from the past based on our improving knowledge of the earth and its ecosystems, but we also recognise that even today our knowledge is far from complete. We also recognise the complexity of the systems we are dealing with. This must mean that we have to tread carefully when putting forward ideas for change and we must allow for flexibility so as to be able to respond to the better understanding we may have in the future.

The discipline charged with the task of controlling and implementing change is that of management. Managers are thought to possess the skills which allow change to occur efficiently and effectively. However, what is the responsibility of management? *Webster's Dictionary* defines the role of management as 'to bring about or contrive' or 'to direct or conduct the affairs of something'. This raises a whole series of questions. It is not clear, in the case of sustainable development, what 'management' is to 'bring about'. We have argued previously that it is a *process* rather than a *destination* and the end goal in terms of what the sustainable world might look like is changing and unstable.

The timescales and complexity of the issues that contribute to sustainability are also major factors. In sustainable development we are talking about long-term issues and a whole variety of things that act together with a complex network of interdependent issues which may well be changing as time progresses. No one manager has control over the whole series of factors and in addition the timescales mean that, even if he or she did have such control, it is almost certain that the management would change over time. This raises the question of who would hold the blueprint for sustainable development that we might design right now. In reality it is likely to be held by a large number of organisations and people who may well be going through several transformations over relatively short periods of time. Who will feel the ownership and responsibility to see the process through?

Part of the role of management must be to bring the stakeholders together and strive for a degree of harmony between them. It must also be about timing and determining the process and trying to get the optimum balance between all the factors making up a sustainable development. But optimum for whom? Each stakeholder will have a different view, no doubt! The manager will also be responsible for the interactions between people and organisations, and for when they should be consulted and when they should act. It is obviously a very complex problem which cannot be viewed in the normal management sense. Indeed, it seems to be more about changing a culture within a community and then establishing a learning environment responsive to that culture which is constantly reviewing its previous decisions as time goes on.

Managers have an important role to play in the process and new management systems are required to deal with such a long-term and complex issue. It is not goal orientated in quite the same way as conventional management operations, at least not at the strategic level. At a tactical level, decisions have to be made and they would follow normal management practice except that the complexity of relationships and ownership of the problem could still be very diverse indeed. The choice of system is critical to what follows. There is a tendency for some prescriptive systems to control in a way that is counterproductive for the learning environment required for continuous improvement. It is when managers have the insight to see that systems cause their own behaviour that these issues can be tackled effectively. These matters will be explored further in Chapter 8.

Implementing management decisions

At some stage in any process that is going to change events some-one will have to make a decision. This statement is not as naive as it sounds. We can define the problem of sustainable development for ever and a day; we can bring out statistics that make clear the degradation of the environment; we can develop systems that are meant to provide a framework in which we can work; but if we do not get to the point where we can make a decision, all will have been in vain. To be able to do this we need to be clear about what decisions need to be made and who will make them. The question is 'Can this be left to chance or does some order need to be brought to the process?'

If it is left to chance there is every likelihood that something will get missed. If we make the process too prescriptive, either the balance between issues will get distorted or we will be led in a specific direction dictated by the system we are following. Neither of these approaches is desirable. We need to create a flexible decision-making environment where all factors are considered and where a structured approach can be taken which has order without regimentation. We need to know we have covered everything, and that all parties are aware of progress and the critical points for 'go' or 'no go' so that we can work in harmony together.

This would suggest that a protocol of some kind is required to achieve such an end within the process of planning, designing and building, and perhaps one of the most valuable approaches is that developed by Cooper *et al.* for a process protocol (see Chapter 8) in terms of the development process for construction (Cooper *et al.*, 2004). A protocol is any rule, code of behaviour or etiquette used to achieve or perform an action. It can therefore be formal or informal but in the majority of cases would contain some clearly agreed approach or standard. In Cooper's Process Protocol there are a number of hard and soft 'gates' in the process through which the decision-makers pass. The 'soft gates' allow progress to be made without all decisions being firm while the 'hard gates' are points in the process where the process itself cannot continue unless a firm decision is made by those engaged at that point in time. It has been suggested that this procedure might be applicable to sustainable development, and the Cooper research team have considered working on a protocol for sustainable construction which can be superimposed upon the overall protocol as already developed and integrated within it. It has already been applied to Disaster Management (see Chapter 8) which is addressing an extreme form of unsustainability where the very fabric of community is being challenged.

There is certainly a case to be made for a generic model that will provide a template for evaluating and implementing sustainable development at all levels in the sustainable development process. In a complex arrangement with a vast array of potential stakeholders, some form of standardisation is essential if all are to know how, and when, they can participate. It would provide a level of transparency which would aid participation and allow all participants to understand the process and the techniques being employed. The danger would be if this became too bureaucratic and slowed down processes just because of the weight of the management overhead involved. It is a balance between getting as close as we can to the right solution and the time and effort required to get there.

Summary

This chapter has attempted to provide a context for the subject of sustainable development within the built environment. It has introduced some of the arguments and has set the scene for what will follow. Sustainable development has been presented as a process that is emerging and evolving to reflect the knowledge that is emerging and evolving at the same time. It has argued for six requirements in the development of models and processes to be considered to address the evaluation of sustainability:

❏ *Working definition*: Here it has been suggested that the WCED definition might be appropriate even though it has inadequacies.
❏ *Shared value system*: We need a consensus around a set of values in order that all stakeholders can participate.
❏ *Robust classification system*: This is needed to provide a structure for discussion within which knowledge-building can take place.
❏ *A set of assessment/measurement tools*: These are required to assess whether progress has been made.
❏ *Management framework*: If humans are to intervene in the process they must operate within a system that they understand, and because of the timescales involved they must develop such systems to be flexible and to provide an active learning environment with a culture of self-improvement.

❏ *Process protocol*: This is required to ensure that all knowledge with regard to sustainable development is addressed at the right time and with the right technique or approach, otherwise some stakeholders will be disadvantaged.

One further issue needs to be explored and that is the question of the time horizon up to which any decision-making is intended to apply. This is a big subject but it is critical to our understanding of process and what can be achieved by any group of decision-makers. This requirement is fundamental to the whole of the evaluation process. Much modern planning can be considered to be short term and without consideration for future generations. It is often dictated by economic criteria prevailing at the time whereas truly sustainable development requires the long-term view. We will return to this in Chapter 2.

Time and Sustainability

At the heart of sustainable development are some assumptions about how long a development is expected to be sustainable for. Over what period are we considering the issue? One answer might be 'forever', another might be 'over a human lifetime' and another might be 'until something comes along which is better or changes the reason for trying to sustain the development'. Underlying all the assessments and evaluations of sustainable development must be some consideration of the time period over which we are making the assessment. Some might argue that as sustainable development is thought to be a *process* it is not necessary to pay too much attention to this matter. It is part of getting all the stakeholders to think in a certain way about the future to avoid leaving future generations in a worse position than we have today. It is therefore as much about culture and the creation of a learning environment as it is about calculation and prediction.

However true this might be, at some stage decisions have to be made about what to build, how to build and how to use the built environment. Finance houses, clients, local authorities and all the other participants who have some power or require accountability in the process will want to know over what time period these assessments have been made. Every decision is made within the context of an assumed time period. It influences the choice of material, the speed at which development occurs, the response to market forces, the design and layout and a whole host of other factors that make up the complexity of the built environment. While our horizon might be the long-term future, we have to make decisions in the here and now.

Evaluating Sustainable Development in the Built Environment, Second Edition
By Peter S. Brandon and Patrizia Lombardi   © 2011 Peter S. Brandon and Patrizia Lombardi

Strangely, it appears not to be something that is a major issue in the literature on the subject. It is hidden from view but is an implicit assumption in many of the techniques employed. A quick review of some textbooks on sustainable development in the built environment has revealed that only a few have a reference to 'time' in their index. This may be a reflection of the nature and youth of the subject. It may reflect the imprecision in the definitions of the term sustainable development or it may be that the lack of structure underpinning the subject prevents us from getting to this level of detail in general discussion. After all, the time period over which the stakeholders will view a decision will vary from one to another. For example:

❑ Political support for development in an area may be limited to the term of office of an elected politician or party.
❑ Finance houses may view the development over the time required to get a pay-back on their investment.
❑ Retail clients may view the development over the number of years they believe they have left before the market moves on elsewhere or the market has grown to the point where they need a new store or a major extension.
❑ A group of citizens may be interested in the development over their lifetime or the lifetime of their children.
❑ Planners may see the development within the lifetime of their 'master plan' or other such strategic document.
❑ Developers may view the development from a financial point of view but also in terms of what is happening in adjacent sites, regions and even other countries and therefore as a response to market conditions (in the markets in which they work) over the time it takes to create the development.
❑ Experts in demography will be interested in the changing age patterns around the development over a specified period related, perhaps, to government horizons.
❑ Lawyers may at one level be interested in the development for the time it takes to sign off a contract, and/or at another level the length of time new legal business will exist, and at another level the implications of changes in the law over a much longer time period.
❑ Valuation surveyors may be interested in the time taken to create an increase in property and land values.
❑ Architects will be interested over the lifetime of their commission but also in the long-term impact of their design as expressed in the building.

It can be seen from even this short list of potential stakeholders that there are a variety of views of the time dimension. If the aim is to create a harmony of view among all the participants, these different levels of interest over different time periods should be recognised as an essential

aspect of the sustainable development process. This raises many questions, of course, such as:

❑ Whose view should take priority in the case of a dispute? Is it the person or organisation who has the longest time interest in the development?
❑ Should the financiers, who take the major financial risk, be considered pre-eminent in the decision-making process? If they are not, will the finance become available to undertake any development?
❑ Should market forces be challenged as, in time, the markets will adjust to the new situation that faces them? However, the time lag may be too great to avoid irreparable destruction to the environment: is this acceptable?
❑ Is it the aim of sustainable development to avoid negative influences on the environment or is it to provide positive influences towards what is believed to be a better way of living?
❑ Are our techniques for evaluation sufficiently sensitive to the way society views sustainable development?
❑ Would it be more sensible to identify potential critical failure points, rather than critical success factors, in the quest for sustainable development?

Each of these questions contains the essence of a research question which at this stage of the topic has yet to be answered. It is not the intention of this chapter to answer them but to explore their nature and provide some context for the techniques and structures that follow.

Innovation and stability

Stewart Brand in the stimulating book *The Clock of the Long Now* (Brand, 2000) has proposed six significant levels of pace and size in the working structure of a robust and adaptable civilisation. From fast to slow, the layers are as identified in Fig. 2.1 with fashion, technical innovation and other quick-change items stimulating change and the lower levels of culture and nature providing a balancing force. In a healthy society, he argues, each level is allowed to operate at its own pace, safely sustained by the slower levels below and kept invigorated by the livelier levels above.

To quote an example, if commerce is allowed to advance unfettered and unsupported by watchful governance and culture, it easily becomes crime, as in some nations and republics after the fall of communism. Likewise, commerce may instruct but must not control the levels below it because commerce is too short-sighted. Brand goes on to say:

'One of the stresses of our time is the way commerce is being accelerated by global markets and the digital and network revolutions.

The fast layers innovate, the slow layers stabilise.
The whole combines learning with continuity.

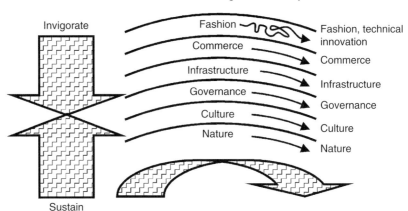

Figure 2.1 The order of civilisation. (Reproduced with permission from Brand, S. (2000) *The Clock of the Long Now: Time and Responsibility: The Ideas Behind the World's Slowest Computer.* Basic Books, New York.)

The proper role of commerce is to both exploit and absorb these shocks, passing some of the velocity and wealth on to the development of infrastructure, at the same time respecting the deeper rhythms of governance and culture'.

He debates the roles of each of the layers in a similar manner.

For our purposes in this book, this useful metaphor provides an indication of the timescales within which civilisations change and work, and their innovative drivers and stabilising forces. When these are not in harmony tensions and breakdowns occur. Nature is seen as the major stabilising force but it is this layer that is under threat because the other facets are imposing themselves upon it in a negative way. It may be a case of *Future Shock* (Toffler, 1985) where the future is coming so fast that the natural evolutionary processes cannot keep up.

The built environment plays a major part in infrastructure and commerce and its impact on those below can be significant. It identifies the physical position of governance, expresses the culture that has created it and imposes itself on the natural world in many different ways.

Perceptions of sustainable development

There is within the human psyche a latent model of the world and the future which understands that within a closed system such as the universe, as time progresses, less energy becomes available to be used and the system falls into decay. Atrophy seems to be the fate of most systems.

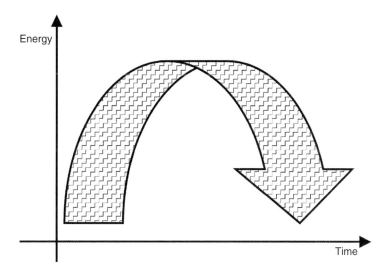

Figure 2.2   Atrophy in closed systems – is our mental model like this for sustainable development?

This model pervades our thinking and we think in terms of something being created, existing for a finite time and during that period of existence probably increasing in energy before reaching a peak and then moving into decline. Figure 2.2 shows this in graphic form.

The conventional wisdom within sustainable development seems to have this model behind it. A development is created, there is growth in that development in both physical and social terms and then it reaches a peak. For a further period of time it remains at this level and then it begins to decline for a wide variety of reasons until eventually it disappears as a recognisable development. This process may take thousands of years or it may be measured in tens of years or even shorter time spans if a major catastrophe should befall the development. The purpose of sustainable development is to halt the downward decline and, if possible, increase the availability of energy represented by social cohesion, physical well-being, biodiversity, appreciation of the habitat and so forth that go to make up a sustainable community, which in turn creates the sustainable physical environment in which the community lives.

Evidence for this pattern of events can be seen in a large number of the cities we see around us. They start as small settlements, grow into larger conurbations with a strong social activity and then decline, often as the result of a downturn in economic well-being of the country or context in which they find themselves. Often this pattern is repeated at the sub-city level with certain suburbs going into decline as crime and poverty begin to establish themselves. Others become fashionable and continue to rise, sometimes creating barriers beyond the financial to entry from unwelcome influences that exist in the poorer suburbs. In time, two societies exist side by side with tension between them, and in some cases this tension is so great that it creates a complete social breakdown which can lead to the demise of both. These events are almost unpredictable until they are well into the decline phase of the graph. The potential for breakdown can be articulated but it is much more difficult to know exactly *when* this might occur.

If we are to address the Brundtland definition (see Chapter 1) of sustainable development (WCED, 1987), we have an obligation to leave the environment in at least the same position, and if possible a better position, for future generations. We should not compromise their ability to make decisions about their future even if it means some short-term sacrifice in the way we behave now. The problem is that it is difficult to get people to accept the concept of self-sacrifice when they are not the beneficiaries. Even in the short term we know that this is true because governments that tax to provide something better a few years ahead, or to aid the redistribution of wealth, often find themselves unpopular and voted out of office. This is where education and public participation have a major part to play. Education is required to develop a different culture with a set of values that reflect sustainable development, and public participation is needed to enable as many stakeholders as possible to be informed and engaged in the planning process that adopts these values.

In many situations there is considerable inertia. Plans are made, budgets are set, political mandates are established and, together with the desire of many for certainty and routine, there is a reluctance to alter the *status quo*. It is not until a real breakdown of social cohesion or security or quality of environment occurs that we see a willingness to alter direction or to make substantial investments. The danger here is that the breakdown may be irreversible and significant damage may have been done which may destroy the community, and the stakeholders may well not be interested in doing anything about it. In the wider dimension of the earth's natural resources, for those resources that cannot be replaced (i.e. they are non-renewable) it will be impossible within any time frame to do anything about it. In other instances, such as the destruction of rainforests and other habitat, it may be possible to reverse the trend but there must be the political will. In the built environment it is difficult to envisage a total loss of the urban infrastructure as it can rise again as it has done for centuries – often one on top of another! Its nature may be forced to change because of the scarcity of the non-renewable resources that make up its physical presence but its ability to emerge again always remains. What will be lost are some of the less physical aspects of the built environment such as its historical and cultural value, its use as a social integrator, its role as a focal point of religious significance, for example. The pattern of sustainable development in the urban context is represented in Fig. 2.3.

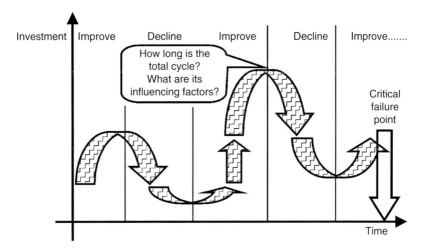

Figure 2.3 Hypothetical cyclical pattern of investment in the built environment over time.

Of course, the investment is not necessarily so abrupt or the decline so rapid as envisaged above, but nevertheless the pattern is recognisable and can even be seen in our personal investment in our homes. We do not usually invest in a new washing machine when the original is still serviceable. Then, later, we may decide to buy a better one if our finances allow it or the decision is forced upon us because the original has completely broken down and is not worth repairing.

In cities the decisions are similar but of course much more complex and bigger in their impact. The decline of docklands in many parts of the world because of a change to container traffic and other forms of transport (a change in the technology) has resulted in considerable expanses of blighted urban landscape. More recently, these land-holdings adjacent to the docks have been seen by developers as an opportunity and have been rapidly developed as new conurbations, revitalising a derelict area. The London Docklands, Salford Quays in Manchester and the Albert Dock in Liverpool are all prime examples in the UK. In Bilbao it has been the Guggenheim museum that has revitalised the whole city and in Sydney, Australia, the opera house has transformed the image of the whole country. These transformations are almost always the result of a political will to get things done. In the early days of Salford Quays, which was originally the old Manchester docks, the local authority tried to sell the site without success. No developer would invest and in fact the developers who were approached were asking for money to take it off the authorities' hands. It was not until a new vision was created by a small number of like-minded individuals with influence, and the government changed its planning policies and began to invest in urban infrastructure, that a new and successful life was given to the area. Now it is a prime development site and has wonderful new cultural buildings, with each new development reinforcing the others success (see Fig. 2.4). An initial outlay of around £30 million has seen an inward investment of over £1 billion. This is now being extended still further with the development of Media City UK, the second largest construction site in Britain after the Olympic Park. It is most unlikely that when the original docks were developed that such a major scheme could be seen in the future.

The question for all these developments is how long they will last before they move into decline. In fact, of course, nobody knows. A serious downturn in the economy creating a lack of tenants, followed by a lack of maintenance and security, could quickly see the beginning of a demise. If war should break out on a large scale, it is again difficult to predict what might happen. Sustainable development can only survive while all the external factors that bear upon the development are in harmony together. A failure in any of the major factors could well bring the whole development into crisis. The aim of sustainable development seems to be to ensure that the overall pattern of investment into an area continues in an upward direction even if we have to accept that there will be fluctuations in the upward graph caused by normal investment cycles. It is worth noting here that investment in this context is being used in its widest sense to include any input of resources, whether it be labour, finance, infrastructure, arts, social welfare or whatever is required to sustain or improve the built environment.

Critical failure points

In the majority of decision-making strategies relating to the built environment, the people making the decision are driven by the 'critical success factors' (CSFs). They look for the returns and the key ingredients that will make the development successful. This is the basis for some of the sustainability indicators that are used. In sustainable development these positive attributes still hold good but at the same time it may be important to give equal attention to the critical failure points. These are the factors which, if they fail or do not exist, could lead to a rapid decline in the sustainability of development in general and possibly the demise of the whole scheme or area. The type of issues that may be of this nature include:

❑ *The loss of a key resource* such as water. In India the city of Fatehpur Sikri near the Taj Mahal lasted only 15 years because the water supply dried up.
❑ *The loss of the major employer* in a region can destroy the local economy and the ability of the community and its infrastructure to survive. Examples of this include some of the towns built around coal mines that closed, or steel works that became part of a concentration of production elsewhere.

Figure 2.4   The regenerated Salford Quays, Salford, UK.

❏ *Pollution of air, land or water*, if on a long timescale, can mean that an area becomes uninhabitable. Examples are toxic chemicals in the land, pollution of sea water depriving the fishermen in an area of their livelihoods, or acid rain destroying forests.

❏ *A breakdown in law and order* which can mean that property values fall and residents become trapped in a cycle of decline; or, if they are financially able, they may move to other places but no one wishes to take the place they have vacated.

❏ *A breakdown in the commitment of a community* due to a challenge to the faith that has been practiced there. Towns in what used to be Yugoslavia identified as Muslim or Christian or towns built around a religious order find themselves vulnerable if the basis of the community is challenged.

It can be seen from the above that most of these issues are related to well-being and the quality of life. Some of them, such as pollution or loss of a key resource, are secondary to the need for a quality of life, however that is defined, although ultimately these issues impinge on the enjoyment of life anyway. It should be possible to overcome these matters but it requires substantial resources or a level of technical competence that the community might not have. It is therefore better for the community to move elsewhere and thus avoid the problem. By moving, their quality of life is expected to improve. Perhaps the biggest shift has been the change from an agrarian to an urban society in the last century and this has been driven by the expectation that life in the city will be more rewarding in one way or another. In many instances this is not borne out in practice as can be seen by the many shanty towns around major cities in the developing world. Nevertheless, it is expected that 80% of the world's population will live in cities by 2050.

In the context of the discussion of 'time' in sustainable development, these factors complicate the issue. We do not know when these movements might occur and in many cases we will not know with certainty the underlying causes. It is therefore difficult in developing a model of sustainable development to prejudge when we can expect a critical failure point to manifest itself. All that we can do is ensure that, as far as our knowledge exists today, the circumstances that might lead to such an eventuality are avoided or mitigated through the process of development. This leads us on to the approaches used in 'risk management'.

The majority of 'failures' are not critical in this respect. They do not result in sudden collapse. In general there appears to be a spiral of decline, a vicious cycle, where a lack of investment, a period of disinterest by the current and potential stakeholders or a lack of economic well-being, in particular, can result in gradual decline. Eventually, the possibility is that it is no longer feasible to create a virtuous spiral that will build the community again and result in a sustainable solution. Again, the timescale for this is unknown. We cannot predict with

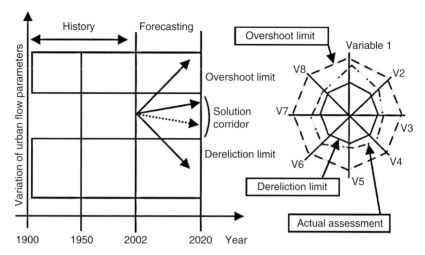

Figure 2.5 Solution corridor within urban regeneration. (Reproduced with the kind permission of Niklaus Kohler from his 2003 Presentation: Cycles of transformation for the city and its culture. *Intelcity Workshop*, Siena (under the auspices of the University of Salford).)

certainty how long this will take and we often do not know when the stage of non-renewal has been reached. So here we have a strong psychological urge to ensure that we create something sustainable, yet we cannot predict the events that will create the environment in which this demise will take place nor can we predict the timescale over which it is likely to happen. The two are of course related.

Kohler (see Fig. 2.5) has shown this diagrammatically in his work on life cycle analysis in the case of cities (Kohler, 2003). He suggests that there might be a corridor of solutions that need to be examined and evaluated over time which any decision-maker should be aware of and keep within. It is possible to overshoot as much as undershoot and the job of the decision-maker is to keep in balance all the contributing factors. Critical success and critical failure are therefore built within this framework. Of course, even with dereliction there is usually the opportunity to build again but the economic, social and other costs are that much larger.

Another view of this problem concerns the changing timescales for renewal within the process of an emerging and evolving city. These complicate the time when decisions *can* be made and in a complex organism such as a city they make the task of addressing the sustainability problem that much more difficult.

Figure 2.6 shows some assumed cycles for physical and other assets in the built environment. In some ways these are similar to the upper layers of the invigorating and sustaining aspects of the order of civilisation in Fig. 2.1.

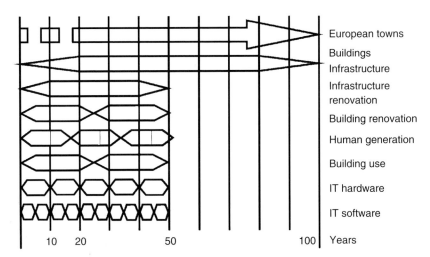

Figure 2.6 Cycles of transformation for the city and its culture. (Reproduced with the kind permission of Niklaus Kohler from his 2003 Presentation: Cycles of transformation for the city and its culture. *Intelcity Workshop*, Siena (under the auspices of the University of Salford).)

These differing transformations suggest that we have to address 'time' in some other way, not as a measure but as a continuum within which we learn and improve. This is not unlike the arguments being put forward by those advocating the concept of the learning organisation within business. Senge (1990) describes 'learning organisations' as:

> 'organisations where people continually expand their capacity to create the results they truly desire, where new and expansive patterns of thinking are nurtured, where collective aspiration is set free, and where people are continually learning how to learn together'.

It appears that the act of learning and sharing the results of learning can lead to a corporate view of the problem and a solution that allows for more creative ideas and a positive attitude to the aims of the organisation. Senge goes on to say that

> '...learning disabilities are tragic in children, but they are often fatal in organisations. Because of them, few corporations live even half as long as a person – most die before they reach the age of forty'.

Perhaps this is also true with regard to corporate action for sustainable development.

This approach requires a move to systems thinking which we shall address later. For now, it is worth noting that a focus on working and learning together is thought to be beneficial to organisations and, as the built environment is an organisation of a sort, there may well be lessons to be learnt for achieving a sustainable development. If we do not do this the cycles described are likely to continue and we can expect failure on a regular basis.

Time in evaluation

Even with a learning organisation approach and the focus on the process, it will not be possible to ignore the effect of time in our evaluation and assessments. As we have said earlier, most of those authorities with financial or political power will want to have proposals justified in order to persuade committees or shareholders or boards or whatever group they are accountable to. This inevitably means that some form of risk assessment has to be made, and this is a recognition that we cannot predict or control all future events.

In economic evaluation the concept of discounting is used to take account of the effect of time on the view of the investor at the present day. In simple terms the view is held that the value of a payment or receipt in the future is worth less now because, in the case of a payment, a smaller sum of money could be set aside now that could grow over time to meet the needs of that payment at the time specified. In the case of a receipt the value to the recipient now is worth less because a smaller sum invested now will accrue at compound interest to the amount to be received in the future. This is shown diagrammatically in Fig. 2.7.

What this graph indicates is that if you are set to receive €100 in 25 years time its value to you now is €29.5 if you expect your investments to produce a return of 5% and €9.2 if you expect a return of 10%. In other words, if you invested €9.2 now in a bank or other financial

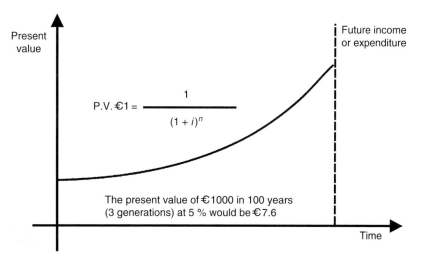

Present value

Future income or expenditure

$$\text{P.V. €1} = \frac{1}{(1 + i)^n}$$

The present value of €1000 in 100 years (3 generations) at 5 % would be €7.6

Time

Figure 2.7   The present value of an amount to be paid or received in the future.

concern and a return of 10% was guaranteed, it would accrue, with interest added, to €100 in 25 years' time. Notice that the higher the interest rate, the lower the value to you now or the smaller the amount that needs to be invested now to accrue to the same figure. The time remains the same but the effect on the supposed value is quite different, depending on the interest rate. It follows that if we were to use a higher rate of interest in our calculations we would be discounting the effect of future transactions more than if we used a lower rate. If in sustainability we want to take a long-term view and encourage this within our calculations, we would use a low rate of interest because this would make future activities appear more important in financial terms.

The choice of interest rate is therefore critical and is more complex than it appears at first. No account has been taken of inflation and this might have a substantial impact on the calculation. It might, for example, eat away at the real benefit from the investment over time. Some would argue that the 'real' rate of interest that should be used is the assumed rate less the inflation rate. Others would argue that inflation can be ignored as it affects both income and expenditure equally. This may or may not be true as differential inflation is quite common. It is also quite clear that long-term periods of stable interest rates and inflation are almost non-existent within the timescales of the built environment.

The time element is also a major consideration. The formula for computing the present value is based on the compound interest formula and is presented as follows:

$$\text{Present value } \text{€}1 = \frac{1}{(1+i)^n}$$

where i = interest rate divided by 100 and n = number of years.

It follows that there is an exponential curve which rapidly discounts future values as time increases. The result is a model of the world, upon which decisions are made, based upon a view that suggests the future is something to be discounted and is of considerably less value than the present. It is mechanistic and uses few variables in its operation. Nevertheless, much of financial investment is based upon it. It has replaced some of the other models such as 'pay back', where the length of time required to pay off the original investment is the criterion, because it is thought to more accurately reflect the logic of the financial markets. However, even on this assumption it may not reflect the real values that investors adopt within their decision-making processes.

Future aversion

It could be argued that when time enters a calculation most people are likely to prefer present over future gains (this could be termed 'future aversion' – we want to limit the risk on future gain) and future losses

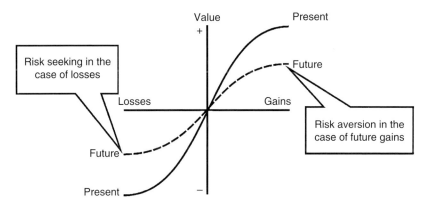

Figure 2.8   Risk aversion related to the future.

over present losses (this could be termed 'future seeking' – we are prepared to take a greater risk to minimise losses). However, there is unlikely to be symmetry between the two, which is plausible on the intuitive grounds that a postponed loss is less aversive than a post-poned gain of a similar amount is attractive (Kahnemann & Tversky, 1984). This is illustrated diagrammatically in Fig. 2.8. In sustainable development, where the emphasis is on reducing future losses, this asymmetry could be important in reflecting the psychology of the decision-maker within the technique.

If there is such a view at work in the minds of the decision-makers, it has relevance to sustainable development and affects the way in which those who are encouraging sustainable development are prepared to argue for different models that allow a longer-term perspective to be addressed. It would suggest a move away from the conventional eco-nomic models to the adoption of a moral imperative which will demand that future values are given significant weight. This could be done in some cases by legislation and regulation that requires minimum stand-ards to be kept – say the reduction in major pollutants, or it could be that business advantage is achieved by taking the long-term view.

There are already instances in banking where banks that take an ethi-cal stance in their investments have managed to increase their perform-ance substantially. However, this may be the absorption of the niche market of those investors sensitive to these issues. Nevertheless, it is a start and with further education in these issues it may be that the minor-ity niche market becomes the mainstream. Directives such as those con-tained in the Agenda 21 documents and adopted by many authorities throughout the world will hasten the take-up of a longer-term assess-ment. There is little doubt that it will require a variety of approaches to ensure that the concepts of sustainable development are included as the norm in addressing decisions in the built environment.

Clever or wise?

Patricia Fortini Brown, in *Venice and Antiquity* (Brown, 1996) draws our attention to the fact that the ancient Greeks distinguished two kinds of time: *kairos*, meaning opportunity or the propitious moment; and *chronos*, meaning eternal or ongoing time. 'While the first … offers hope, the second extends a warning'. *Kairos* is the time of cleverness, *chronos* the time of wisdom. Our dead and our unborn reside in the realm of *chronos*, murmuring warnings to us presumably if we would ever look up from our opportunistic, *kairotic* seizures of the day. Today we live in the golden age of *kairos*, where opportunity is all, the cult of the individual is paramount and the corporate sense that will allow us to engage with time is hard to come by. This has its zenith in economic evaluation where the views of shareholders in corporations often seems to dictate a short-term perspective in policy matters and where the evaluation methods heavily discount the value to future generations.

In 2008 and 2009 even this expectation was challenged. In the rush to get rich quick many of the existing rules of financial prudence were waived or suspended and the result was that the confidence in the whole financial system corroded. The major developed nations found themselves having to prop up the ailing financial institutions otherwise the whole of the economic and social fabric would be undermined. The systems which led to this debacle were unsustainable and could lead to an unsustainable future for many. The credit crunch brought home to nations, government and businesses the interrelationships which exist to achieve sustainable development and how fragile some of these relationships are.

Practical assessment of 'time'

This discussion has revealed some of the issues relating to 'time' within decision-making. It has not, however, put forward a proposal that can be used on a day-to-day basis to address the matter. This is because no one method exists. In fact when the situation is analysed fully it is realised that it is difficult to obtain a universal view of timescales for something as varied and complex as the built environment. Boulding (1978) diagnosed the problem of our times as 'temporal exhaustion': 'If one is mentally out of breath all the time from dealing with the present, there is no energy left for dealing with the future'. She proposed a simple solution: expand our idea of the present to 200 years – 100 years forward and 100 years back. A personally experienceable, generations-based period of time, this reaches from grandparents to grandchildren – people for whom we feel responsible – thus allowing human nature to support the longer-term perspective. From our grandparents and parents we distil our values and through our

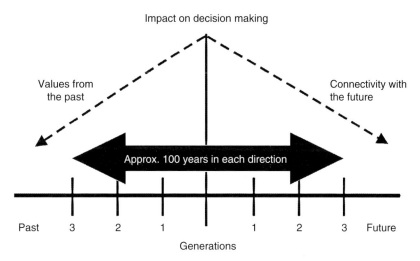

Figure 2.9 Impact of generations on decision-making.

children and grandchildren we connect with the future. This is shown diagrammatically in Fig. 2.9.

Whatever scale we choose, it would seem that a philosophy is more appropriate than a range of techniques. It is more about behaving within a framework in a way that is conducive to the objective to be achieved. One of the attempts to outline a philosophy such as this in a simple way, that all could understand, was Alex Gordon's '3 Ls' concept: 'Long life, Loose fit, Low energy' when designing buildings (Gordon, 1974). It had no quantitative measures but provided a frame of reference within which it was possible to begin to collect quantitative evidence and then seek improvement. It enters the realm of the learning organisation where the call for improvement becomes the watchword of the organisation – in this case society. The questions asked are then:

❏ 'Will this building development last a long time or longer than previous developments?'
❏ 'Will it be easily adaptable to change in the future to avoid using up non-renewable resources either in extraction or in use?'
❏ 'Will it use less energy in extraction, manufacture and operation than similar types of building?'

Once we get into this frame of thinking we begin to devise the techniques and measures appropriate to this view of the world. It provides a belief system which those who adhere to this belief can respond to and justify their behaviour. If it becomes the mantra of the many, it becomes politically unacceptable to follow a different path and it is adopted within the culture. In the '3 Ls' concept, two of the drivers have time as a key feature and so it begins to permeate the thinking of the many. What seems appropriate for a building soon becomes the view of the planners and the local authorities and begins to have significance for the district and then the city. A virtuous circle has begun.

Perhaps the closest to a view about how to approach the question of 'time' is the methodology employed in the study referred to in Chapter 8. This was a competition to set out a plan for a sustainable city for 100 years time and was won by the City of Vancouver. Those undertaking the study had to address the question of time in a very positive way. Targets for the future were set by the team and then it was necessary to discover a process by which these could be achieved including milestones relating to time for the whole of the 100-year period. As such, they had to address many of the issues raised in this chapter in a very practical way. The encouraging aspect of the exercise was that as the stakeholders began to look beyond the immediate future they began to leave the 'baggage' of the present behind and were able to think more freely. If this is the case it could be argued that we need more of this type of study because it encourages improvement without the constraints of the future and allows a wider group to gain consensus around the problems faced by an urban environment in achieving sustainable development.

The luxury of the 'time' horizon

The discussion in this chapter has argued the case for a longer time period in which to consider sustainable development than presently seems to exist in the developed world. Short-term financing and meeting the needs of stakeholders are often quoted as the reason why we can't extend our horizons. Financiers and investors want quick returns and sustainable development needs time to establish itself. Even if we could persuade people to think long term and consider the needs of future generations in the developed world, and there are signs that this is happening, the Developing World might consider this a luxury of the rich.

If someone is living at subsistence level and the question is one of whether he or she will survive, then considering the needs of future generations appears absolutely irrelevant because it may well be that the present generation will not survive. Long-term thinking becomes a luxury which only the wealthy can contemplate.

Various figures suggested for South Africa, a very mixed group of First and Developing world peoples, forecast that by 2010 deaths from AIDS will leave 2 million children as orphans. If this is true the repercussions for the country are enormous. Not only is there the problem of assisting these poor children but there is also the social impact of large numbers of children, many of them living on the streets, who to stay alive may turn to other activities that may be antisocial. In addition, it means by implication that a vast swathe of those who work and provide the economic wealth of the country (the parents of these children) will be dead or incapacitated. It is thought that around 17% of the population of South Africa is HIV positive. The impact on the economy and its ability to provide social services for the orphans will be devastating. This problem will impact within a decade, not within a generation. The timescale over which decisions have to be made is extremely short and taking the long-term view, which may still be a good thing to do, is almost impossible. Survival becomes the order of the day.

This is in a country where many communities have been able to live sustainably for scores of generations. However, the integration of outside cultures, and the wealth within those cultures, has led to aspirations that go beyond rural living and that often create an unsustainable society as the mistakes of the western economies are repeated, within much shorter periods, in the Developing World environment.

These aspirations for wealth can lead to the repetition of First World mistakes at a time when the First World is coming to terms with those mistakes and attempting to take action. Does the First World turn back and retreat into a more primitive but nevertheless sustainable way of living and meet the developing nations half-way, or is there some other way in which the aspirations, already realised by western economies, can be achieved by the developing nations? It is a critical issue and a visit to some of the nations with high economic growth will show that the mistakes are often being repeated.

When the West points a finger, the developing nations cry hypocrisy. It is often seen as a way of penalising the developing world when the West has reaped the benefit of exploitation in the past. For the disadvantaged world it can appear to be a restraint on their growth and a means by which the West can avoid competition – economic power is being used to exploit them still further.

Approaches to Evaluation 3

Chapter 1 provided an outline of the issues related to sustainable development and suggested that certain needs must be met. It is the intention of this book to put forward a structure that can address some of these issues although it is recognised that there is much work to be done in creating the tools which will allow the complete set to be implemented. For some time it has been recognised that unless some evaluation can take place it will be impossible to judge whether progress has been made. But progress towards what?

In the previous discussion it was recognised that sustainable development is a *process* and not a destination. It is something ongoing which is at the same time a learning activity whereby behaviour is modified as we learn from our actions and the growth of knowledge. It follows, therefore, that it is likely to be imprecise in terms of measurement and evolving in terms of content. This would suggest that it might be useful to concentrate on the structure by which knowledge is gained and classified in order that new knowledge can be identified and placed within an appropriate framework. This will allow relationships to be expressed that will address the complexity of the multi-criteria and multi-dimensional nature of the problem. Sustainable development rests on the *harmony* between the needs of stakeholders, and they require a framework within which they can address the issues that affect them.

Underpinning the framework must be an understanding of what we are trying to achieve and what we need to do to get there. The driving force is often the environmental agenda and therefore it is the value systems pertaining to this agenda that provide the foundation for the

Evaluating Sustainable Development in the Built Environment, Second Edition
By Peter S. Brandon and Patrizia Lombardi   © 2011 Peter S. Brandon and Patrizia Lombardi

approaches taken by many researchers and practitioners in the field. There are a large number of these and most are partial in terms of the total sustainable agenda. For example, some just address the energy issues, others the issues of pollution or contamination, and some just focus on conservation or historical development. These are not *wrong* in any sense but it must be recognised that they fulfil only part of the agenda for a sustainable development. There are also some which are more fundamental and provide a generic approach. It is worth looking at a few of these to see how they might impact on our future proposals in the book.

The Natural Step

The Natural Step approach was originated by Dr Karl-Henrick Robert in Norway in the 1980s and in 1991 he attempted to describe the basic environmental laws that would form the basis of a sustainable society. These arose from a scientific consensus of what was required to maintain the earth's systems. This consensus focused on what were called 'system conditions' and these became the primary focus of the Natural Step creators. The Natural Step emphasises that the only long-term sustainable approach in which business and society can operate is within the earth's natural cycles. It accepts that answers to the wide and complex environmental problems facing society are not clear so it returns to basic science as the foundation of a consensus view (Robert, 2002).

The scientific principles are:

❑ Matter and energy cannot be destroyed (first law of thermodynamics and the principle of the conservation of matter).
❑ Matter and energy tend to disperse (second law of thermodynamics) so that sooner or later all matter introduced by man will be released into the natural system.
❑ Material quality can be characterised by the concentration and structure of matter – we never consume energy, only its exergy (i.e. we decrease its order, purity and structure).
❑ Net increases in material quality on earth can be produced by sun-driven processes. Disorder increases in all closed systems (second law of thermodynamics), therefore an exergy flow from outside the ecosphere is needed to increase order.

In this frame of reference 'quality' represents the value of a resource. Higher quality means a material is more useful, e.g. 'concentrated' iron is more valuable than iron ore, and so on. Throughout evolution, energy from the sun has driven natural processes which have provided a continual increase in quality, e.g. concentrated hydrocarbons. Current industrial society reverses this process with the loss of material quality being waste and pollution. Fortunately, nature constantly tries to produce quality by reprocessing and reconcentrating waste into more valuable resources in a cyclical process. Recent industrialisation has imposed a linear process in which quality is consumed faster than it is produced in nature (Jackson, 1996; Stahel, 1996).

From an understanding of nature's fundamental cyclic principles, the authors of the Natural Step believe that this can be accomplished through four basic sustainable conditions. These provide the framework within which assessment and monitoring can take place. The four conditions are:

(1) *Materials from the earth's crust must not be systematically increased in the atmosphere.* In practice this means the extraction of fossil fuels, metals and other minerals no faster than their redisposition into the earth's crust – in other words radically decreased mining and use of fossil fuels and minerals.

(2) *Materials produced by society must not systematically increase in the ecosphere.* In practice this means the production of substances no faster than they can be broken down and reintegrated into the cycles of nature and the phasing out of persistent man-made substances not known in nature, e.g. CFCs.

(3) *The physical basis for the productivity and diversity of nature must not be systematically diminished.* In practice this means the harvesting and manipulation of ecosystems that preserve productive capacity and diversity in order to husband the capacity of nature to reconcentrate and reconstruct waste in a way that maintains the productivity of the land and sea.

(4) *There must be a fair and efficient use of resources with respect to meeting human needs.* In practice this means that society's values should allow sufficient stability to achieve the other three conditions by doing more with less through a much more resource-efficient lifestyle in the wealthy sections of society.

These are, of course, important guiding principles and they provide an effective sounding board for much of the discussion on sustainable development. They also provide a context within which business can judge its efforts and they have been used by a large number of organisations that are sensitive to the environment or see long-term business advantage in addressing sustainability issues. The Natural Step suggests that organisations are not expected to achieve long-term goals immediately. Firms are encouraged to move systematically towards the goals by making investments that will provide benefits in the short term while also retaining a long-term perspective. Organisations can use the Natural Step framework to map out a series of steps that will eventually lead to sustainability. It is often appropriate to start with the 'low-hanging fruit' and to take the steps that are easiest and that will achieve results that will help move the organisation towards its goals. This pragmatic approach has been attractive to a large number of organisations.

Dr Robert's approach has been endorsed by over 50 of Sweden's leading scientists and has been backed by a number of large Swedish industrial concerns including Electrolux, Scandic, IKEA, OK Petroleum, Gripen, SJ (Swedish rail), Bilspedition and over 60 local municipalities.

In America, The Interface Corporation, the world's largest manufacturer of commercial carpet tiles, was one of the first companies to embrace the concept. In just a few years it had revised its processes and products in line with this approach and had saved approximately $76 million. It has since been joined by a number of other American companies including Home Depot, Nike, Mitsubushi Electric (USA), Collins Pine (Forest products), Placon, IKEA and MacDonald.

In the UK the principles underlie 'Forum for the Future' led by Jonathan Porritt and worldwide the Natural Step organisation now includes over 10 000 professionals and 19 networks from all disciplines.

These firms and organisations appear to recognise that viewing sustainability issues through a framework that has a strong environmentally friendly future perspective is good for their business and their relations with the community. They see the process as gradually moving in a strategic way towards a vision rather than solely trying to solve problems caused by the mistakes of the past. The method claims that the potential benefits of doing this include reduced expenses for resources and waste disposal, avoidance of future liability, enhanced innovation and improved internal morale and motivation.

In practice the approach has been of benefit to many, but it is not easy to know what would take priority for the shareholders if there were a conflict between short-term profit and long-term environmental payoff. It will depend on the commitment of the organisation to The Natural Step principles and how far they are prepared to examine their trading activities to meet these goals.

In particular, the last principle of meeting human need is difficult for any organisation to determine, let alone to action. At the national level, the distribution of wealth is something that is debated continuously in most democratic countries but the evidence in most economies is that those who have get richer while those who have not get relatively poorer. Is this sustainable in the long term? In time this is likely to lead to a loss of social cohesion. A firm which might be trying to contribute to meeting the needs of all its stakeholders might find it difficult to address this issue in any meaningful way. This is true for any organisation irrespective of the structures and frameworks within which it chooses to work. It is, however, a fundamental aspect of the WCED definition of sustainability (i.e. meeting current and future needs) and the themes of the Rio World Congress.

The concept of community capital

Another way to look at sustainability is through the concept of 'capital'. This term is familiar to those engaged in financial markets and refers to the accumulated wealth, usually (but not exclusively) of a company. However, it can also be applied to other facets that contribute to a wider definition of wealth.

Maureen Hart, in her *Guide to Sustainable Community Indicators* (Hart, 1999), suggests the following as being contributors to what she calls *community capital*:

❑ *Built and financial capital*: Manufactured goods, equipment, buildings, roads, water supply systems, jobs, information resources and the credit or debt of a community.
❑ *Human and social capital*: The people in society, their skills, education and health and their ability to cooperate and work together.
❑ *Natural capital*: The natural environment, which includes natural resources (both renewable and non-renewable), the services that the ecosystem provides and the life-enhancing qualities of nature.

All of these types of capital are necessary for communities to function. All three types of capital need to be managed by a community. All three types of capital need to be cared for, nurtured and improved over time. Hart (1999) goes on to suggest that this can be represented diagrammatically as a pyramid (Fig. 3.1).

The base of the pyramid is the *natural capital* which relates directly to The Natural Step systems but is extended to include those matters that a community finds attractive or beautiful. The second layer of the pyramid relates to human and social capital and has two blocks, people and connections. This begins to extend the concept of sustainability much further than the Natural Step. *Human capital* is each individual's personal skills and abilities, physical and mental health and education. Social capital is the connections in the community and the ways in which people interact and relate to each other. The simplest connections are connections to family, friends and neighbours and we can then proceed on to the larger scale where we form connections through community organisations, links to government and the ability to form commercial organisations to create goods and services to satisfy the needs of the community. Finally, the remaining level of the pyramid is *built capital* which provides the physical infrastructure and supplies the needs that allow the other levels to flourish. It includes roads, transport, factory buildings, houses and basic necessities such as food and clothing together with luxury goods such as dishwashers, cars, telephones and computers.

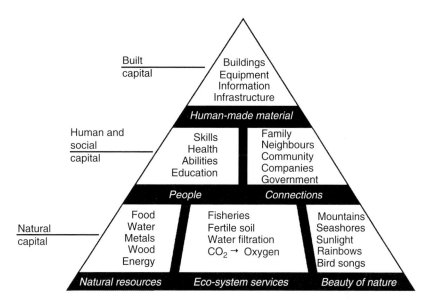

Figure 3.1 Sustainable community indicators. (Reproduced with permission from Hart, M. (1999) *Guide to Sustainable Community Indicators*, 2nd edn. Sustainable Measures (formerly Hart Environmental Data), North Andover, MA.)

Money is not included as money is just a medium by which we exchange goods and services. We do not have to use money as we could exchange by barter, for example.

The three forms of capital are measured in different ways and this is what makes them difficult to compare when trying to make value judgements. A value can be given to a house or car or share of stock in monetary terms. It is much more difficult to place a monetary value on those items that appeal to the human senses or contribute to a sense of well-being. A mountain view, a clean beach, the ability to read, contentment in a child and an open and free government are all of value to the community but are difficult to capture in monetary terms, although some try to do this through techniques such as cost–benefit analysis. In trying to get harmony between stakeholders and even between the priorities you might hold as an individual, it is very difficult to know what weight to place on one feature rather than another.

Nevertheless the concept of capital would appear sensible. The driving force behind the sustainability debate has been the loss of natural capital through human intervention in the environment and the pollution created by this intervention. In our daily lives we try to live off the interest that we gain from investments rather than lessen the capital, which, when invested, earns that interest. If we eat into our capital we will have less interest to enjoy, and eventually we will find we have no capital from which to gain income. Extrapolations of what is happening to our planet as we use up the non-renewable resources are forecasts of what is likely to happen to our natural capital. It will eventually disappear and we will be able to get no return. We are not always sure we can find an alternative that will give the same service or satisfaction.

The concept of *community capital* takes this a stage further. It recognises that people's quality of life also depends on other matters which are not just about food and shelter and our access to natural resources but about how we can assimilate, create, interact, celebrate, care for and enjoy ourselves. In turn these things have an impact on what we demand from the man-made environment and consequently what will be taken from natural capital to satisfy these wants. Where these things are in balance we do not use up our capital at a faster rate than we can replace it. Where they are out of balance it can lead to disaster or extreme difficulties. This book is largely about the built environment and its contribution to sustainable development. It is therefore largely addressing the top of the pyramid and how we create systems that allow us to monitor whether natural capital and the response to demand are in equilibrium. However, it must also take into account the communities that create the demand and how development is contributing to the satisfaction of these wants in a sustainable way. This raises another issue: it is possible to invest and to create more capital. Most communities will want to improve their position rather than stay where they are. The Brundtland definition of sustainability (see Chapter 1) recognises this and specifically mentions meeting the needs of future generations. The question is whether this improvement can be achieved without depletion of the capital base.

At the present time there are many examples throughout the world of communities giving up their natural capital and thus degrading their community capital. The obvious ones are the depletion of the rain forests in Brazil, the depletion of fish stocks in the North Sea, and the pollution of air, land and water in many places. It could also be argued that human capital is being degraded in some communities through poor health promotion (e.g. the spread of AIDS), insufficient and inadequate education, poor training for employment and so forth. In some cases the legal and financial infrastructure is not sufficiently robust to support the values of society or the need to conserve non-renewable stocks of resources. All these factors have a contribution to make to sustainable development.

At the level at which this book is considering sustainable development, that is, at the largely urban level of the built environment, these larger matters of community capital are viewed from the local perspective. However, some of these issues are global in their nature, affecting other communities way outside the community that is making the decision to deplete the natural or other capital. Each local community will be making an impact on the world outside and cannot ignore the interdependence between itself and others.

The concept of community capital is one that is useful in any deliberation on sustainable development and it is important that any structure or evaluatory system attempts to preserve capital wherever possible. Again, it provides a conceptual framework which allows us to explore sustainable development in a useful way.

The ecological footprint

So far we have addressed approaches that build on the broad issues of the environment and the way in which an understanding of capital can be used to test judgement and explain the concept of sustainable development. These are compatible approaches where one extends the other. Another approach is to look at the impact that an individual or an individual development has on the environment and/or the community in which they live or are developed. This is sometimes referred to as the *ecological footprint*. A footprint is of course a measure of the amount of space that a person uses to stand upon the earth's surface. It follows therefore that an ecological footprint is a measure of the amount of space a person uses in the ecosystem. To take a simple example, imagine yourself living in a glass dome that covers you and some land around you. If the dome is too small you will quickly run out of air to breathe, and if it were a little larger you might have enough air but might run out of water or food. If you include enough space to provide all your needs such as energy for heat, electricity and transportation, housing materials, food, clothing, etc. as well as enough land to assimilate all the waste that you generate and to convert all the carbon dioxide to oxygen, the result would be your ecological footprint.

The size of your footprint depends on the amount of resources you consume. Someone who travels by foot or by bicycle has a smaller footprint than someone who travels by car. It could be that someone who lives in a small well-insulated house has a smaller footprint than someone who lives in a large, poorly insulated house although the ecological impact of the extraction processes for the insulation and quality of materials, known as their *embodied energy*, would have to be taken into account. In the developed world it is lifestyle issues that are playing an increasingly large part, including food menus requiring the transport of ingredients from across the world, leisure activities and methods of transport.

Some of the figures generated by this form of assessment are quite staggering. It is estimated that the average American's ecological footprint is over 13 acres. This compares with a world average of 4.68 while in India it is 1.04. Figure 3.2 shows this in diagrammatic form. However, even with the existing population and the amount of productive land, there is less than 4 acres available per person on the whole earth! If everyone consumed as much as the average American we would need

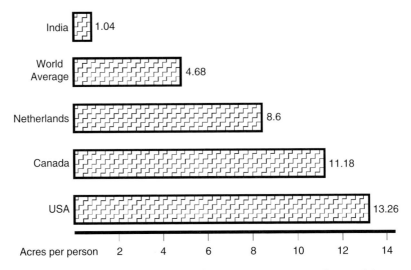

Figure 3.2 The ecological footprint of countries. (Source: Wackernagel & Rees, 1995.)

two more earths. It is clear that this level of consumption would not be sustainable if every one on earth were acting in this way. It would require a major reduction in the earth's population just to allow this kind of behaviour to continue if the wealth and lifestyle aspirations of those in the Developing World are to be realised. Alternatively, the developed world has to seek new ways of achieving its quality of life without endangering the planet on which the activity takes place. It would require a change in lifestyle that uses natural resources without degrading or destroying the ability of the ecosystem to continue to provide those resources and services indefinitely (Wackernagel *et al.*, 1993).

Imagine now looking not at the individual but at the impact of a new building or development. What would it take to bring the building or development into operational being and what would be the impact on the ecosystem? This would include all the energy required for the extraction of materials, the transportation of materials and labour, the infrastructure for the construction process, the materials for the components, the communication links, the water supply and so on. Then you would have to consider the running and organisational costs of the building and all the activities and heating/cooling, etc., that were needed to meet the occupiers' demands. Finally, you would have to consider the issues related to demolition and disposal as well as the disposal of waste over the lifetime of the property. The ecological impact could be vast.

In construction and building the notion of footprint is well understood. This is the area of the planet's surface directly covered by a building's ground floor plan. However, its ecological footprint is not so well established. In one sense it could be argued that every building is an act against nature (Cooper & Curwell, 1998). A building directly makes some proportion of the earth's surface organically sterile by covering it over, rendering that area of soil incapable of producing those natural resources that require the interaction between soil, sun and water. As a result, in ecological terms the building is a parasite, what Rees (1992) describes as 'a mode of pure consumption' which calls on an extensive external resource base to sustain the life that it houses.

It follows that a building's footprint is very much larger than the physical footprint it occupies. It will require other activities to support it, many of which will be elsewhere and distant, and each of these will have its own ecological footprint. These may grow into economic or cultural dependencies which may develop instability or new power structures when acting together with other aspects of a global economy. These in turn may create social unrest and lead to conflict and more wastage and pollution. For a large building as for a city, the ecological footprint may extend across the planet, drawing in materials from developed and developing countries. This problem of boundaries and interdependence makes the development of an assessment tool based on the footprint very difficult.

For a city or building to be described as sustainable its ecological footprint should closely match or be smaller than its physical footprint. This is achievable only by using the minimum of resources, by obtaining them locally and by minimising the amount of resulting pollution and waste to a level that can be disposed of safely within the confines of the site or community. This is the concept behind the autonomous building or city. However, autonomy is too unsophisticated and restrictive to effectively define sustainable urban development in modern complex market economies. The idea of replacement or renewal is better. This accepts that resources are finite and, combined with man's ingenuity and technology, can supply a given maximum at any one time. Finite resources are being drawn upon too heavily so we must replace the natural capital that is used by any particular development. This idea is supported by the concept of total cost accounting, in which the external costs of environmental degradation of the production process are represented in the internal costing of products and services – which in turn is reflected in the 'polluter pays' principle (see Costanza, 1991). These ideas have the attraction that a number of traditional ways of assessing 'progress' such as money, energy, labour content, etc., can be used to assess sustainable development (Cooper & Curwell, 1998).

A major problem with this approach, as pointed out by Haberl *et al.* (2004: 200), Van Kooten & Bulte (2000: 264) and Pearce (2005: 482) is that the true carrying capacity of the biosphere cannot be calculated, measured or predicted with any accuracy. Bossel (1998: 73) further criticises aggregate indicators like the ecological footprint for possibly 'hiding serious deficits in some sectors which threaten the overall health of the system'. The idea of aggregating all environmental impacts into a simple index such as hectares per capita has also been criticised as 'resource reductionism' open to the same flaws found in economic measures such as the gross domestic product (Doughty & Hammond, 2004: 1229). Rees & Wackernagel (1996) argue, however, that while the ecological footprint does not provide a perfect measure of urban sustainability, it can be used to assess the status quo of the sustainability gap (the difference between the footprint and the carrying capacity), to test scenarios built on different development pathways and/or technology choices, and to monitor progress through time series studies (Du Plessis, 2009).

Another major criticism of checklist-type indicator systems and aggregate indicators as a means of studying urban sustainability is that they cannot capture the systemic and dynamic nature of urban processes (Bossel, 1998: 74). Attempting to introduce such a systemic understanding is the concept of urban metabolism, which builds on the understanding of the city as an ecosystem with inputs of energy and materials and outputs in the form of waste products (Newman, 1999: 220; Du Plessis, 2009).

Monetary (capital) approach[1]

There are other approaches to measuring sustainable development. Among them, the capital [monetary] approach has found a lot of attention. It attempts to calculate national wealth as a function of the sum of, and interaction among, different kinds of capital, including not only financial capital and produced capital goods, but also natural, human, social and institutional capital. This requires that all forms of capital be expressed in common terms, usually in monetary terms.

The frameworks for sustainable development indicators based on this approach vary, but, in general, they all try to identify first what development is, and, second, how development can be made sustainable. This draws attention 'to what resources we have at our disposal today, and towards the issue of whether we manage these in ways that make it possible to maintain and further develop the resource base over time'.

Explicit in the [monetary] capital approach is the notion of substitutability between different types of capital, which is indeed a complex issue. There are clear examples of substitutability – machines for human labour, renewable for non-renewable sources of energy, synthetics for some natural resources. Future technological innovation and human ingenuity may greatly expand the scope. However, there may also be assets that are

---

[1] This and the following three sections are partly taken from: *Indicators of Sustainable Development: Guidelines and Methodologies* © United Nations, 2007. Reproduced with permission.

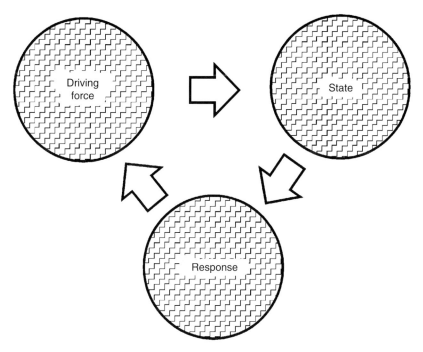

Figure 3.3 Driving force–state–response model.

fundamental and for which no substitution is possible. This could include, for example, a reasonably stable climate or biological diversity.

There remain many challenges to using monetary indices. Among them is disagreement about how to express all forms of capital in monetary terms; problems of data availability; questions about substitution; and the integration of intra-generational equity concerns within and across countries. Nonetheless, the concept of using capital as a way to track sustainable development could be a powerful tool for decision-making, and work in this area is continuing.

The driving force–state–response model

In the driving force, state and response (DSR) framework (Fig. 3.3), a variation of the previous pressure–state–response model (OECD, 1994), later expanded to the driver–pressure–state–impact–response (DPSIR) framework, human activities and external forces (the drivers) are seen as producing pressures that can induce changes (impacts) in the state of the biophysical and socio-economic environments and thus on the state of human settlements. Society then responds to changes in pressure or state with policies and programmes intended to prevent, reduce or mitigate pressures and their impacts. These responses in turn produce new pressures.

DPSIR is still the most well-known framework for organising indicators (see Chapter 4); it is also the principal framework used for developing environmental impact analyses across Europe (see Chapter 5). Driving force indicators describe processes or activities that have a positive or a negative impact on sustainable development (e.g. pollution or school enrolment). State indicators describe the current situation (e.g. nutritional status of children or land covered by forests), whereas response indicators reflect societal actions aimed at moving towards sustainable development.

This model was used for classifying the indicators set proposed by the Commission on Sustainable Development (CSD) under the UN Sustainable Development Programme, and it will be better illustrated in Chapter 4. Whereas variations of the pressure-state-response framework continue to be used in more environmentally oriented indicator sets, the revision of the CSD indicators in 2001 discontinued the DSR framework mainly because it was not suited to addressing the complex inter-linkages among issues; the classification of indicators into driving force, state or response was often ambiguous; there were uncertainties over causal linkages; and it did not adequately highlight the relationship between the indicators and policy issues.

Issues or theme-based frameworks

Issue- or theme-based frameworks are the most widely used type of frameworks, especially in official national indicator sets. In these frameworks, indicators are grouped into various different issues relating to sustainable development. The issues or themes are typically determined on the basis of policy relevance. Most countries in all regions of the world that have developed national sustainable development indicators have based them on a thematic framework. This is also true of regional strategies and indicator programmes, such as the indicators used in the Baltic 21 Action Programme, the Mediterranean Sustainable Development Strategy and the Sustainable Development Indicators for the European Union.

The main reason for the prominence of thematic frameworks is their ability to link indicators to policy processes and targets. This is intended to provide a clear and direct message to decision-makers and facilitates both communicating with and raising the awareness of the public. A thematic framework for indicators is also well suited to monitor progress in attaining the objectives and goals stipulated in national sustainable development strategies. It is flexible enough to adjust to new priorities and policy targets over time. Unfortunately, these themes are not always homogeneous across nations; therefore comparison and benchmarking exercises among countries and regions are not always possible using these kinds of frameworks.

Accounting frameworks

Indicator systems based on accounting frameworks draw all indicators from a single database allowing for sectoral aggregation and using consistent classifications and definitions. The most prominent example in this regard is the System of Integrated Environmental and Economic Accounting (SEEA) pioneered by the United Nations Statistical Commission with the International Monetary Fund, the World Bank, the European Commission and OECD. The SEEA extends national accounting to environmental aspects through a satellite system of accounts. It is, thus, clearly linked to the standard system of national accounts (SNA). The SEEA includes accounts expressed in monetary terms as well as accounts in physical terms. It allows for the construction of a common database from which some of the most common sustainable development indicators in the economic and environmental spheres can be derived in a consistent manner. Several countries are using the SEEA, and it is in the process of being proposed as an international statistical standard.

Integrated national account frameworks such as the SEEA were not set up specifically to address sustainable development and therefore do not take into account all the dimensions of sustainable development, especially the social and institutional ones. Nevertheless, some of these concerns are being addressed through efforts both to expand the system by incorporating human capital and to explore the possibility of linking the frameworks with social accounting matrices (SAM) which have been developed in consistency with the national accounts.

Implementation of the SEEA would improve systems of sustainable development indicators embedded in capital frameworks as well as those based on thematic frameworks. In the case of capital frameworks, the SEEA facilitates moving from modelled and estimated data towards directly obtained capital measures.

An example of such implementation, is the material and energy flow accounting (MEFA) proposed by Haberl *et al.* (2004: 201) which consists of three components: Material Flow Accounting (MFA), Energy Flow Accounting (EFA) and Human Appropriation of Net Primary Production (HANPP) (ibid.: 204). According to the author, this is able to link 'socio-economic dynamics (e.g. monetary flows, lifestyles or time allocation) to biophysical socio-economic stocks and flows and these, in turn, to ecosystem processes'.

Frameworks of assessment methods' tool kits

A number of frameworks have been developed in recent decades by target research projects (e.g. BEQUEST, CRISP, LUDA, Sustainability-Test, etc.) or specific networks (e.g. CIB – *Conseil International du*

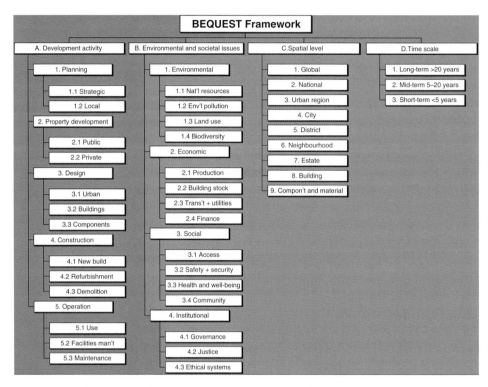

Figure 3.4 The BEQUEST framework. (Source: Deakin *et al.*, 2001. Reproduced by permission of *The International Journal of Life Cycle Assessment.*)

Bâtiment) with the aim of providing a basis for planning and structuring built environment assessment methods' tool kits (see also Chapter 5).

These frameworks (and relative tool kits) seek to provide a comprehensive classification system of assessment methods, procedures and indicators with the aim of supporting decision-making and providing easy access to relevant and structured information. For instance, the BEQUEST – Building Environmental Quality Evaluation for Sustainability through Time – (a project funded by the European Union 4th Framework Programme, 2001) framework relates four main dimensions of urban development: the development activity, environmental and social issues, spatial level and timescale (see Fig. 3.4).

Development activity comprises a number of activities and sub-activities, that is, planning (strategic and local), property development (public and private interests), design (urban, building and components), construction (new build, refurbishment and demolition) and operation (use, facilities management and maintenance). Each represent separate processes where more sustainable development thinking, good practice and assessment can be applied.

Environmental and social issues comprise various human activities which create effects which have an impact on whether development is more or less sustainable. These activities are created by, or are consequences of, sources of environmental, economic and social stress. Environmental stresses include depletion of natural resources, pollution, excessive land use and a consequent loss of biodiversity. Economic stress is often a cause and effect of loss of production, decaying building stock, and/or of inadequate finance or incentives. Transport and utilities are important industrial sectors that affect and are affected by other economic sectors. Social stress may include lack of access to facilities, inadequate safety and security, poor health or general loss of well-being which is often associated with poor sense of community. Good governance is necessary to create equality of access to resources along with social participation and judicial means of redress; these are all part of the institutional framework necessary to support sustainable development. All these aspects, and the spiritual dimensions of life, are ethical constructs.

Spatial levels: Urban development can take place at various spatial levels from the scale of the whole city down to that of the individual building and its material components. Equally, the environmental effects or other socio-economic implications can be felt from local to global levels. A planning proposal can lead on to various new industrial and commercial consequences for the environment, economy and society from the level of the whole city down to the neighbourhood scale. The provision of new buildings can effect the extraction of raw materials and the manufacture of components, which in turn can create emissions that can have effects on the environment from the local to global scale and so on.

Timescale: The timescale used by BEQUEST, that is, short-term 0–5 years, medium-term 5–20 years and long-term more than 20 years, represents the normal scale used in economic and strategic planning.

This framework, which has also influenced the development of other similar frameworks such as the LUDA – *Large Urban Distressed Areas* (see Fig. 1.11), and CRISP – Construction *and City Related Sustainability Indicators*, has been criticised by several authors. Kohler (2002), in his critique of the BEQUEST project, points out a number of the weaknesses. The first is a reliance on aggregation methods for the assessment of different interventions in what is in essence a complex, dynamic system. The second is that many of these assessment methods are not only data intensive, but the criteria and indicators themselves have not been validated. However, the biggest lack in this approach is that it does not easily lend itself to a systemic understanding of the city, as the formulaic approach by its nature remains a mechanistic, as opposed to a systemic, solution to introducing considerations of sustainability into urban development processes (Du Plessis, 2009).

As reported by Du Plessis (2009: 86), the danger of such an approach was brought to light by Forrester (1969) who argued for a dynamic systems' approach to cities, as interventions that attempt to solve problems from a linear cause-and-effect premise can result in responses that only cause further problems. First, an attempt to relieve one set of symptoms may only create a new mode of system behaviour that also has unpleasant consequences. Second, the attempt to produce short-term improvement often sets the stage for long-term degradation. A mechanistic checklist approach would therefore prevent decision-makers from understanding the possible interactions between decisions made in different parts of the urban system, resulting in unintended and possibly unfavourable consequences in other parts (e.g. building a factory to provide jobs resulting in contamination of water sources and air pollution). The recognition that urban sustainability requires an approach that would consider the relationships between the parts of a city, was also raised by the BEQUEST team (Hamilton *et al.*, 2002: 110) and will be further expanded in this book which proposes a new approach to urban sustainability that looks at the city as a (multi-modal) system (see Chapters 5 and 6).

Summary and conclusions

From the above, it can be seen that the dominant approach to the study of urban sustainability has been in the main mechanistic and reduc-tionist fields and this in turn ignores the systemic relationships between problems, and the dynamic processes of change that characterise exist-ence. Even when there is an intuitive appreciation of the city as a sys-tem, this has not yet been fully translated into approaches that study urban sustainability. In addition, current approaches to studying urban sustainability can be criticised for losing focus on the essential sustain-ability question of how to develop a healthy human–nature relation-ship. Most of them have been based on dimensions and criteria derived from untested, ideologically based assumptions about problems and remedies, and negotiated through political consensus processes.

On the other hand, the above conceptual frameworks for indicators are recognised to be helpful in order to focus and clarify what to meas-ure, what to expect from measurement and what kinds of indicators to use. Most of these concepts are useful, particularly in terms of the envi-ronment. They provide us at a very strategic level with conceptual cri-teria which we can apply to a new or existing development to ascertain whether or not the development is going to be sustainable. In the case of the Natural Step and the ecological footprint, they are looking at the issue of sustainability through the filter of the environment and the reasons why people behave in a certain way to cause these things to happen are largely ignored. It is the end result that is the focus and not the processes leading to such an eventuality. Of course when these are used in practical decision-making they act more as checks and drivers on the processes and measures used to judge them. It is a little like assessing the result of a general parliamentary election for a new government. The end result is clear but the reasons *why* people voted in a particular way need much further analysis and a great deal of knowledge of the factors that concerned people at the time. This in turn requires an understanding of their culture and the framework within which they live their lives. This framework includes the value systems that they hold dear and the legal and ethical framework that reflects these values. None of these issues is overtly reflected in the two systems although it could be argued that the concern for the environment and the preservation of the human species are strongly represented.

The concept of community capital takes the matter a stage further. It looks at a much wider range of issues which ultimately have an impact on the way human beings intervene within the environment. However, it looks at them as capital which in this context means the wealth and resource available to be used at any point in time. Is this resource being depleted or is it being enhanced? Will future generations be able to use this resource for their benefit or will it diminish or disappear and not be available to them? In the case of the natural capital this could be disastrous unless renewable alternatives are found or space freight travel occurs and we can mine other planets. Since both of these are unknowns, we can assume that in our timescale for decision-making space travel, at least, is not part of the equation. We cannot easily predict how technology will develop to create alternatives so it may not be sensible to build any strategy for sustainability on this expectation. We could have damaged our planet beyond repair before the alternative is produced to satisfy our needs.

Nevertheless, the introduction of community capital is very helpful since it begins to address the *processes* by taking us into the realm of human behaviour, values and judgement – the very things that decision-makers have to deal with when making practical decisions. However, there are still limitations. It is still monitoring the end result and not the interrelationships which take us to the point where capital is created or diminished. The processes are implicit in the system but not explicit. It is a little like looking at the value of your house and not considering the multitude of processes, decisions and external factors that act together to reach the finite sum we call house value. The concept of the value of the house is largely an economic one but it derives from supply and demand. Demand will reflect society's values in terms of accommodation requirements (bathrooms, kitchens, etc.) and also location, perhaps the most important variable for most house prices. The supply side will provide what society demands, whether that is brick external walls, two bathrooms, a level of heating or cooling to provide comfort, gold-plated taps or whatever. Society, on the other hand, may wish to control some of these issues so it produces planning laws or gives powers to local authorities or introduces anti-pollution legislation which limits what can be done.

The strength of the relationships between this mass of variables and the way they interact is important. In addition, the concept of capital gives little indication of what affects what and by how much. Obviously, these are major issues which any structure is going to find difficult to address. However, perhaps we should be striving for something which keeps all these concepts intact but takes them still further in providing an understanding of relationships and how they impact on sustainability. It needs the widest possible terms of reference because practically anything that occurs in the world can be said to have some impact on the question of sustainability and sustainable development. In Chapter 6 we try to put forward another framework which attempts to provide further illumination of this question.

For the moment we will leave the matter of structure, process and interrelationships and will focus on the evaluations we may think are appropriate for assessing progress in sustainable development. Evaluation tools are critical for such monitoring but they are also important for setting targets for the future and for gauging the importance of the variables which contribute to the concept of sustainability. Without them it is hard to rank, prioritise, measure and act in a sensible and auditable way.

Indicators and Measures

As illustrated in Chapter 3 the diversity of sustainable development theories and the core values of the authors have resulted in the development of different frameworks. The main differences among them are the ways in which they conceptualise the key dimensions of sustainable development, the interlinkages among these dimensions, the way they group the issues to be measured, and the concepts by which they justify the selection and aggregation of indicators. This chapter will specifically focus on indicators for measuring progress towards sustainable development.

Why evaluate?

If we are to evaluate sensibly we need enough information to enable us to make prudent and good decisions. It is possible to measure many things to several decimal places but the extra benefit obtained from measuring to this level of detail diminishes rapidly beyond a certain point. In fact, in some cases it is counterproductive to have too much detailed information since it can confuse, can give a false impression of accuracy when the underlying data from which it is abstracted is not measured with precision, and can add to the computation problem. Imagine all the detailed information that goes into the calculation of ecological footprint outputs. We could present the accumulated data to many decimal places but, firstly, many of the inputs would be fairly coarse measures; second, the data would probably be out of date now;

Evaluating Sustainable Development in the Built Environment, Second Edition
By Peter S. Brandon and Patrizia Lombardi   © 2011 Peter S. Brandon and Patrizia Lombardi

and third the conversion to 'carrying capacity' is not a precise art. However, the output is not devalued by a broad approximation. It *indicates* the comparative values between societies and allows us to draw a reasonable conclusion.

To take another example from everyday life, we do not require a very precise measurement of the amount of gasoline or petrol left in the tank of our car when we are taking a journey. The purpose of the measure is to tell us when to fill up again to avoid running out of fuel. We know that when the tank gauge shows it is empty, with or without a warning light, we will have enough petrol to get to a reasonably close petrol station. When it is half-full we can gauge roughly when we will need to fill up again on a long journey. The indicator has to be timely to be useful. It would not be of much use if the petrol or gas indicator only showed the position at the start of the journey and did not keep the driver informed along the way. It also has to be understandable in that it must convey the information quickly and effectively. Petrol gauges can come in different forms such as a dial or an electronic presentation but they have the same purpose. These rough indicators, the measures used and the methods of presentation are sufficient for the purpose for which we use them. If, on the other hand, we wanted to undertake a test of the fuel efficiency of the car we might need to measure every drop of petrol used and the precise distance covered.

Indicators therefore are presentations of measurements to suit a particular need. They are pieces of information that summarise the characteristics of systems or highlight what is happening in a system. Indicators simplify complex phenomena and make it possible to gauge the general status of a system. An indicator helps you understand where you are, which direction you are going in, and how far you have to go. It both assesses the current situation and gives advice for the future. Indicators can alert you to a problem before it becomes critical and in some case can help the user recognise what needs to be done to resolve the problem. Sometimes it is useful to bring many indicators together to provide a composite assessment of what is happening and this is called an *index*. However, an index is an indicator in its own right, simplifying the complexity of the indicators that form its constituent parts.

According to the European Environment Agency (EEA) indicators can be described as communication tools that: (a) simplify complex issues making them accessible to a wider audience (i.e. non-experts); (b) can encourage decision-making by pointing to clear steps in the causal chain where it can be broken; (c) inform and empower policy-makers and laypeople by creating a means for the measurement of progress in tackling environmental progress (EEA, 2007). It is the capacity of the indicator to reach its target audience that determines its success. The essentials of all good indicators are therefore as follows:

❏ They must be *relevant* and fit for the purpose for which they are intended.
❏ They must be *reliable* so that you can trust the information the indicator is providing.
❏ They must be *easy to understand* even by the people who are not experts in the field.
❏ They must be based on *accessible data* so that the information is available while there is still time to act.

However, because sustainable development is a multi-stakeholder process, indicators must communicate to a variety of different actors, and the additional preferred characteristics of a good indicator are as follows (Lombardi & Cooper, 2007a; Lombardi *et al.* 2009):

❏ They must be *transferable/comparable* across spatial scales and stakeholder interest.
❏ They must be *complementary* – displaying multi-scalar reciprocity.
❏ They must be able to account for both tangible and intangibles aspects of sustainable development.
❏ They must be useful to *show transition to knowledge society* – showing or distinguishing between, for example, just being a 'good neighbour' and being socially beneficent, for example, by leading a local virtual interest group.
❏ They must be demand driven by stakeholders (cities, citizens, businesses, built environment professionals) from the bottom-up as well as top-down.

Traditional versus sustainable development indicators

The reader will be aware of the very large number of indicators that abound in the world today. All the developed nations have a long history of collecting information that could be useful to them in making strategic decisions and in particular for advising government on policy issues. The areas where these indicators proliferate most are in the economic fields where the economic performance of a government is critical to its survival in office and in advising the financial and trading markets on where to invest. These may be measures of, for example, trends in employment, inflation, level of investment or gross national product (GNP). Gradually these measures are being brought into line so that comparisons can be made across national boundaries.

Other sectors are also producing similar sets of measures that gauge how they are performing. For example, the health services may want to measure life expectancy or waiting lists at hospitals or cost efficiency per patient. The education services may want to measure the cost per pupil, the performance of school children in standard tests or the league tables on school performance in a particular area. The transport departments may want to examine the congestion in an area judged by the number of cars passing through a checkpoint or the number of passenger miles travelled on public transport. With increased accountability the number of indicators has grown enormously. It is important to realise that most of these indicators are derived from some kind of model which a group of people, usually designated as experts, have decided is the appropriate way to measure or evaluate a particular feature. There can be arguments for different measures depending on what end result is required.

Sustainability raises another set of issues which may not be reflected in these traditional measurements. For example, the economies of most nations are measured in terms of GNP. This drives the agenda of most governments and is thought to be a gauge of prosperity. However, sustainability wants to look at the quality of life over the longer term. It is more concerned with long-term prosperity and the underlying issues that reflect this quality of life. Normal GNP measures may not reflect these issues. For example, a country that has a large number of car accidents may well see its GNP grow because these accidents place extra demand on the health services and extra demand for new cars or car repair services. These push up the GNP but it would be difficult to argue that this aids sustainability or adds to the quality of life. On the other hand, if a large number of citizens decided to walk to work the population would be fitter and would place less demand on the health services, but the GNP would go down.

To take some other examples, a traditional indicator might use the cost of electricity as a measure for energy but to use this as a cost of consumption, without regard to the effects on the energy use, would not assist in indicating an improvement or otherwise of sustainability. If the cost is lowered it is likely to increase consumption which might not be desirable from a natural resources or air pollution perspective.

Another indicator might be the median income of a family, which is frequently used as an indicator of economic well-being. By definition, in any community half the people earn less than the median and half earn more. What this measure does not do is link the economic well-being of the community with the social or environmental well-being of that community. So if, for example, the median value rises by 5% but inflation rises by 10%, the economic well-being of the community has declined in comparison with other communities in terms of what is normally required to live at a certain standard. A better measure might be to see whether the median income allowed a person to survive at a certain level based on the average cost of basic needs of that community within its social context. Another problem might be that the rise of

5% is a result of using up non-renewable resources and is thus at the expense of the environment. Here, a measure which looks at the percentage of the population whose income comes from the non-sustainable use of resources might be a better one.

This brief introduction to the problem raises a number of issues of which two are key to further development. Firstly, where will we get the data for these new measures when the world has spent the last century or more developing and recording against a set of measures that are now thought to be inappropriate, at least to the sustainability agenda? Second, how many of these indicators do we need to use to be reassured that we are indicating in a reliable manner whether a development is sustainable or not?

The first point is easy to respond to, but less easy to implement. At some stage in the past our society was faced with just this issue when determining its current set of indicators. It managed over time to develop and add new ones so that we find ourselves with the range we have today. The same will happen with sustainability indicators, provided there is the political will to ensure that sustainability becomes a key issue in all policy making. For instance, it has been recognised that user involvement is important in the designing and acceptance of the sustainability indicators. Stakeholders may have local knowledge that can contribute to more effective indicators. Participation also ensures relevance to the decision-making process, political commitment, and ownership of the results. Participatory processes can reveal conflicting social interests, values and preferences that must be taken into account (Sunikka, 2006).

The question of data capture is less obvious but this will depend on the growth in integrated systems and tools such as remote sensing which may allow automatic capture of information and analysis that can then be made widely available. There is no doubt that we are moving in this direction, sometimes with concern over the kind of information being captured and also the privacy of this information.

Technically many of the problems have been solved. Perhaps the main issue now is how far society is prepared to go in making transparent the way its citizens behave? Issues of privacy and individuality become important in this matter. A clear example concerns the business community. Although many corporate reports now include information on environmental and social performance that could be used for indicators, it is still difficult to get businesses to share the information they collect. Some information is seen as confidential because it provides a commercial advantage, and businesses are not motivated to share negative information that might damage their reputation or profitability. Yet much of the effort to move towards sustainability involves identifying and reducing problems such as pollution. This is an important gap that must be filled, particularly for small and medium enterprises that are responsible for the bulk of business activity.

There will still be a very large number of indicators, perhaps the majority, which relate to social and political issues that are difficult to capture. In addition, if we do use measures we sometimes forego the richness of human culture and society and consequently lose something significant in terms of sustainable communities. Issues such as aesthetics and heritage can come into this category. How is it possible to measure these and capture their full meaning to a society?

Not only that, but our perspective on these matters changes quite quickly and what is an appropriate view now will not necessarily be shared by future generations. You only have to look at how society values buildings over time. At one point it wants to pull them down to build a 'brand new modern' future, then shortly afterwards it wants to preserve them as part of its common heritage, signposts to the past and a sharing of its common roots. In addition, the public view of what is a beautiful building also changes as fashions come and go.

There is still significant work that needs to be done on incorporating the general public into the policy processes. While the link to science, and the ability to identify and track material issues through indicators, has become more sophisticated, there are still difficulties associated with setting standards or fixed indicators, even within fairly small geographical envelopes. This is because the significance of the environment varies with geography, and because cultural differences result in concern over different matters. A review of a number of Eurobarometer survey results since 2000 show this quite conclusively (European Commission, 2005 for example).

A further problem concerns the difficulty in identifying indicators that accord with the majority of the population (Sveiby & Armstrong, 2004). The fact that methods of capturing this information vary widely, and different methods are effective in different cultures, makes this variation within populations even more difficult to quantify. Attitudes and behaviour patterns shift markedly in populations, sometimes within a short period of time, making longer-term monitoring a difficult proposition. So far, the elementary question of whether the European economy is moving towards sustainability or away from sustainability cannot be answered because there is still not a consensus on the indicators and the integrative framework to be used.

To ascertain all these factors in the sustainable development debate will require new methods and a totally different view on the data with which we work.

Generic and specific questions

Whatever approach we adopt, we have to recognise that it will never be complete nor will it capture every possible nuance that relates to whether something is sustainable or not. It will be a useful (we hope!)

contribution or indicator but it will not be precise. There is also another important issue that we need to address: how many indicators do we need? If we have too many the systems fall into disuse because human beings cannot spend the time collecting and analysing them or they suffer from fatigue or they think it is economically not worthwhile. If we have too few we run the risk of missing a really important feature that goes to the very root of whether a particular development, in the case of the built environment, is going to be sustainable. There have been many attempts to provide a comprehensive list of indicators but there are severe problems. The UN Report on the State of the Indicators (United Nations, 2001) suggested that many people are designing many indicators without verifying them as there are no data collections related to the chosen indicators and consequently many of the indicators are not being used.

There appears to be no consistency in the choice of indicators among the various groups trying to evaluate sustainability, and no consensus as to what the indicators should contain and what should be the method of assessment. Of course something like this has happened in a wide variety of disciplines as each discipline has emerged. It is not possible to wave a magic wand so that suddenly everyone agrees and an instant structure and set of measures is created. There needs to be considerable dialogue and debate and a real wish to seek a common ground. Unfortunately it is human nature to hold on to the measures you have invested in and developed, even though something better might be preferred by others. At some stage a powerful authority needs to endorse a particular approach so that the others will follow and create such a strong critical mass that it is difficult not to change. In the case of sustainable development that authority is currently the United Nations, as we shall see later. However, it is by no means dominant and there are still hundreds of different systems being used throughout the world.

This does raise another question. At what level of detail is agreement to be sought? Surely there are generic questions to which we can all give our assent. We can then leave the second-order questions that follow to an evolutionary process of refinement and selection. For example, if one of the key questions for a sustainable development is 'What level of commitment and vision is there from all the stakeholders to the proposals being postulated?', we could leave the other questions that tease out the detail behind this generic question to the particular community undertaking the development and its own set of priorities. In the UK, for a new commercial scheme on a derelict brownfill site, we might ask about the political support, the planning authority support, the financial support and so forth. On the other hand, if we were evaluating the regeneration of a historic area as our development we might want to ask these questions but also to ask about the views of the community on the preservation of the area, the vision of the national historic commissions interested in this work and the Arts and other councils.

In fact because of the complexity and interdependence between factors and the external implications for most development, it would be impossible to devise a robust scheme at this second level which could be used by all. We would find that the list would get longer and longer as each proposal identified how it was different from others that preceded it and why it therefore should have a different set of questions and different evaluation criteria. These would then have to be added to the list. This probably paints too black a picture as in time there would be sufficient consensus around a set of issues, at least for a particular type of development. It does, however, illustrate the difficulty. It also illustrates where we should be placing our effort at this time: on the big generic questions around which we should be able to gain a consensus. To do this we need a robust structure within which to frame these questions and this book tries to contribute to the debate with the proposals in Chapter 6.

International indicators

There has been a strong desire among all those addressing the issues of sustainability to provide a set of indicators that can form the basis of an agreed set of parameters for sustainable development. Given the preceding discussion it is clear that these indicators will need to be at a high strategic level, allowing more detailed work to take place at the next level down in tailoring the indicators to the needs of local and cultural circumstances. Of the many that have been developed there can be little doubt that those developed by the United Nations (UNCSD, 1996; United Nations, 2007) are likely to have the most authority and to be implemented most widely as a result. Indeed the intention of such indices and indicators is to gain widespread support and use in order that the concept of sustainable development can be included in all national agendas, allowing for international comparison.

It would be true to say that there is still some debate about the indicators to be adopted and some of the developed nations of the world would argue that those currently listed are simplistic and do not reflect the complexity of the problem. They also believe there can be trade-offs between the indicators such as the planting of forests to compensate for CO_2 emissions. Nevertheless, the indicators identified by the United Nations have widespread acceptance and form the basis of many of the other indicator lists found across the world. They were grouped under a number of categories of sustainable development, that is, social, economic, environmental and institutional aspects (known in literature as 'the four pillars').

The model on which they were based is the driving force–state–response framework illustrated in the previous chapter.

In the revised, third edition of the Commission on Sustainable Development (CSD) indicators, under the UN Sustainable Development Programme, the division of indicators along the lines of four 'pillars' of sustainability is no longer explicit. This change aims to emphasise the multi-dimensional nature of sustainable development and to reflect the importance of integrating its pillars.

In this newly revised set of indicators, the UN makes explicit reference to the Millennium Development Goals (MDG) derived from the United Nations Millennium Declaration which was adopted by 189 nations in 2000. This has set goals and targets to be achieved by 2015 on the basis of the global situation during the 1990s.

These goals are as follows (see also the revised MDG monitoring framework presented by the Secretary-General of the United Nations in 2007, available at: http://mdgs.un.org/unsd/mdg/Default.aspx):

(1)   Eradicate extreme poverty;
(2)   Achieve universal primary education;
(3)   Promote gender equality and empower women;
(4)   Reduce child mortality;
(5)   Improve maternal health;
(6)   Combat HIV/AIDS, malaria and other diseases;
(7)   Ensure environmental sustainability;
(8)   Develop a global partnership.

The newly revised CSD indicators contain a core set of 50 indicators. These core indicators are part of a larger set of 96 indicators of sustainable development. The introduction of a core set helps to keep the indicator set manageable, whereas the larger set allows the inclusion of additional indicators that enable countries to do a more comprehensive and differentiated assessment of sustainable development. The indicator set retains the thematic/sub-thematic framework that was adopted in 2001, that is, Poverty; Governance; Health; Education; Demographics; Natural hazards; Atmosphere; Land; Oceans, Seas and coasts; Freshwater; Biodiversity; Economic development; Global economic partnership; Consumption and production patterns (for more details, see: United Nations, 2007).

It is clear that these indicators work at a very high strategic level for the nation as a whole. Indeed since 1993 governments have been preparing national reports for submission to the CDS in order to help countries monitor their own progress and share experience and information with others, and to serve as an 'institutional memory' to track and record national actions undertaken to implement Agenda 21.

It would be possible to bring these indicators into the local understanding of sustainability but in most developed countries the local situation would mirror the national situation and it would be difficult to know where to draw the boundaries for data capture. Political boundaries for local authorities are useful but may reflect a rather arbitrary historical precedent. For a new development within the built environment a whole series of other measures might be more appropriate such as the number of vacancies in local schools at different age levels, the number of pupils going on to university education, the age profile of the local population and so forth. This illustrates the point that while we might be able to accept the generic heading we will almost certainly have to develop more sensitive local indicators for a particular situation in a particular locality.

Sustainable Development Indicator (SDI) sets across Europe differ strongly with respect to their size (Hametner & Steurer, 2007). While some countries have a small set with about 20 (headline) indicators (such as France, Germany and Norway), others use rather comprehensive sets with more than 100 indicators (such as Italy, Latvia, Switzerland and the UK). Some of these latter countries also use a smaller number of headline indicators for communication purposes with the general public; and a second, more detailed and extensive set of indicators for specialist use. One advantage of using sets of indicators is that the changes across several dimensions of sustainable development can be separately analysed. Its drawback is that it is difficult to make simple statements regarding the direction of the changes, since the various indicators may move in different directions.

The EU SDI framework themes 'economic development' and 'climate change and energy' are the ones that are addressed most coherently. 'Public health' is another prominent issue in all national SDI sets analysed. In contrast, countries obviously use few or different indicators for the themes 'good governance' and 'global partnership'. This conforms with the revised EU SDI set from 2007 that no longer contains a headline indicator for 'good governance'. As Eurostat's 2007 monitoring report points out, 'good governance is a new area for official statistics, which is reflected in the lack of robust and meaningful indicators on this topic' (Eurostat, 2007b: 268).

Aggregated indicators[1]

The development of a single, composite index implies selecting a number of different components and combining them into a single unit. The obvious advantage of a single set of indicators is that it is straightforward to see if the indicator improves or deteriorates from one period to the next. Furthermore the trade-offs between the different components included in the index (e.g. environmental, social and economic aspects) can be explicitly assessed when calculating the

---

[1] This section is partly taken from: *Indicators of Sustainable Development: Guidelines and Methodologies* © United Nations, 2007. Reproduced with permission.

index. However, the complexities in defining a common matrix for the aggregation are daunting. Composite indices also risk oversimplifying a complex system, and may give potentially misleading signals. In addition, even when using a single index, it will often be necessary to decompose its changes into the various components, to identify which factors contributed most to the observed change.

There have been several efforts to develop aggregated indicators to capture elements of sustainable development. Most aggregate indicators are primarily used for raising public awareness and receive notable attention in the media. Rather than offering a comprehensive view of sustainable development, many of these indicators are specifically focused on the environmental dimension of sustainable development and resource management.

Examples of such indicators include the United Nations 'Human Development Index' (HDI); the World Conservation Union (IUCN) 'Wellbeing Index'; the World Economic Forum (WEF) 'Environmental Sustainability Index' (ESI); the Environmental Performance Index (EPI), the World-Wide Fund for Nature (WWF) 'Living Planet Index'; and Redefining Progress 'Ecological Footprint' and 'Genuine Progress Indicator' (GPI). For instance, the ESI, integrates 76 data sets – tracking natural resource endowments, past and present pollution levels, environmental management efforts and the capacity of a society to improve its environmental performance into 21 indicators and finally into a single index. The EPI aggregates 16 indicators related to resource depletion, pollution, environmental impact and energy efficiency into an index aimed at measuring policy impact.

More comprehensive aggregated indicators on sustainable development include the Adjusted Net Saving and the GPI, developed by the World Bank. It is calculated by subtracting monetary values for resource depletion and damage caused by air pollution from traditional net savings derived from national accounts, and adding expenditures on education. This indicator is also included in the set of CSD indicators in the economic development theme. The GPI, developed and maintained by Redefining Progress, modifies GDP by adding economic contributions of household and volunteer work, but subtracting factors such as crime, pollution and family breakdown in order to arrive at a measure of well-being. It is related to the Index of Sustainable Economic Welfare (ISEW) developed by Daly & Cobb (1989).

A recent index has been developed by UN-HABITAT to measure progress in achieving good urban governance: the Urban Governance Index (UGI). This is being developed in line with the campaign's advocacy and capacity building strategies with a twofold purpose. At the global level, the index will be used to demonstrate the importance of good urban governance in achieving broad development objectives, such as the Millennium Development Goals and those in the Habitat Agenda. At the local level: the index is expected to catalyse local action to improve the quality of urban governance. The structure of the index reflects four core principles of good urban governance promoted by the Campaign as the overall organising framework for the Index: effectiveness, equity, participation and accountability. The index can then be used to test for correlation between the quality of urban governance and issues such as urban poverty reduction, quality of life, city competitiveness and inclusiveness. For more details, see: http://www.unhabitat.org/. However, as Eurostat's 2007 monitoring report points out, 'good governance is a new area for official statistics, which is reflected in the lack of robust and meaningful indicators on this topic' (Eurostat, 2007b: 268).

All these indicators face significant challenges to aggregation related to data availability, methodologies, selection of variables and, in the case of indexes, weighing of the variables. Nonetheless, this ongoing work represents important attempts to aggregate a broad range of variables in order to convey a message that is easy for both decision-makers and civil society to understand.

Discussion

The modern SDI process started at the Rio Earth Summit in 1992. Since that time, many data sets have been developed, to the extent that most national sustainability programmes report progress against indicators that have been derived from a domestic selection process. The indicator sets discussed above are just those being proposed by United Nations initiatives. There are literally hundreds of lists of indicators being developed by a very large number of organisations for a variety of different purposes at different spatial scales.

Recent surveys estimate that there are now over 600 formal or recognised full sustainable indicator sets in use, and many more that have been informally developed, or have been created as a subset of the larger agenda (Horner, 2004; Therivel, 2004; Kazmierczak et al., 2007). A large number of indicators are most frequently used at international level within assessment tools for buildings, neighbourhoods or cities. Chapter 5 will specifically deal with assessment methods and tools for sustainable development. Examples of indicators systems, indices and tools which have been developed for measuring the Sustainable Development and Knowledge Society at different spatial levels, are provided in Table 4.1.

The large number of indicator systems available at present illustrates the important role that indicators and assessment methods play in the study of urban sustainability (Lombardi & Cooper, 2007a,b, 2009; Alwaer & Clements-Croom, 2009; Lombardi et al., 2010). However, using indicators as a means for measuring or assessing the sustainability of cities and practices intended to improve sustainability is being criticised for several reasons.

Table 4.1 Overview of indicators, indices and rating systems at different spatial scale.

Global	Global Competitiveness Report (World Economy Forum), Transnationality Index (UNCTAD), Globalisation Index (A.T. Kearny), Globalisation Index (World Market Research Centre), Global Warming Potentials (IPCC), …
National	ESI (Environmental Sustainability Index), Sustainable national product (SNP), Human development index (HDI), Sustainable economic welfare index (ISEW) (Daly & Cobb, 1989), Emergetical return of investment (Odum & Odum, 1980), Ecological footprint (Rees, 2004), Information Society Index (for KS), WEF (Economic Competitiveness), GIS (Innovation), CPI (corruption perception), HANPP (Human Appropriation of Net Primary Production), Happy Planet Index (HPI), MIPS (Material Input per unit of Service), …
Regional	WWF Sustainability Checklist, Ecological footprint; …
City	Agenda 21, BRE Sustainability Checklist, Community Sustainability Assessment, SPARTACUS (System for Planning and Research in Towns and Cities for Urban Sustainability), SEEDA (South East England Development Agency) Sustainability checklist, SCALDS (Social Cost of Alternative Land Development Scenarios), CITY Green, Quality of Life model, PLACE3S (Planning for Community, Energy, Economy and Environment Sustainability), Citizen Engagement matrix, Democracy indicators, CASBEE (Comprehensive Assessment System for Built Environment Efficacy) for Urban Development, ECOTECT, DOE 2.2, …
Community	Agenda 21, UK Audit Comm Qu-o-L; LEED™ (Leadership in Energy and Environment Design) for Neighbourhood, HQE^{2}R (Sustainable Renovation of Buildings for Sustainable Neighbourhoods), Safety indicators, …
Organisation	GRI, G3, UPBEAT (University Partnership to Benchmark Enterprise and Associated Technologies), IAM (Intangible Assets Monitor), WBCSD Global Water Tool, …
Infrastructure	CEEQUAL (Civil Engineering Environmental Quality Award Scheme)
Buildings	SB (Sustainable Building) Tool, CASBEE (Comprehensive Assessment System for Built Environment Efficacy), LEED™ (Leadership in Energy and Environment Design), PromisE, SPeAR, EcoCal, BREEAM, HK-BEAM, SBAT (Sustainable Building Assessment Tool), EcoQuantum, HQE, SuBETool, Qualitel, EcoEffect, EcoProP (Eco-efficiency indicators for buildings), LiderA, Økoprofil, Legep (Tool for Integrated Lifecycle Performance of Buildings), Green Star, Sustainable Buildings Climate Index (UNEP); Building Design Advisor, Minnesota Sustainable Design Guide,…
Materials	ECOPOINTS/ECOProfile; …

Note: The above list does not aim to be exhaustive.

One of the main concerns is the way in which indicators are developed through often 'ad hoc' processes without a structured framework or consensus on what urban sustainability is (Alberti, 1996; Mitchell, 1999; Bossel, 1998; Lundin & Morrisson, 2002; Lombardi & Cooper, 2009). A further concern is that detailed indicator systems 'are often difficult to operationalize...as precise empirical evidence is not always available or accessible' (Finco & Nijkamp, 2001: 296).

According to Du Plessis (2009), a further problem with aggregate indicator systems is that they break up the problem of urban sustainability into smaller, simpler sub-problems that can then be reduced to specific ratios, for example, energy use per square metre, people per hectare, or number of parking spaces per tenant. This reductionist approach was criticised as early as the 1960s by Jane Jacobs for attempting to turn a problem of disorganised complexity into 'problems of simplicity' that can then be resolved in isolation (Jacobs, 1992[1961]: 438).

As discussed by Bossel (1998), Brugmann (1999), Meadows (1999) and, recently, by Birkeland (2005), many larger-scale applications of indicator systems, including current indicator-based building assessment systems prioritise retrospective analysis over future orientated design; their use encourages measurable and therefore mechanistic approaches at the expense of more innovative systems that defy simplistic measurement; analysis that aggregates measurements obscure total resource flows and systemic interactions and discourage solutions that build on synergies and symbiosis; and data-driven processes come at the expense of mapping systems dynamics (Du Plessis, 2009). This view is supported by Schendler & Udall (2005) who, in their review of the Leadership in Energy and Environmental Design (LEED) rating system, conclude that an indicator-based rating system rewards point-mongering but not integrated design or innovation.

Finally, perhaps most critically, many of the indicators reflect the specific interests of their authors, they are *blunt to say the least* (Bossel, 1998; Sveiby, 2004; Adams, 2006). Even much-used statistics rely on assumptions that are often hidden when we draw our conclusions. In other words, often the decision determines the indicators chosen. As such the development of indicators is 'a dialectic process that goes hand in hand with the development of policies' (Foxon *et al.*, 1999: 146), and not necessarily the product of an empirically derived understanding of what would constitute sustainability in the particular domain in which the indicator is to be used for assessment.

Literature in the field has highlighted the importance of user involvement in indicator design and acceptance (Lombardi & Cooper, 2007b; Alwaer *et al.*, 2008a,b; Alwaer & Clements-Croom, 2009). Stakeholders may have local knowledge that can contribute to more effective indicators. Participation also ensures relevance to the decision-making process, political commitment and ownership of the results. Partici-patory processes can reveal conflicting social interests, values and preferences that must be taken into account. The issue of how to rec-oncile the centralised approaches needed to produce standard compa-rable indicators with the decentralised nature of most decision-making affecting sustainability has not been sufficiently explored, yet (Lombardi *et al.*, 2010).

Summary

As discussed above, a number of sustainability indicator systems exist that can be used at a global, national, regional, city, community, organisation, building or material level. Many of them are applied to assess the state-of-the-art or to monitor the trend from a selected per-spective.

In broad terms the categories identified by the UN do provide a baseline from which to work. However, while the UN indicators pro-vide an indication of the positive and negative impacts of human inter-actions on sustainable development it could be argued that they are not integrated with each other. Each indicator has an influence on another and there is therefore a problem associated with a lack of dis-crete measurement which may mean that too much or too little empha-sis is given to one measure. For example, the economic indicators have an impact throughout the system. If unemployment is low and incomes are high, many of the indicators for poverty will have little impact. However, the economic well-being of a community will also have an impact on what shelter can be provided and what tenure will be expected. It will also affect what can be done to tackle the environmen-tal issues (as many of them require substantial investment) and even perhaps the institutional frameworks within which the total system can operate. This interdependency can create problems in weighting various indicators when deciding what actions to take to improve mat-ters. It may be clear that the economic activities are of such overriding importance that if these are dealt with all other aspects will follow. On the other hand, a rise in economic levels can lead to a major rise in con-sumption which in turn can have an impact on waste, pollution and all those other downside issues. There will be more cars, more packaging, more travelling and so forth. This is why we need to be careful with the indicators that are chosen.

The danger is that we use the measures that already exist but find them inadequate in assessing sustainable development issues. They are attractive because of the fact that they exist already but they can send the wrong signals and distort the behaviour patterns of the decision-makers. In these early years of establishing a new way of looking at development it is inevitable that there will be a period of transition from the old to the new. The speed at which new indicators are accepted and used and the data collected to make them meaningful will depend on the political will of each nation and of the world community.

In the next chapter, we will come back to indicators by analysing how most of them are used at international level within assessment tools for buildings, neighbourhoods or cities.

Assessment Methods 5

In order to make progress, assessment methods must be adopted for determining whether the environmental capacity required for the city of tomorrow and its cultural heritage exists. These tools must be able to evaluate whether the forms of human settlement that surface from urban development processes are, in social terms, sustainable (Deakin *et al.*, 2002a, 2007). Evaluation methods are also required to assess whether progress has been made towards sustainable development and, finally, to justify any decision that might be made now or in the future.

'Evaluation', in this context, is generally defined as 'a technical–scientific procedure for expressing a judgement, based on values, about the impacts of a policy or of an action on the natural and built environment, or for assessing the effects of these impacts on the community' (Bentivegna, 1997: 25). The monitoring of progress is also important because unless we can evaluate what contributes to sustainability it will be very difficult to judge whether a sustainable environment has been created (Brandon, 1998).

Recent surveys reveal that the evaluation methods currently in use are many and there is no agreement among scholars on the theoretical framework within which they can be placed (Horner, 2004; Curwell *et al.*, 2005; Deakin *et al.*, 2007). Additional surveys show that opinion about the potential of environmental assessment is currently divided between those who believe it can promote sustainable development (Bergh *et al.*, 1997; Brandon *et al.*, 1997; Nijkamp & Pepping, 1998), and those who feel existing approaches, exemplified by revealed preference techniques (e.g. contingent valuation methods), are unable to

Evaluating Sustainable Development in the Built Environment, Second Edition
By Peter S. Brandon and Patrizia Lombardi   © 2011 Peter S. Brandon and Patrizia Lombardi

evaluate non-market goods and services and hence are inappropriate for sustainability assessment (Guy & Marvin, 1997).

According to Deakin and Lombardi (2005b) this division of opinion is important for two reasons. Firstly, it illustrates that the scientific community is divided about the quality and value of assessment methods, and second, it undermines the confidence of the professional community in the validity and usefulness of these methods (Pugh, 1996; Cooper, 1997; Cooper & Palmer, 1999).

The authors of this book believe that environmental assessment methods can be used to promote sustainable urban development, and that the root cause of the problem is the absence of a systematic approach towards the assessment of all the activities in the urban development cycle related to significant sustainability issues (Cooper & Curwell, 1998; Curwell *et al.*, 1998). This opinion receives support from the literature (e.g. Hardi & Zdan, 1997; Devuyst, 1999; Devuyst *et al.*, 1999; BEQUEST, 2001; Deakin *et al.*, 2002a, 2007; Curwell *et al.*, 2005a,b; Vreeker *et al.*, 2008).

Techniques for evaluation and monitoring are required to be fair and transparent so that the inputs and outputs are not favouring one particular view or, if they are, that all parties are aware of this limitation. There are in fact very few, if any, techniques that are completely neutral in their advice. Therefore, it is important to know whether an assessment, if it takes place, is confined by the techniques employed to assess the problem. It might be confined to those aspects that are easy to measure. Measures that are easy may not produce the right result.

According to Francescato (1991), there is a distinction between *measurement* and *assessment*. Measurement involves the identification of variables related to sustainable development and the utilisation of technically appropriate data collection and data analysis methods. It mainly deals with sustainability indicators rather than with processes and methods. On the other hand, assessment involves the evaluation of performance against a criterion or a set of criteria. Both performance and criteria can only be defined by a value-based judgement. They are not empirically verifiable. Indeed the term 'performance' must denote a goal-orientated behaviour, that is, a behaviour rendered meaningful by the existence of a criterion that specifies when a goal has been attained.

A major objective of this book is to offer a new framework which is able to make the value-based judgement, mentioned above, intelligible in a consistent manner, and thus to explain the complexity underlying a decision. It is also required to help recognition where limitations and gaps exist in current assessment methods. This will be illustrated in the next chapter.

Since different assessment techniques are required for different dimensions, and for the micro and macro scales, it is also clear that sustainability assessment of the urban environment may need to be a procedure or process that uses various techniques rather than one integrated method (Mitchell, 1996; BEQUEST, 2001; Deakin *et al.*, 2001; Lombardi, 2001; Bentivegna *et al.*, 2002).

This chapter specifically focuses on the assessment methods available, and their classification and use for evaluating sustainable development in the built environment. It also addresses their main limitations, in order that all participants can engage properly within the process (Bentivegna, 1997). However, this chapter will not deal with the problems of sustainability indicators and their classification systems as these were discussed in Chapters 3 and 4.

A directory of assessment methods

A directory of assessment/measurement tools is one of the key requirements to be considered in the development of models and processes to address the evaluation of sustainability. These are sometimes known as evaluation 'tool-kits'.

A number of inventories of assessment methods are currently available for evaluating sustainable development in the built environment. A useful web-book of Advanced Tools for Sustainability Assessment is proposed by the 'SustainabilityA-Test' EU project (FP6 – STREP Priority; area: Global Change and Ecosystems, http://ivm5.ivm.vu.nl/sat/). This includes a database of more than 50 common assessment tools, including: participatory tools, scenario tools, multi-criteria tools, cost–benefit and cost–effectiveness analysis tools, accounting tools, physical analysis tools and models.

A different classification of assessment methods is provided by the recent ECO^2 Cities study (Suzuki *et al.*, 2009), suggesting the following categories: (a) methods for collaborative design and decision-making (these are operational and process methods that help cities undertake leadership and collaboration). (b) Methods for analyzing flows and forms (e.g. materials flow analysis, ecological design, scenario GIS). The combination of analytical methods helps cities to reveal the important relationships between spatial attributes of cities (forms) and their physical resource consumption and emissions (flows). (c) Methods for investment planning assessment (accounting methods, life cycle costing and proactive risk mitigation and adaptation). The fundamental purpose of all these methods is to simplify the process of analysis, assessment and decision-making, providing practical ways for cities to take leadership, collaborate, and analyse and assess various scenarios and projects.

Other studies and projects undertook similar surveys of assessment methods, including the already mentioned LUDA project – *Large Urban Distressed Areas* (Fig. 1.11), which took forward and implemented the BEQUEST project – *Building Environmental Quality Evaluation for Sustainability* (Fig. 3.4). The latter undertook a survey of 61 assessment methods, tools and procedures currently made use of by planners,

Table 5.1   List of assessment methods, tools and procedures.

1. Analysis of Interconnected Decision Areas (AIDA)
2. Analytic Hierarchy Process (AHP)
3. ASSIPAC (Assessing the Sustainability of Societal Initiatives and Proposed Agendas for Change)
4. ATHENA (life cycle impact assessment of building components)
5. BEPAC (Building Environmental Performance Assessment Criteria)
6. BRE Environmental Assessment Method (BREEAM)
7. BRE Environmental Management Toolkits
8. Building Energy Environment (BEE 1.0)
9. Building Environmental Assessment and Rating System (BEARS)
10. Building for Economic and Environmental Sustainability (BEES 2:0)
11. Cluster Evaluation
12. Community Impact Evaluation
13. Concordance Analysis
14. Contingent Valuation Method
15. Cost Benefit Analysis
16. Eco-Effect
17. Eco-Indicator'95
18. Eco-Instal
19. Economic Impact Assessment
20. Ecological Footprint
21. Eco-points (a single unit measurement of environmental impact)
22. Ecopro
23. Eco-Profile (a top-down method for environmental assessment of existing office buildings)
24. EcoProP (a requirements management tool)
25. Eco-Quantum (Eco-Quantum Research and Eco-Quantum Domestic)
26. ENVEST (tool for estimating building life cycle environmental impacts from the early design stage)
27. EIA – Environmental Impact Analysis
28. Environmental Profiles (BRE Methodology for Environmental Profiles of Construction)
29. EQUER
30. ESCALE
31. Financial Evaluation of Sustainable Communities
32. Flag Model
33. Green Building Challenge, currently changed in Sustainable Building (SB) Tool
34. Hedonic analysis
35. Green Guide to Specification (Environmental Profiling System for Building Materials Components)
36. Hochbaukonstruktionen nach ökologischen Gesichtspunkten (SIA D0123)
37. INSURED
38. Leadership in Energy and Environmental Design Green Building Rating System (LEEDTM)
39. Life Cycle Analysis (LCA)
40. Mass Intensity Per Service Unit (MIPS)
41. MASTER Framework (MAnaging Speeds of Traffic on European Roads)
42. Meta Regression Analysis
43. Multi-Criteria Analysis
44. Net Annual Return Model
45. OGIP (Optimierung der Gesamtanforderungen ein Instrument für die Integrale Planung)
46. PAPOOSE

Continues

Table 5.1 *Contd.*

47. PIMWAQ (minimum ecological levels for buildings and ecological degree of development projects)
48. Project Impact Assessment
49. Regime Analysis
50. Quantitative City Model
51. Planning Balance Sheet Analysis
52. Risk Assessment Method(s)
53. SANDAT
54. Semantic Differential
55. Social Impact Assessment
56. SPARTACUS (System for Planning and Research in Towns and Cities for Urban Sustainability)
57. SEA (Strategic Environmental Assessment)
58. Sustainable Cities
59. Sustainable Regions
60. Transit-orientated Settlement
61. Travel Cost Theory

architects, engineers and surveyors to build environmental capacity in all the planning, design, construction and operation stages of the sustainable urban development process (Deakin & Lombardi, 2005a,b; Deakin *et al.*, 2007) (see Table 5.1) and has classified them in terms of 'pre-' and 'post-Brundtland' (see Table 5.2).

The pre-Brundtland directory includes most of the assessment methods in use. They can be traced back to cost–benefit analysis and the critique of the discounting principle upon which this technique of analysis is based (Pearce & Markandya, 1989; Pearce & Turner, 1990; Rydin, 1992). Their development can also be linked to the emergence of hedonic and non-market techniques of analysis such as the contingent value and travel cost method of environmental assessment described below (Brooks *et al.*, 1997; Powell *et al.*, 1997). The pre-Brundtland approach tends to identify impacts (using checklists or matrices, for example) and evaluates development using techniques such as logical frameworks, fiscal analyses, cost–effectiveness analysis and multicriteria assessments. Cost–benefit analysis was also widely used to evaluate outcomes from these techniques, with environmental (non-market good) evaluations using revealed or expressed preference techniques including contingent valuation, hedonic pricing and the travel cost method (see, for example, Pearce & Markandya, 1989).

Since Brundtland and the Agenda 21 (UNCED, 1992) call for the integration of environment and development in decision-making, the science of assessment has been placed under greater scrutiny by environmentalists and critical distinctions have been drawn between ecocentric (those focused on the concept of nature) and anthropocentric

Table 5.2   Classification of assessment methods and tools.

Pre-Brundtland environment in general	Post-Brundtland forms of life cycle assessment	
	Environmental appraisal	**Environmental impact assessment**
Cost–benefit analysis Contingent valuation Hedonic pricing method Travel cost method Multi-criteria analysis	Compatibility matrix Eco-profiling Ecological footprint Environmental auditing Flag method Spider analysis	Community impact evaluation ASSIPAC BEES (Building for Environmental and Economic Sustainability) BREEAM (Building Research Establishment Environmental Assessment Method) LEED™ (Leadership in Energy and Environment Design) CASBEE (Comprehensive Assessment System for Built Environment Efficacy) CASBEE (Comprehensive Assessment System for Built Environment Efficacy) Eco-points Sustainable Building Tool MASTER Framework Meta-analysis (Pentagon method) NAR model Quantitative City model SPARTACUS Sustainable City model Sustainable communities Sustainable regions Transit-orientated settlement

(Adapted and integrated by the authors.
Source: Deakin *et al.*, 2002a; Deakin & Lombardi, 2005a; Deakin *et al.*, 2007.)

(those based around humankind) techniques of analysis (Rees, 1992; Pearce & Warford, 1993). The role of the natural environment as the fundamental support system for all economic and social development is now being increasingly recognised in all forms of assessment. This recognition has led to the development of many methods that focus on energy and material flows, addressing both resource usage and waste arising across a wide range of urban activities. This has in turn led to the development of multi-criteria analysis as a key method in environmental assessment. Examples include ATHENA, a tool for the life-cycle impact assessment of building components, BREEAM and BEES, which address material flows and impacts associated within individual buildings, and the ecological footprint and environmental space methods which can express consumption patterns of cities, regions or countries relative to clearly defined environmental sustainability thresholds (Breheny, 1992; Selman, 1996).

As illustrated in Table 5.2, these assessment methods may be grouped in two major classes: *environmental in general* and those augmenting into various forms of *life-cycle assessments* (Deakin & Lombardi, 2005a,b). The 'environment in general' methods tend to focus on assessments of eco-system integrity. Examples of this class include cost–benefit analysis and multi-criteria analysis. The forms of 'life-cycle assessment' have been sub-classified as *environmental appraisal* and *environmental impact assessments* (complex and advanced evaluations).

The forms of environmental appraisal include the production of a compatibility matrix, the use of eco-profiling measures and environmental auditing techniques. The environmental impact assessments include project, strategic, economic, social and community evaluations, BEES, BREEAM, CASBEE, eco-points and the sustainable building tool. It also includes the MASTER framework, the Pentagon model, the quantifiable city model, SPARTACUS, the sustainable city model, sustainable region, sustainable community and transit-orientated settlement models as advanced forms of environmental assessment.

Several of the latter are complex computer-based urban models integrating extant models of individual urban processes, often within a Geographical Information System (GIS), with other decision–making techniques (e.g. Delphi, multi-criteria analysis) used to evaluate alternative development options within a sustainability framework. They are distinct from conventional urban models in that they are orientated towards sustainable development processes rather than having an objective to further the understanding of urban land use or demographic or transportation processes. All these methods tend to focus on building the environmental capacity needed to not only qualify the integrity of ecosystems but to evaluate the equity, participation and futurity of the economic, social and institutional issues underlying the built environment and the city of tomorrow (Deakin *et al.*, 2002a).

All these methods are used in two ways: to assess the environmental capacity of a specific stage of the urban development process (e.g. planning, design) and, in a more general way, to qualify and evaluate whether the planning and design of the urban development is sustainable. The use of the methods in this more general way illustrates the growing interdisciplinary nature of the assessment exercise.

Methods that assess the planning policy commitment to sustainable development can be applied at the city-regional, district and neighbourhood scale. These levels of analysis are also typical of the methods adopted to assess the planning and design of major infrastructure projects. Methods that assess the design, construction and operational aspects of various buildings relate to the whole building, components and materials as major levels of analysis.

With regard to the time dimension, methods are available to assess urban activities across short, medium and long (>20 years) time periods. However, often the political pressures for urban regeneration means that decisions that reflect evaluation conducted over the short term are taken (<5 years) with little or no consideration of the long term and particularly the inter-generational effects. Thus, as with the design, construction and operation of buildings, short-term considerations often apply and dominate the appraisal in question (see, for example, Curwell & Lombardi, 1999).

An outline summary of the main assessment methods, tools and procedures in use

In this section a short description of the best-known procedures, tools and more assessment methods in use is given, together with their main limitations. These include examples for each of the classes suggested in Table 5.2, pre-Brundtland (or 'environment in general') and post-Brundtland (or 'life-cycle assessments'). It also gives a description of the main evaluation procedures or 'statutory instruments' (Deakin *et al.*, 2007) of environmental assessment methods for evaluating sustainable development included in Table 5.1, that is, environmental impact analysis (EIA) and strategic environmental assessment (SEA). In particular, all the following are described:

Statutory instruments

EIA –   Environmental impact analysis
SEA –   Strategic environmental assessment

Pre-Brundtland

CBA –   Cost–benefit analysis
CVM –   Contingent valuation method
HPM –   Hedonic pricing method
MCA –   Multi-criteria analysis

Post-Brundtland

CIE –   Community impact evaluation
ANP –   Analytic network process
LCA –   Life cycle assessment
BREEAM –   Building Research Establishment Environmental Assessment Method
CASBEE –   Comprehensive Assessment System for Built Environment Efficacy

The reader can find a short explanation of additional methods, procedures and tools, among those included in Table 5.1, at http://research.scpm.salford.ac.uk/bqtoolkit/index2.htm, http://www.luda-europe.net/hb5/select.php; http://www.sue-mot.org.uk/ and http://ivmb.ivm.vu.nl/sat/, http://crisp.cstb.fr/db_ListIS.asp, http://www.aggregain.org.uk/sustainability/sustainability_tools_and_appro aches/index.html, and http://www.smartcommunities.ncat.org/lan duse/tools.shtml.

EIA – environmental impact analysis

EIA is a comprehensive procedure which involves different dimensions of a planning problem such as social, administrative and physical. It has been developed and is used as a means to identify potential damaging effects of proposed developments.

This procedure was born in the USA in 1969 under the National Environmental Policy Act (NEPA) for land use planning. Later, the EEC introduced a common directive to all Member States (85/337/CEE), amended in 2003 (Directive 2003/35/EC), which imposed the application of this EIA to all those projects having strong impacts on environmental resources.

More recently, the United Nations Economic Commission for Europe has recommended the extension of EIA principles to policies, plans and programmes (see SEA, below).

More specifically, EIA is the process of assessing the physical and social impacts of projects. The main aim is to ensure that the environmental implications of decisions are taken into account before the decisions are made. The main purpose is to inform decision-makers and stakeholders about the environmental impacts of a proposal before a decision is made. The process involves an analysis of the likely effects on the environment, recording those effects in a report, undertaking a public consultation exercise on the report, taking into account the comments and the report when making the final decision and informing the public about that decision afterwards. IAIA/IEA (1999) describes the following steps as being part of an EIA process:

- Screening is the process of determining whether an EIA is required for a specific project.
- Scoping is identifying the impacts that are likely to be important.
- Examination of alternatives is the process of determining the environmentally most desired policy option.
- Impact analysis is the process of identifying and predicting the effects of the proposal.
- Mitigation and impact management is the process of establishing measures (or mechanisms) to minimise negative effects.

- Evaluation of significance is the process of evaluation if the impacts that cannot be mitigated are acceptable as compared to the benefits stemming from the proposal.
- Environmental impact statement (EIS) report needs no further explanation.
- Review of the EIS is the process of assessing the quality of the report.
- Decision-making is approving or rejecting the proposal.
- Follow up is the process of monitoring impacts and the effectiveness of mitigation measures as well as reflecting on the EIA to strengthen future applications.

As such the EIA provides the framework for applying all kinds of assessment tools, such as cost–benefit analysis, multi-criteria analysis and various participatory tools (see: Sustainability-test web-book at http://ivm5.ivm.vu.nl/sat/?chap=28).

Strengths and weaknesses

The strength of EIA is that the procedure ensures that environmental impacts are being considered at some point in the decision-making process. Unfortunately, there are still a number of methodological problems associated with non-monetary methods and, more generally, with EIA procedures, such as the following: difficulties in predicting impacts, lack of definition and measurement, monitoring of ongoing environmental change, absence of specific methods, and consultation and participation. At the moment, the analysis is usually limited to a list of environmental factors that do not take into account the complexity of interdependence with the human system.

For further details

❏ Department of the Environment (1993) *Environmental Appraisal of Development Plan: A Good Practice Guide*. HMSO, London.
❏ Warner, M.L. & Preston, E.H. (1984) *Review of Environmental Impact Assessment Methodologies*. US Environmental Protection Agency, Washington, DC.
❏ Zeppetella, A., Bresso, M. & Gamba, G. (1992) *Valutazione ambientale e processi decisionali*. La Nuova Italia Scientifica, Rome.
❏ Bettini, V. (1996) *Elementi di ecologia umana*. Einaudi, Turin.
❏ IAIA/IEA (1999). Principles of Environmental Impact Assessment. Best practice. International Association for Impact Assessment (IAIA) in cooperation with Institute of Environmental Assessment (IEA). USA/UK.
❏ Sheate, W.R., Byran, H., Dagg, S. & Cooper, L. (2005). The relationship between the EIA and SEA directives. *Final Report to the European Commission*. Imperial College London, United Kingdom.

❏ A great number of useful references to EIA-related publications and reports can be found at: http://ec.europa.eu/environment/eia/eia-support.htm; http://www.iaia.org/Non_Members/Activity_Resources/Key_Citations/environm.doc. Furthermore, there is a scientific journal dedicated to EIA: http://www.elsevier.com/locate/eiar.

SEA – strategic environmental assessment

SEA is an integrated assessment approach for policies, plans and programmes as it extends the process of EIA beyond specific projects. The European Commission has long espoused the desirability of extending EIA from projects to higher tiers of action and began consultations on an SEA directive in 1991. This is a consequence of the growing belief that project EIAs may occur too late in the planning process to ensure that all the relevant alternatives and impacts are adequately considered (Therivel *et al.*, 1992; Wood, 1995).

The statutory arm of the SEA Directive on the assessment of the effects of certain plans and programmes on the environment – the EU Directive 2001/42/EC – was implemented in all European Member states as of July 2004. This directive is intended to complement Directive 97/11/EC, which requires an environmental assessment of specific types of project. Its objective is to provide a high level of protection for the environment and contribute to the integration of environmental considerations into the preparation and adoption of plans and programmes with a view to promoting sustainable development.

In comparison with EIA, the focus of evaluation is essentially on development plans' strategies and policies. These are shaped and influenced by many driving forces such as economic, social and political priorities. Individually, or as whole, they can have a significant positive or negative impact on the environment. SEA can be seen as the process by which such impacts are identified and alternative courses of actions are proposed with the aim of considering the impacts at the earliest possible planning stage.

As with project EIA, SEA involves all the following phases:

- 'Screening', investigation of whether the plan or programme falls under the SEA legislation.
- 'Scoping', defining the boundaries of investigation, assessment and assumptions required.
- 'Documentation of the state of the environment', effectively a baseline on which to base judgements.
- 'Determination of the likely (non-marginal) environmental impacts', usually in terms of direction of change rather than firm figures.
- Informing and consulting the public.
- Influencing 'decision-taking' based on the assessment.

- Monitoring of the effects of plans and programmes after their implementation.

The skill of the assessor comes to bear in selecting an appropriate mix from all the different approaches, tools and techniques available.

A considerable range of methods are available, including specific techniques for air quality, health risk and tools such as the Policy Impact Matrix. This allows identification of the impact of each policy on the country's environmental stocks.

Strengths and weaknesses

The main advantages of using environmental assessment at the strategic level are as follows: SEA gets in earlier so that the strategic actions can influence the type of projects to be implemented. It deals with impacts that are difficult to consider at the project level such as the cumulative impacts of multiple projects and large scale impacts (e.g. on biodiversity or global warming). In addition, SEA promotes a better consideration of alternatives since it affects the decision-making process at a stage where more alternatives are available for consideration. It incorporates environmental and sustainability considerations in strategic decision-making. Finally, it facilitates public participation: at a minimum, by providing one opportunity for the public to comment on a strategic action before it is formally agreed; at best, by allowing the public to be actively involved throughout the strategic decision-making process.

However, SEA does have some limitations. It takes time and resources. It relies on various quantitative data that cannot necessarily be provided for an urban area or a district. It is a relatively new process, and so the mechanisms, that is, for baseline data, public participation, etc. may not yet be in place to adequately carry out it. In addition, SEA has to deal with uncertainties from a local up to a global level, which may occur throughout the course of the strategic action (often taking years), for example, floods, technical changes. Thus, it needs to be responsive, adaptable and quick; so potentially is not as detailed and scientific as one might like. Finally, social and economic aspects are usually neglected; this procedure does not take into account problems with multiple causations as can be found, for instance, in urban distressed areas.

For further details

- ❏ Therivel, R., Wilson, E., Thompson, S., Heaney, D. & Pritchard, D. (1992) *Strategic Environmental Assessment*. Earthscan, London.
- ❏ Therivel, R. & Partidario, M.R. (eds) (1996) *The Practice of Strategic Environmental Assessment*. Earthscan, London.
- ❏ European Environmental Bureau (EEB) (2004) Strategic Environmental Assessment: Background; Legal500.com, Strategic

environmental assessment; UK Environment Agency: SEA: Good practice guidelines.

❏ ODPM (2003) SEA Guidance for Planning Authorities; Institute of Environmental management and assessment (IEMA). What is Strategic Environmental Assessment? http://www.unece.org/env/eia/sea_manual/links/report_quality.html

❏ World Bank. Information on SEA development worldwide, and methods and tools for monitoring and evaluation. Available at: http://www.worldbank.org/eapenvironment/sea-asia

CBA – cost–benefit analysis

CBA is a well-known appraisal technique widely applied by both public and private organisations to aid the decision-making process in an early stage of a project's development. The main purpose of undertaking project appraisal at an early stage is to determine the viability of a project development to decide whether or not to build. Project appraisal can also help to establish cost limits or boundaries in order to determine the availability of funding and resources in undertaking the proposals (Ding, 1999).

CBA sets out to measure and compare the total costs and benefits of different projects that are competing for scarce resources by means of a market approach. It is concerned with which alternative gives the best return on capital. Thus it can be used to determine which of the possible projects to finance in order to maximise the return from a given amount of capital or public resources.

There are two types of CBA: economic and social. Economic analysis involves real cash flows that affect the investor. Social analysis involves real and theoretical cash flows that affect the overall welfare of society. Discounted cash flow analysis is used to make judgements about the timing of cash inflows and outflows on rates of return. Most experts agree that timing is fundamental to the correct evaluation of projects involving differential time periods in the payment and receipt of cash and that discounting makes allowance for the financial impact over time (Ashworth & Langston, 2000).

The main components of CBA are project costs and project benefits. Project costs are all expenditures incurred by the developer in completing the project. They are broadly divided into development and operation costs. The development costs refer to the expenditure for the construction of a project. They include land acquisition costs, relocation costs, construction costs and other statutory charges. Operation costs begin when the project finishes on site and continue up to the end of its lifespan. They refer to the energy consumed during the operation period, regular maintenance and repair, major repair work and regular cleaning. However, total project cost should go beyond just the cost incurred and also include costs to the public and the community in terms of environmental quality and impacts. Nevertheless, these costs are often ignored and not included in the project cash flow.

Project benefits are the revenues received from a project development and depend on the attitude of the developer towards the development. If the developer intends to use the completed project, benefits are derived from the selling of goods and services produced by it or revenue from renting out the completed project in the market place. However, the intended use of the project may be for the developer to utilise the building for his own activities, and the benefits from the development may be in terms of a better working environment and increased productivity. Nevertheless, project benefits should also go beyond the actual benefits expressed in monetary terms to take into account environmental issues such as a better living environment, leisure facilities and better traffic arrangements. From an economic point of view, project implementation may include productivity and employment opportunities in the region. However, it is difficult to place a money value on these social benefits (Ding, 1999).

The two most common capital budgeting tools used as selection criteria in CBA are net present value (NPV) and internal rate of return (IRR). Both rely on the existence of costs and benefits over a number of years, and lead to the identification and ranking of projects. Literature on the deficiencies of CBA as a major tool in project evaluation indicates that it neither theoretically nor empirically accounts in a satisfactory way for ecological sustainability objectives. Alternatives have been suggested either to replace CBA completely with another technique that does not need to value environmental cost, or to supplement CBA with a technique that can measure environmental cost in other than monetary terms.

Strengths and weaknesses

The main strength of CBA lies in the systematic way that the technique deals with costs and benefits and thus provides a common metric for ease of comparison. It allows for comparing options and choosing the one with the maximum net benefits (benefits minus costs). Non-market measurements of externalities and other such intangibles leave the technique open to criticism. It raises questions about the distribution of costs and benefits and the equity of development in terms of willingness to pay for or accept. Such intangibles are normally dealt with by contingent valuation method (see next method, below).

Recently assessment methods like community impact analysis (CIA) have tried to solve the major problems that CBA faces, such as the accounting for distributional equity. The concerns about the equity and the non-participatory nature of the technique also apply to more applied versions of the planning balance sheet for CBA, in terms of economic, social or environmental impact assessment (EIA). Each of these techniques also has the added problem of fragmenting the assessment process and not representing sustainability as an exercise in balancing the economic, social and environmental impacts (Deakin et al., 2007).

For further details

❑ Marshall, A. (1949) *Principles of Economics*, 8th edn. Macmillan, London.
❑ Walras, L. (1954) *Elements of Pure Economics*. Allen & Unwin, London.
❑ Misham, E.J. (1964) *Welfare Economics; Five Introductory Essays*. Random House, New York.
❑ Pearce, D. (1983) *Cost Benefit Analysis*. Macmillan, London.
❑ Dasgupta, P. & Pearce, D.W. (1972) *Cost-Benefit Analysis: Theory and Practice*. Barnes & Noble, London.
❑ Pearce, D.W., Atkinson, G. & Mourato, S. (2006) *Cost-Benefit Analysis and the Environment. Recent Developments*. OECD Publications, Paris
❑ Boardman, A., Greenberg, A., Vining, A. & Weimer, D. (1996) *Cost-Benefit Analysis: Concepts and Practice*. Prentice Hall, Upper Saddle River, NJ.
❑ Environment Agency (EA) (2003) *Integrated Appraisal Methods. Final Report*. EA, Bristol.
❑ Gramlich, E. (1990) *Guide to Benefit-Cost Analysis*. Prentice Hall, London.

CVM – contingent valuation method

CVM is a direct method of eliciting valuations from customers by questioning their stated willingness to pay (WTP) for an environmental improvement, or their willingness to accept (WTA) compensation for a fall in the quality of the environment. It has been used for over 40 years in studies of recreation and the environment as a means of obtaining monetary estimates of individuals' preferences for goods, such as clear air, landscape and water quality, which are not traded in the marketplace and thus do not attract a price.

CVM is based on Hicksian measures of utility: welfare change is estimated as the money income adjustment necessary to maintain a constant level of utility before or after the change in provision of the environmental good or service being investigated. In practice, estimates are generated through the use of a questionnaire survey. Here, respondents are presented with a hypothetical scenario in which they are asked to estimate their WTP or WTA compensation for a given level of provision of environmental quality.

The construction of the hypothetical scenario and the design of the questionnaire are both critical to the successful application of the methodology. In practice, the method works best when respondents are asked about things with which they are familiar and when the valuation question is based on a payment mechanism that seems reasonable (Brooks *et al.*, 1997).

This approach is well suited for public goods, such as improvement in environmental quality delivered by a public programme, and non-market private goods, such as reductions in health risks.

Strengths and weaknesses

A major strength of CVM is that it is the only valuation technique capable of measuring 'non-use values', that is, the value that people place on certain goods or natural resources even if they do not use them nor plan to do so in the future. Such non-use values can account for a large fraction of the total value of a good, and are usually attributed to (1) people's desire to preserve natural resources for future generations (bequest value), (2) pure existence values and (3) the desire to conserve a resource in case the individual wishes to use in the future (option value). Another advantage is the method's flexibility, in the sense that it can be used to value a wide array of goods, as long as they are described appropriately and in a realistic fashion to the individuals being surveyed.

The method is appropriate for valuing relatively small changes from the current situation, but should not be applied to valuing entire ecosystems. In addition, it may not be appropriate with goods that the consumers are unfamiliar with or with cases that require some expert knowledge.

For further details

- ❏ Mitchell, R.C. & Carson, R.T. (1989) *Using Surveys to Value Public Goods: The Contingent Valuation Method.* Resources for the Future, Washington, DC.
- ❏ Cummings, R.G., Brookshire, D.S. & Schulze, W.D. (1986) *Valuing Environmental Goods: An Assessment of the Contingent Valuation Method.* Rowman & Allanheld, Totowa, NJ.
- ❏ Bishop, R.C. & Heberlein, T.A. (1979) Measuring values of extra-market goods: are indirect measures biased? *American Journal of Agricultural Economics,* **12**, 926–932.
- ❏ Hanemann, W. M. (1994) Valuing the environment through contingent valuation. *The Journal of Economic Perspectives,* **8** (4), 19–43.
- ❏ Simons, R. & Winson-Geideman, K. (2005) Determining market perceptions on contaminated residential property buyers using contingent valuation surveys. *Journal of Real Estate Research,* **27** (2), 193–220.

❏ Diamond, S. S. (2000) Reference guide on survey research. In: *Reference Manual on Scientific Evidence*, 2nd edn. Federal Judicial Center. Retrieved from Internet: www.fjc.gov/public/pdf.nsf/lookup/sciman00.pdf/$file/sciman00.pdf

HPM – hedonic pricing method

HPM was developed by Rosen (1974), on the earlier consumer theory of Lancaster (1966). It aims to determine the relationship between the attributes of a good and its price.

It is strongly rooted in microeconomic consumer theory and takes as its starting point that any differentiated product unit can be viewed as a bundle of characteristics, each with their own implicit or 'shadow' price. Thus the price of a given property in the built environment can be viewed as the sum of the shadow prices of its characteristics.

Hedonic models are most commonly estimated using regression analysis, although more generalised models, such as sales adjustment grids, are special cases of hedonic models.

A large number of hedonic studies considering the effect of the environmental and neighbourhood variables (such as a forest or a site of special scientific interest; countryside characteristics or the impact of surrounding properties; location and proximity to a high-pressure gas pipeline or aircraft flight path) on house prices have been undertaken. There also exists a significant body of research into the impact architectural style and historic sites have on property valuation.

Strengths and weaknesses

HPM allows one to examine multiple environmental and policy stressors. In addition, it is based on market data. However, the method suffers from econometric identification problems. It is very sensitive to both the choice of functional form and the definition of the extent of the market. Some difficulties also exist with correlation.

For further details

❏ Rosen, S. (1974) Hedonic prices and implicit markets: Production differentiation in pure competition. *Journal of Political Economy*, **82** (1), 34–55.
❏ Lancaster, K.J. (1966) A new approach to consumer theory. *Journal of Political Economy*, **84**, 132–157.
❏ Nelson, J. (1978) Residential choice, hedonic prices, and the demand for urban air quality. *Journal of Urban Economics*, **5**, 357–369.
❏ Ekeland, I., Heckman, J. & Nesheim, L. (2002) Identifying hedonic models. *American Economic Review*, **92** (2) (May), 304–309.

❏ Triplett, J. (2004) *Handbook on Hedonic Indexes and Quality Adjustments in Price Indexes: Special Application to Information Technology Products.* DSTI/DOC(2004)9, OECD Publications, Paris.

MCA – multi-criteria analysis

MCA attracts increasing attention from all around the world as one of the most important alternatives to CBA in decision-making. Due to the fact that environmental impacts are difficult to assess in economic terms within a market approach framework, the MCA techniques of weighting and ranking are investigated and applied to value these impacts in non-monetary terms.

In general, MCA is a family of techniques designed to manage decisional processes typically characterised by many assessment criteria, alternatives and actions. The main advantage of MCA is that it makes it possible to consider a large number of data, relations and objectives (often in conflict) which are generally present in a specific real-world decision problem, so that the decision problem can be studied from multiple angles.

Attaining a solution in a multi-actor and multi-criteria problem is a far from easy task. The presence of several conflicting criteria excludes the existence of an 'optimum', that is, a solution presenting the best score according to all criteria taken into account. Each alternative solution presents advantages and disadvantages, while preferences can vary according to the relative importance attributed to the various criteria in the 'ideal' solution, that is, the alternative having the best performance for all the criteria selected is usually not feasible, and a compromise between realistic solutions is necessary.

The robustness of a MCA result depends on the (un)certainty of the information feeding into the selected criteria, on the priorities given to the criteria (the weights or importance) and the extent to which these weights are commonly agreed upon by stakeholders. Sensitivity analysis can be used to check the robustness of the result for changes in scores and/or weights.

A large number of MCA methods exist to rank, compare and/or select the most suitable policy options according to the chosen criteria. These methods distinguish themselves through the decision rule used (compensatory, partial-compensatory and non-compensatory) and through the type of data they can handle (quantitative, qualitative or mixed).

The concept of compensability is an important factor in these decision rules. Compensability refers to the possibility of compensating what is considered to be a 'bad' performance of a criterion (for example a high environmental impact) with a 'good' performance of another criterion (for example a high income). According to the extent different criteria can be compensated by other criteria, three main types of methods can be distinguished in MCA: compensatory, partial-compensatory and non-compensatory methods.

Within a compensatory method a weak performance of one criterion can be totally compensated by a good performance of another criterion. Within a partial-compensatory method a limit is set to the allowance to compensate weak performances by good ones. A non-compensatory method finally does not allow compensation at all.

In principle each criterion to order policy alternatives can be measured qualitatively or quantitatively. Some MCA methods are designed to process only quantitative information on criteria (weighted summation). In practice, this disadvantage is not very significant because the pluses and minuses used for qualitative assessments are often derived from underlying classes of quantitative data. With a well-chosen method of standardisation such as goal standardisation, this underlying quantitative scale can be used in the weighted summation of these scores. Other methods are designed to process qualitative data (Dominance method, Regime). Finally there is a group of MCA methods that can handle data according to the way it is measured (those with a tick mark under the heading 'mixed data').

In conclusion, the method chosen to apply MCA depends on the decision rule preferred and the type of data available (Lombardi, 1997).

Strengths and weaknesses

MCA is set up to look at the trade-offs between changes in the various assets in question. It has the potential to be used more extensively than others. However, MCA does not permit a decision rule of doing nothing as with the CBA (Pearce, 2005). In addition, it tends to assume all alternatives are discrete (not interdependent) and each option can be pursued without inequitable effects on the distribution of income. Additional methodological difficulties are related to working with multivariate criteria, calculating forms of ranking (usually known as performance) indexes and weighted scores to lead decision-making.

For further details

- ❏ Figueria J., Greco S. & Ehrgott, M. (eds) (2005) *Multiple Criteria Decision Analysis. State of The Art*. Springer, New York.
- ❏ Munda, G. (2005) Measuring sustainability: A multicriteria framework. *Environment, Development and Sustainability*, **7** (1), 117–134.
- ❏ Roy, B. (1985) *Méthodologie multicritère d'aide à la décision*. Economica, Paris.
- ❏ Voogd, H. (1983) *Multi-Criteria Evaluation for Urban and Regional Planning*. Pion, London.

ANP – analytic network process

Inside the large 'family' of MCA methods, the analytic network process (ANP) is a most advanced network version of the analytic hierarchy process (AHP). It consists of clusters, elements, interrelationship between clusters and interrelationship between elements. It allows interactions and feedbacks within and between clusters and provides a process to derive ratio scales priorities from the elements.

Synthetically, the methodology involves the following three main stages.

(1) Structuring the decision-making model. This activity involves an identification of both the elements constituting the decision problem and their relationships. The network model is constituted by various groups (clusters) of elements (nodes), and alternatives or options from which to choose. Literature on ANP shows that there are two possible modelling approaches to ANP: the BOCR (benefits, costs, opportunities, risks) approach which allows simplification of the problem structuring by classifying issues into traditional categories of cost and benefit; and a free-modelling approach, which is not supported by any guide or predetermined structure (Saaty, 2000; Saaty & Vargas, 2006).

(2) Developing pairwise comparison of both elements and clusters to establish relations within the structure. In this step, a series of pairwise comparisons are made by participants to the decision-making process (usually experts, managers and citizens' representatives) to establish the relative importance of decision elements with respect to each component of the network. In pairwise comparisons, a ratio scale of 1–9 is used (named, fundamental scale or Saaty's scale). The numerical judgements established at each level of the network form pair matrixes which are used to derive weighted priority vectors of elements (Saaty, 1980).

(3) Achievement of the final priorities. To obtain the global priority vector of the elements, including the alternatives, the mathematical approach encompasses the use of three kind of 'supermatrices': an initial supermatrix of elements (containing all the priority vectors obtained from the previous stage 2); a weighted supermatrix (obtained by multiplying the initial supermatrix with the weights of the clusters); a 'limit' supermatrix which contains the global priority vector, that is, a long-term stable set of weights (obtained by raising the weighted supermatrix to limiting power).

Strengths and weaknesses

The ANP is the only decision support method which allows to deal systematically with all kinds of dependencies and feedback.

This representation of the problem is more appropriate when dealing with complexity.

However, the BOCR approach for problem structuring is often inadequate to support planning or design alternative choices because it falls into reductionism; while the free-modelling approach is often difficult to be applied in complex decision-making problems. The next chapter will present a new problem structuring approach, named Multi-modal framework which is able to answer this problem since it explains complexity without falling into reductionism and/or subjectivism (Basden, 2008; Lombardi, 2009). Case study 2 in Chapter 7 will provide an application of this method.

Another weakness of ANP is that it is time consuming: it may require the submission of hundreds of pairwise comparison questions to the decision-making participants, depending on the complexity of the network structure.

Finally, the method has not completely solved the problem of *rank-reversal*, that is, the change of the order in the final ranking when one adds one alternative or criterion to the model. This problem was quite problematic in the previous Analytic Hierarchy Process.

For further details

❏ Saaty, T.L. & Vargas, L.G. (2006) *Decision Making with the Analytic Network Process*. Springer Science, New York.
❏ Saaty, T.L. (2000) *Fundamentals of Decision Making and Priority Theory with the Analytic Hierarchy Process*. RWS Publications, Pittsburgh.
❏ Lombardi, P. (2009) Evaluation of sustainable urban redevelopment scenarios. *Proceedings of the Institution of Civil Engineers. Urban Design And Planning*, **162**, 179–186.

CIE – community impact evaluation

CIE is a method that results from the adaptation of cost–benefit analysis to urban and regional planning. Its fundamental feature is that it provides the measure not only of the total costs and benefits but also of their impact on different sectors of the community, enabling the equity and social justice implications of the decisions to be taken into account (Lichfield & Prat, 1998).

The method was originally developed by Lichfield in 1956, with the name of the Planning Balance Sheet or PBS (Lichfield, 1996). PBS was explicitly devised to overcome the fact that many social costs and benefits are not easily measured in monetary terms, so that the results of any social benefit analysis was always liable to objections that some costs or benefits were incorrectly valued. Thus the approach stopped short of assigning values to many cost and benefits, simply indicating where they should be placed on the balance sheet, either as assets or liabilities. CIE further indicates which sections of the community are likely to gain or lose from planning, so taking the distribution effects into account (Brooks *et al.*, 1997).

Strengths and weaknesses

A major strength of CIE is that it emphasises the role of the community and enhances stakeholder participation in the sustainable urban regeneration process. However, problems arise in the selection of data used for evaluating and classifying societal impacts.

For further details

❑ Lichfield, N. (1996) *Community Impact Evaluation*. UCL Press, London.
❑ Lichfield, N. & Prat, A. (1998) Linking ex-ante and ex-post evaluation in British town planning. In: *Evaluation in Planning: Facing the Challenge of Complexity* (eds N. Lichfield, A. Barbanente, D. Borri, A. Kakee & A. Prat), pp. 283–298. Kluwer Academic Publishers, Dordrecht.
❑ Lichfield, N. (1988) *Economics in Urban Conservation*. Cambridge University Press, Cambridge.

LCA – life cycle assessment

Life cycle assessment is a systematic set of procedures for compiling and examining the inputs and outputs of materials and energy and the associated environmental impacts directly attributable to the functioning of a product or service system throughout its life cycle. The life cycle is considered to include the consecutive and interlinked stages of a product or service system, from the extraction of natural resources to the final disposal. There are four interlinked components of LCA:

(1) Goal definition and scoping: identifying the LCA's purpose and the expected outputs from the analysis; determining the boundaries in terms of what is and is not to be included in the analysis and assumptions based upon the goal definition;
(2) Life cycle inventory: quantifying the energy and raw material inputs and environmental releases to air, land and water associated with each stage of the life cycle;
(3) Impact analysis: assessing the impact on human health and the environment associated with the consumption of energy and raw materials and the associated environmental releases, as quantified by the inventory;
(4) Improvement analysis: evaluating the opportunities to reduce energy, material inputs (e.g. through resource efficiency measures

or recycling) and the environmental impacts at each stage of the product life cycle.

LCA's rigorous methodology is based on ISO 14040 and BS EN ISO 14041–43. Software tools exist for evaluations of buildings, for example, BEES – Building for Environmental and Economic Sustainability or BRE – Building Research Establishment (see below).

Strengths and weaknesses

LCA allows clear comparisons between product systems, leading to greater understanding of the way in which environmental impacts are generated. A number of weaknesses are: the lack of general consensus on the metrics for measuring environmental impact; the lack of a systematical consideration of the economic and social impacts; the costly and time-consuming procedure which may limit the use of the techniques in both the public and private sectors.

For further details

❏   Edwards, S. & Bennett, P. (2003). Construction products and life-cycle thinking. *UNEP Industry and Environment* (joint edition combining Sustainable Building & Construction). UNEP, **26** (2–3), 57–62.
❏   Environment Agency (EA). (2003). *Integrated Appraisal Methods. Final Report*. EA, Bristol.
❏   Graedel, T.E. (1998) *Streamlined Life-Cycle Assessment*. Prentice Hall, New Jersey.
❏   ISO (2000) *Life Cycle Assessment – Principles and Guidelines*. ISO CD 14 0402. International Standard Organization, Geneva.
❏   Handbook 5, *The LUDA Assessment Decision Support System*. http://www.luda-europe.net/hb5/files/method_descriptions/pdf/new/life_cycle_assessment.pdf

BREEAM – Building Research Establishment Environmental Assessment Method

BREEAM is a scheme for environmental labelling of buildings developed by the Building Research Establishment (BRE) in collaboration with a number of private sector sponsors. The basis of the scheme is a certificate awarded to individual buildings stating clearly the performance of the building against a set of defined environmental criteria. The scheme is voluntary and self-financing. Assessment is carried out by independent assessors licensed by BRE.

The first version, launched in 1990, was for new office buildings assessed at the design scheme stage. This was updated in 1993 to reflect developing knowledge and experience gained in the operation of the scheme. Other design stage schemes have been launched for super-markets, new houses, light industrial buildings and others.

The scheme embraces a large range of environmental issues grouped under three main headings:

(1) *Global issues*, which include CO_2 emissions resulting from energy use, acid rain, ozone depletion due to chlorofluorocarbons/ HCFCs, natural resources and recyclable materials, storage of recyclable materials and designing for longevity.

(2) *Local issues*, which include transport and cyclists' facilities, water economy, noise, local wind effects, overshadowing of other buildings and land, reuse of derelict/contaminated land and ecological value of the site.

(3) *Indoor issues*, which include hazardous materials, natural lighting, artificial lighting, thermal comfort and overheating and ventilation.

Issues receive individual, discrete credits. A credit signifies that the design satisfies the criteria for the issue concerned but there is no attempt at weighting the diverse issues. A summary of the performance is included; this is expressed as a single rating of 'fair', 'good', 'very good' or 'excellent', based on a minimum level of credits achieved in each of the three classes of environmental issues. This rating is simply a measure of the balance of the design approach across the three classes. A rating of 'excellent' indicates a high standard of performance across the range of impacts, although there may still be scope for further refinement.

Similar schemes to BREEAM are LEED™ in USA, HQE by the CSTB (Centre scientifique et technique du bâtiment) in France and SBTool, formerly known as GBTool, as an international project. The latter is the software implementation of the Green Building Challenge (GBC) assessment method that has been under development since 1996. The GBC process was launched by Natural Resources Canada, but responsibility was handed over to the International Initiative for a Sustainable Built Environment (iiSBE) in 2002.

The BREEAM standard is now being exported to regions such as the Gulf (BREEAM Gulf) and Europe. On June 2009, it was announced that the BRE had signed a Memorandum of Understanding to work together with the French CSTB and its subsidiary CertiVéA to develop a pan-European building environmental assessment method. The CSTB are one of the organisations behind the French Haute Qualité Environnementale (High Environmental Quality) standard, which has similarities to BREEAM. It is hoped that this will eventually result in the development and promotion of a common assessment method throughout the European Union, aligned with the work of the international Sustainable Building Alliance, a network whose overall objective is to develop common metrics for the key issues and allow comparisons between the different rating schemes.

Strengths and weaknesses

BREEAM and other similar rating methodologies have the potential to turn the generic concept of sustainability into action. These permit a ranking of buildings in terms of ecological performance. Today, however, the international community is still very far from achieving a standardised set of indicators, while international institutions are still trying to develop a generic indicator for measuring and monitoring sustainable development. The many existing measures vary enormously both in their complexity and in their application.

A further problem of current indicator-based building assessment systems, as discussed previously in Chapter 3, is that these prioritise retrospective analysis over future-orientated design; their use encourages measurable and therefore mechanistic approaches at the expense of more innovative systems that defy simplistic measurement (Schendler & Udall, 2005; Du Plessis, 2009).

For further details

❑ Birtles, T. (1997) Environmental impact evaluation of buildings and cities for sustainability. In: *Evaluation in the Built Environment for Sustainability* (eds P. Brandon *et al.*), pp. 211–223. E & FN Spon, London.
❑ Prior, J. (ed.) (1993) *Building Research Establishment Environment Assessment Method (BREEAM), Version 1/93: New Offices*. Building Research Establishment Report, 2nd edn.
❑ Cole, R.J., Rousseau, D. & Theaker, I.T. (1993) *Building Environmental Performance Assessment Criteria, Version 1: Office Buildings*. The BEPAC Foundation, Vancouver.
❑ Cole R. & Lorch L. (eds) (2003) *Buildings, Culture & Environment*. Blackwell, Oxford.

CASBEE – Comprehensive Assessment System for Built Environment Efficacy

CASBEE is a recent built environment assessment tool developed in 2001 as a collaborative government, academic and industry (building designers, contractors, subcontractors, utilities, building owners) project with the support of the Ministry of Land, Infrastructure, Transport and Tourism in Japan. It is managed by the Japan GreenBuild Council (JaGBC)/Japan Sustainable Building Consortium (JSBC) who is continuously updating the CASBEE system.

Currently, all the following CASBEE certifications are available: for New Construction; for New Construction (Brief version); for an Existing Building; for Renovation; for Heat Island; for Urban Development; for an Urban Area + Buildings; for a Home (Detached Houses) (http://www.ibec.or.jp/CASBEE/english/index.htm).

CASBEE corresponds to a 'family' of tools which encompass the whole building life cycle process. It includes: CASBEE for Pre-design, CASBEE for New Construction, CASBEE for Existing Building and CASBEE for Renovation, to serve at each stage of the design process. Each of them is intended for a separate purpose and target user, and is designed to accommodate a wide range of uses (offices, schools, apartments, etc.) in the evaluated buildings.

Potential CASBEE-certified buildings are assessed by both their environmental efficiency and their impact on the overall environment. In this assessment system, the quality of the building (Q) is addressed in relation to the environmental load (L) giving a factor of building environmental efficiency (BEE). The ranking assigns separate scores for Q and L and ultimately gives an assessment of BEE, based on those results. Each of these areas are broken down into greater detail, and ranked in order, from Excellent (S), Very Good (A), Good (B+), Fairly Poor (B−) and Poor (C).

According to the CASBEE For New Construction 2008 Technical Manual, this approach is employed because 'higher marks for improving load reduction quality' is easier to understand than 'higher marks for load reduction' as an assessment system, just as 'improvements in quality and performance earn higher marks'.

CASBEE covers the following four assessment fields: (1) energy efficiency, (2) resource efficiency, (3) local environment and (4) indoor environment. These four fields are largely the same as the target fields for the existing assessment tools such as BREEAM or LEED (Leadership in Energy and Environmental Design), but they do not necessarily represent the same concepts, so it is difficult to deal with them on the same basis.

Environmental quality (Q) consists of the indoor environment (including acoustics, lighting, thermal comfort and air quality), service quality (including adaptability, flexibility and durability − not present in tools like BREEAM or LEED) and the outdoor environment. Environmental load (L) consists of energy, materials and off-site environment. Compared with other existing tools, in the outdoor environment, for instance, there is a fundamental difference in terms of the absence of biotopes in the assessment (no compensation for green space) and the limitation to urban environment, including the reduction for the heat island effect (Kawazu *et al.*, 2005).

Finally, although this tool is the equivalent of BREEAM or LEED Platinum certification in the United States, achieving the highest level of sustainability differs slightly in the two countries, both in philosophy and process. For example, in energy a building achieves an excellent rating easier in BREEAM and CASBEE 25% compared to LEED 50%. The process of obtaining CASBEE certification differs from LEED also. LEED certification starts at the beginning of the design process, with review and comments taking place throughout the design and construction of a project. Though CASBEE's latest version for New Construction ranking uses pre-design tools, certification consists more of site visits after the building is completed.

Strengths and weaknesses

Compared with existing building rating tools, the main innovation of CASBEE is the concept of Building Environmental Efficiency (BEE). This, originally derived from eco-efficiency, establishes the connection between the quality and quantity of environment, and expresses the goal of sustainable buildings: through minimum environment impact to get maximum quality improvement (Tian, 2005). A further strong point of CASBEE is the visual way it can show factor × improvement.

Finally, the tool has been jointly developed by all stakeholders and therefore it is positioned as central in Sustainable Building development (Klinckenberg & Sunikka, 2007). CASBEE has become a definition of sustainable building and its quality assurance in Japan where the use of the tool is encouraged in several policy documents, for example, the Ministry of Land, Infrastructure, Transport (MLIT) Action Plan (2008) and the Kyoto Protocol Target Achievement Plan (Matsuo, 2006). Here, the tool is integrated to other policy tools and certificates are used in the market transformation strategy to address purchasing behaviour (Sunikka-Blank, unpublished). For instance, in some cities CASBEE is used as a judging tool for subsidies given to housing projects (Osaka City) and for a lower interest mortgage (Kawasaki City, Sapporo City and Kitakyushu City, Nagoya).

One of the major weaknesses of this approach is that it is time consuming. Expert interviews provided by Sunikka-Blank (unpublished) indicate that, in practice, the use is limited due to the excessive criteria – with its six elements and numerous subcategories the assessment normally takes 3–7 days although a simpler version can be done in 2 h, where it is possible for local governments to feed in data on local climate and policy priorities.

Further weaknesses have been highlighted by Tian (2005) in relation to the not always clear relationship between Q and L which affects the impartiality of the assessment. The large number of qualitative criteria in CASBEE affects the degree of discretion of the results.

For further details

- ❏ http://www.ibec.or.jp/CASBEE/english/index.htm
- ❏ Endo, J., Murakami, S., Ikaga, T., Iwamura, K., Sakamoto, Y., Yashiro, T. & Bokagi, K. (2005) Extended framework of CASBEE; designing an assessment system of buildings for all lifecycle stages based on the concept of eco-efficiency. *Proceedings of The 2005*

World Sustainable Building Conference (SB05Tokyo), Tokyo, 27–29 September 2005.

❏ Kawazu, Y., Shimada, N., Yakoo, N. & Oka, T. (2005) Comparison of the assessment results of BREEAM, LEED, GBTool and CASBEE. *Proceedings of the 2005 World Sustainable Building Conference* (SB05Tokyo), Tokyo, 27–29 September 2005.

❏ CASBEE Osaka (Comprehensive Assessment System for Building Environmental Efficiency for Osaka City).

❏ http://www.globest.com/news/1386_1386/insider/178149-1.html

The evaluation methods and procedures previously described belong to different scientific disciplines and technical fields, such as economics, engineering, technology and planning. Most of them are able to deal with different sustainable development issues at the same time (e.g. multi-criteria analysis) but some can only deal with one or a few of them (e.g. financial appraisal). None is able to tackle all the sustainable development issues in a comprehensive manner (Deakin *et al.*, 2002a; Horner, 2004; Deakin & Lombardi, 2005a,b).

According to Horner (2004) and Deakin & Lombardi (2005b), the environmental dimension of sustainable development has the greatest coverage among the main assessment methods in use. Here, issues such as resource consumption, pollution and impacts on biodiversity and people's health are considered, using methods that include cost–benefit analysis and revealed/expressed preference techniques (contingent valuation, travel cost and hedonic pricing), building scale methods (BREEAM, LEED™, SB Tool, CASBEE), and methods to evaluate infrastructure and particularly planning policy. The latter is addressed by EIA, SEA and community impact analysis (CIE).

The social and economic sustainable development elements address, respectively, considerations relating to the financing of the infrastructure and utilities required for the desired urban development, access to services, people's safety and security, and aesthetic issues. With the application of the pre-Brundtland 'environment in general' methods, both economic and social analyses are confined to the planning, property development and design stages (thus addressing assessment of policy, programme and infrastructure provision), and do not address the construction of projects, or the installation of operations. Conversely, the 'post Brundtland' methods attempt to address social and economic issues in addition to their environmental focus, although this treatment is piecemeal.

It is apparent that these life-cycle assessment methods often address social or economic issues using approaches from the former group. Examples can be found in the sustainable city models, in the mix of formal life-cycle assessment and CBA (e.g. Glasson *et al.*, 1994; Lichfield, 1996; Therivel, 1998), in meta-analysis of policy planning and infrastructure design (Bergh *et al.*, 1997), and in the transformation of multi-criteria assessments into regime analysis, flag method, spider analysis and analytic network process so as to resolve environmental problems arising from alternative economic and social structures relating to sustainable development (Bizarro & Nijkamp, 1997; Deakin *et al.*, 2002a).

Another observation that can be drawn from this transformation of environmental evaluation methods, as pointed out by Deakin *et al.* (2007: 13–14), is related to the way in which the 'hard' (environment) and 'soft' (economic and social) components of sustainable development form part of the assessment methodology. For instance, with BEES, the biophysical aspects of the ecosystem are the main issues. Assessment methods integrating the biophysical and the social (environmental, economic and social) issues, include BREEAM and the sustainable city model. 'Such assessment methods are trans-disciplinary, cutting across traditional disciplines in the interests of advancing a methodology capable of providing evaluations which are more integrated in nature'.

A major problem with approaches based on economic utility theory, such as cost benefit analysis, which are widely applied in spatial planning is that the long-term effects of human actions are often ignored. Opposite approaches based on argumentation and rhetoric or nominalistic theories (Zeppetella, 1997; Khakee, 1998), such as multi-criteria analysis methods avoid the dangers of reductionism by acknowledging the views and wishes of all and sundry. However, there are still some problems; for example, there is no standard by which to arrive at consensus. In addition, there is the danger, in practice, that 'those who shout loudest get heard', while less articulate groups and those who cannot represent their rights, such as animals or young children, tend to get ignored unless their cause is championed by others (Lombardi & Basden, 1997).

Deakin *et al.* (2002a) have also shown that a number of gaps exist in relation to many interrelated activities of the urban development process, such as in scientific and human development and institutional development. Perhaps the most obvious 'gap' evident is the relative absence of methods addressing institutional issues such as governance, justice and ethics with respect to development. Unfortunately, there is evidence to indicate that methods addressing these issues experience extreme difficulty in dealing with the complexity of institutional structures and the range of stakeholder interests this introduces into assessment. Thus methods to assess the capability of institutional structures to promote sustainable development remain poorly developed, despite the evident need for them (Deakin *et al.*, 2001; Deakin & Lombardi, 2005b).

Although MCA methods have often proved able to provide a guide for selecting suitable planning and design solutions in evaluation, they lack content and a conceptual framework or theoretical guide that can help designers and decision-makers to structure the problem of sustainability in the built environment. Consequently, the selection of the most appropriate criteria to be used in the evaluation process is often developed on an intuitive basis or in a non-optimal manner (see case studies n.1 and 3 in Chapter 7; also Nijkamp, 2007).

In the next chapter a new framework will be illustrated, which is flexible and able to take into account various situations and planning and design problems. This includes an ordered list of aspects which guides the identification of relevant criteria for evaluating sustainable development in an urban context and, at the same time, is easily checked by users.

Although, initially, this approach was not understood by the authors (Brandon & Lombardi, 2005) as an alternative final method for problem solving in planning and construction, it has been recently identified as 'Multi-modal Human Cosmonomic Modelling' and classified within the cluster of 'systems', in a recent survey of assessment methods (Deakin *et al.*, 2007: 10–11).

Summary and conclusions

This chapter has examined some of the major evaluation methods currently in use for assessing the sustainable development of an urban settlement or a building. It has been noted that there are a wide variety of evaluation approaches to sustainable development in planning, design and construction but little agreement among scholars on the theoretical framework to be used. For instance, developers of assessment models for sustainability at the urban scale, such as the Quantifiable City Model by May *et al.* (1997), mostly take into account socio-economic and physical aspects of a sustainable development, while environmental assessment methods at the building scale, such as BREEAM in the UK (1993) and BEPAC in Canada (1995) concentrate on the environmental and ecological issues related to sustainability and quality of life.

All the methods are constrained and limited and take into consideration only a few of the many aspects required for developing sustainable solutions. Most evaluations are mainly technical and economic and there is not a mechanism or tool that is able to take into account all sustainability issues in a comprehensive manner.

Decision-making for sustainable development requires holistic approaches and a change from current methods both in the emphasis and in the criteria by which development is judged. There needs to be a movement towards environmental protection and social/economic objectives. It needs to build social consensus as well as to improve technical performances. Among others, Nijkamp (1991), Brandon *et al.* (1997)

and Lichfield *et al.* (1998) suggest that an appropriate evaluation approach should have a number of characteristics, as follows:

❑ *Include all the relevant effects* generated by urban projects on the environment in the long term.
❑ *Provide information* on the social, economic and environmental consequences of a design process through time.
❑ *Integrate different evaluation approaches* and scientific disciplines (a *multi-disciplinary* approach) required to verify the socio-economic and environmental compatibility of urban projects.
❑ *Take into account the different viewpoints*, objectives and interests of decision-makers, stakeholders and citizens within a participation process (a *pluralistic* or *multi-person* approach).

Since the time when Agenda 21 (UNCED, 1992) called for the integration of environment protection and socio-economic development in decision-making, impact assessment has advanced considerably (Deakin *et al.*, 2002b). Within the EU, EIA has been introduced as a statutory instrument (directive 85/337/EEC and amendment 97/11/EC), and the critique of EIA as solely a project-specific assessment approach (e.g. Glasson *et al.*, 1994) has led to its extension to plans and programmes under the proposed EU SEA directive. This shift in emphasis is significant as it requires the development of procedures for the procurement and assessment of plans, programmes and projects able to satisfy the policy commitment to sustainable development (O'Conner, 1998; Devuyst, 1999; Selman, 2000).

According to Deakin *et al.* (2002b), a further key gain has been the evolution of methods that attempt to assess the impact of development in terms of material and energy flows, across most stages of the urban life cycle. These present opportunities to assess developments with respect to ecological limits, although in practice few are able to achieve this at present. While this suggests that much progress has been made post-Brundtland to improve the theory of assessment, it is recognised that the practice of assessment lags well behind. New methods remain largely experimental, with relatively few applications in practice. Meanwhile, many of the methods currently in widespread use fail to make assessments that adequately address the issues underlying the sustainable urban development process (Cooper, 1997, 1999; Cooper & Curwell, 1998; Curwell *et al.*, 2005; Deakin *et al.*, 2007).

The review of assessment methods and procedures reported in this chapter have pointed out several critical points, as follows.

❑ Firstly, those sustainability issues that are poorly addressed by available assessment techniques have been identified. Method 'gaps' are significantly evident in the social and institutional aspects of sustainable development. Method developments are required in this area, but perhaps the difficulty current methods have in dealing with the complexity of institutional structures and associated stakeholder interests presents the greatest challenge (Deakin *et al.*, 2002b; Deakin & Lombardi, 2005b).

❏ Developments also need to encourage the integration of assessment methods with other assessment techniques alluded to earlier as being beyond the scope of this chapter. In particular, there remains considerable scope for integration of assessment methods with sustainability indicators, and with urban sustainability models (Deakin *et al.*, 2002b; Vreeker *et al.*, 2008). Both attempt to address the urban system holistically, but the former presents essential sustainability benchmarks while the latter presents the opportunity to seek preferred development alternatives for complex urban systems which are otherwise difficult to assess (Mitchell, 1999).

❏ A further aspect, which has been suggested by Mitchell (1996), Deakin *et al.* (2002b) and Therivel (2004), is the need to ensure that the emerging sustainable development assessment techniques are applied and audited. Methods must move quickly beyond the experimental phase and be applied in practice, so that conventional techniques are replaced by those that better address sustainability concerns. This may require the application of multiple methods (conventional and experimental) in parallel to accelerate the learning process and identify how both theory and practice can be improved. Critically, such applications will require greater use of auditing and post-assessment monitoring to determine how well methods perform.

❏ Finally, research is required into methods of assessing the aggregate effect of policy and urban developments on urban sustainable development. This could take the form of assessment method integration as in the above-mentioned emerging models, or development of unifying frameworks and analytical procedures as argued for by Hardi and Zdan (1997) and Devuyst (1999) and illustrated by Curwell *et al.* (1999). However, in practice the effectiveness of both approaches will rely on the development of adaptive management structures within decision-making institutions, so that they are able understand, respond to and foster improvement of the sustainability assessment procedures (Deakin *et al.*, 2002a).

The above results have also been confirmed by the reviews of assessment methods and tools provided by the SUE-MOT studies (Horner, 2004; Therivel, 2004), under the EPSRC's Sustainable Urban Environment research programme.

In the next chapter a new structure to assist the selection of assessment techniques and sustainability indicators will be illustrated. This aims to overcome most of the shortcomings highlighted in the previous chapters in relation to current frameworks and approaches, so as to address sustainable urban development issues in a pragmatic and integrated manner. It specifically aims to address the need for a holistic and a systemic approach which is needed for sustainable urban development. This means that the most significant elements and linkages in the system are addressed, and the 'technical' aspects of assessment, and the 'soft' institutional systems that direct and respond to them, evolve together.

A Proposed Framework for Evaluating Sustainable Development

Previous chapters have provided a basis for viewing sustainable development and have tried to establish some guiding principles. They have also looked in outline at some of the approaches that are being taken by others and their success or otherwise.

One of the major requirements identified in Chapter 1 was the need for structure. This is not a new problem for an emerging discipline. Every new avenue for study has to go through the process of giving the subject form. This allows the subject to progress and encourages the building blocks of knowledge to be developed in a coherent and systematic way so that the full meaning and extent of the subject can be discussed and shared by those working in the field, and subsequently by those who will use and be the beneficiaries of the system. If there is not a commonly agreed structure the following problems can arise:

❏ The topic loses coherence and understanding is difficult.
❏ It is difficult to share knowledge in a meaningful way.
❏ Vocabulary can be too diverse. The same topic can be described in different ways and meanings are not shared.
❏ It is difficult to build knowledge in a systematic way.
❏ Viewed by those who are outside the system (as well as those inside), the subject appears to be ill-formed and it may even be dismissed as unimportant or irrelevant or insufficiently thought through.
❏ Collection of data becomes problematic as standardisation is difficult because of the different competing structures all trying to do the same thing.

Evaluating Sustainable Development in the Built Environment, Second Edition
By Peter S. Brandon and Patrizia Lombardi © 2011 Peter S. Brandon and Patrizia Lombardi

❑ There is little theoretical underpinning for the subject as a whole. It rests on a collection of apparently unrelated topics that cannot be linked together.
❑ A reductionist view prevails and this can mean that the holistic approach is lost.
❑ Sustainable development at the present time suffers from many of the above problems and therefore can often be seen by sceptics as having little substance. A framework or structure does help enormously in people's understanding of what is included in a topic and this in turn can give it more substance than a series of ad hoc studies. This chapter attempts to provide such a structure from what the authors believe to be a useful theoretical base.

The need for a holistic and integrated framework

Decision-making for sustainable development in the built environment requires new approaches that are able to integrate and synthesise all the dimensions of an urban system (or a building) and different points of view, in a holistic manner (Deakin et al., 2001).

Much of the early work on sustainable development in the built environment was focused on the ecological dimension of the problem, as reflected in the policy agendas of various local authorities. On the other hand, the softer and more 'fuzzy' dimensions of sustainable urban development (e.g. political, social, cultural, aesthetic and so forth) are still poorly addressed in decision-making, while contemporary analytical tools do not handle them adequately.

As already pointed out in a previous chapter, recent surveys of environmental assessment (Deakin et al., 2001; Horner, 2004; Therivel, 2004; Curwell et al., 2005a,b; Deakin et al., 2007) have examined how the methods are currently being used. Only in 'life-cycle assessment' is there evidence to suggest that the assessments augment environmental capacity to include equity, public participation and futurity within the sustainable development issues of the economic and social structures in question (i.e. the economic and social structures underlying the city of tomorrow and its cultural heritage). Even with this group of methods, there is clear evidence to show that the methods experience noticeable difficulties in dealing with the complexity of institutional structures and the range of stakeholder interests that this introduces into any such assessment (Nath et al., 1996; Lombardi, 2001).

At present, there is a need for greater integration at the level of local decision-making. This is often emphasised in the literature through the concept of what is sometimes called 'co-evolutionary interdependence' between the physical environment and the human environment (Faucheux et al., 1996; Faucheux and O'Conner, 1998; O'Conner, 1998;

Capello *et al.*, 1999; Du Plessis, 2008). This approach suggests that the development of the environmental, economic and social dimensions is all complementary. There is a serious lack of understanding regarding the complex dynamic interactions and feedback effects of socio-economic–technological activities and the earth's ability to sustain itself. For example, the impact of social organisation on the built environment and subsequently on its sustainability is not well understood.

A further problem is that experts use a specialised and codified vocabulary that is not common to all the disciplines and stakeholders involved in the planning process. Each discipline brings its own agenda, its own classification system and its own techniques to the problem. Often the disciplines are unwilling (or unable) to consider the views represented by others because there is not a common language or a systematic methodology that will allow a fruitful dialogue to take place (Lombardi & Brandon, 1997). Consequently, there is still a need to incorporate sustainable development principles and criteria in current decision-making processes.

Devising strategies for the sustainable development of cities is difficult, not just because the nature of a city is complex, but also because the concept is ambiguous, multi-dimensional and generally not easy to understand outside the single issue of environmental protection. Mitchell (1996) suggests that effective urban sustainable development strategies and sustainable development plans can best be identified by ensuring that decision-makers and developers are adequately briefed on sustainable development issues, local characteristics and community needs. This process requires the application of a suitable operational framework, and an evaluation method or approach that is able to guide developers through the decision-making. However, at the moment, such a structure for organising the information required in decision-making is not yet available or agreed on among the different disciplines and fields of activities.

The lack of an agreed structure that can help decision-making processes achieve greater sustainability is a major problem. This chapter suggests an integrating mechanism or framework which could bring together the diversity of interests necessary to assess the impact of the built environment and urban design on urban sustainable development. This framework could be used by all stakeholders in the development process including political and technical decision-makers, public local control officers, planners and designers, citizens, lawyers and financial advisers, enabling them to check a design or a plan in the context of sustainable development and to learn from it. It should be able to assist the process of devising sustainable planning strategies, ensuring that all sustainable development aspects and quality-of-life issues are included and nested into each other. It also provides a structure that can be used at different levels of detail, thus providing a vehicle that all stakeholders can engage in but contribute to at different levels of complexity.

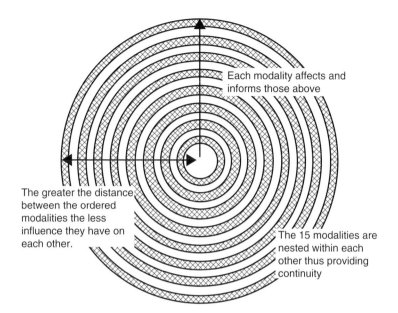

Figure 6.1 Features of the framework.

The basis for this framework is the work of the Dutch philosopher Herman Dooyeweerd (1894–1975) who developed what he called a 'Theory of the Cosmonomic Idea of Reality' (Dooyeweerd, 1955). This theory attempts to integrate all of the aspects of the universe in a meaningful form to help explain structure and relationships in a holistic way. At the very least it provides a checklist of things to examine in order to establish whether a development is sustainable. At best it provides a means of explaining the interdependence between aspects of the urban environment and can be linked to the wider sustainable development agenda. Its holism allows an integrated view of the issue and also assists in explaining what is meant by, and what contributes to, sustainable development (see Appendix A).

As stated earlier, there is the added advantage that this approach is simple in concept and can be used effectively by all stakeholders at different levels of understanding (see Fig. 6.1). The underpinning philosophy, however, is complex and is based on a Christian view of the world not unlike the value systems adopted by the Western democracies. However, in informal conversations with people from other cultures and faiths it has proved to be acceptable as a way forward since it recognises all issues in which human beings are engaged with the universe. The interpretation of content may differ but the structure remains the same.

The theoretical underpinning of the framework

The challenge for political and technical actors (planners, designers and urban authorities) is to devise strategies and policies, urban plans and projects that can guide cities and other aspects of the built environment along a more sustainable development path. At present, there is a lack of a decision-support framework, system or tool, which is both comprehensive and holistic, to harmonise the different aspects of sustainable development in planning and design. This section introduces a possible approach to this problem.

As stated earlier, the framework is supported by Dooyeweerd's theory of the 'Cosmonomic Idea of Reality' (Dooyeweerd, 1968, 1979). This has recently been postulated in a number of studies related to cybernetics, information systems and organisation learning, mainly because it offers an extremely useful checklist to guide systems development and usage, ensuring that not only one but all aspects of human life, from the quantitative to the highest-level value system, are present in the design. In addition, it has been studied and developed by other contemporary authors such as Hart (1984), Clouser (1991), Kalsbeek (1975), de Raadt (1991, 1994, 1997), Griffioen (1995) and Basden (unpublished, 1996, 2008), who have illustrated some of its benefits for understanding and explaining how social systems and institutions work.

A particular feature of the theory is its ability to explain complexity without falling into reductionism and/or subjectivism. This feature suggested that the theory would be useful in structuring sustainable development in the built environment, overcoming one of the problems of current tools (see Chapters 3, 4 and 5).

The theory is complex, but broadly the 'Cosmonomic Idea of Reality' proposes a list of dimensions of reality, named *modalities*, which can be useful for understanding the 'functioning' of a complex system or entity such as the built environment or a local community. The list of modalities identified by Dooyeweerd and their meanings is provided in Table 6.1. The third column of the table illustrates the meaning of each modality in the context of sustainable development. Both the original name of the modalities and the proposed definition are used in Table 6.1.

In simple terms, a *modality* can be defined as an irreducible area of the functioning of a system or entity. It is characterised by a nucleus of meaning and it has its own law, or set of laws, which not only guides but enables entities (people, animals, trees, houses, etc.) to function in a variety of ways. For example, the laws of physics provide the functioning of materials while the laws of biology regulate the functioning of trees. More complex entities, such as local communities, are guided by several other modalities whose laws are less determinative and

Table 6.1   The list of modalities and their meaning.

Modality	Meaning	Proposed definition in the context of sustainable development
Numerical	Quantity	Numerical accounting
Spatial	Continuous extension	Spaces, shape and extension
Kinematics	Movement	Transport and mobility
Physical	Energy, mass	Physical environment, mass and energy
Biological	Life function	Health, biodiversity, eco-protection
Sensitive	Senses, feelings	People's perceptions towards the environment
Analytic	Discernment of entities	Analysis and formal knowledge
Historical	Formative power	Creativity and cultural development
Communicative	Information	Communications and the media
Social	Social intercourse	Social climate and social cohesion
Economic	Frugality	Efficiency and economic appraisal
Aesthetic	Harmony, beauty	Visual appeal and architectural style
Juridical	Retribution, fairness	Rights and responsibilities
Ethical	Love, morality	Ethical issues
Credal	Faith, trustworthiness	Commitment, interest and vision

more normative since their fulfilment is contingent on people's inclination to follow these laws, for example, the law of justice or the law of ethics.

The philosophy of the 'Cosmonomic Idea of Reality' has not placed the 15 modalities in an arbitrary order: the earlier modalities serve as a foundation for the later (Dooyeweerd calls this 'the cosmic order of time') (Kalsbeek, 1975). For instance, the economic modality is dependent on the social, the social on the lingual, the lingual on the historical and so on. In other words, the 15 modalities are nested inside one another and each modality affects and informs those above.

This interrelation between the modalities (*dependency relation*) defines their position in the list. The consequence of this order is also felt in terms of the influence they are able to exert on each other. For instance, we often use the laws of mathematics (numeric modality) to understand economical processes (guided by the economic modality) but the results are much more effective if we use a modality closer on the list such as the social one. In other words, the greater the distance between the ordered modalities, the less influence they have on each other. Figure 6.1 graphically illustrates these concepts. A more detailed description of the theory is provided in Appendix A.

The modalities can be better illustrated by an example related to the built environment.

The built environment explained by the modalities

The built environment represents a meaningful subset of the whole topic of sustainable development (Brandon, 1998). It is part of the physical system and is intrinsically linked to both the environmental (physical) and the human (social and economic) systems. For example, urban density, mobility and lifestyles are usually reflected in the demand for space and the flow of resources (Breheny, 1992).

Literature on sustainable urban development emphasises the need to have the three systems – environmental, social and economic – functioning in an integrated and coherent manner. This is important if we are aiming to achieve a stable or improving level of well-being in the local community in the long term (quality of life) and a reduction of negative effects, such as pollution in the biosphere (environmental quality).

As a physical entity, the built environment has spatial extension, mass and energy. It is subject to the laws of thermodynamics (energy) and others, such as the law of gravity, the laws of physics and the rules of geometry. Its fundamental characteristics include building materials and components, layout and form of the building and the structure of the ground on which it is built. In the 'Cosmonomic Idea of Reality', these are all issues of the spatial and physical modalities whose laws regulate and guide the functioning of buildings, materials and components.

The built environment represents the physical context in which individuals spend their time living, dwelling, working and recreating. Unlike other manufactured products, it is unequivocally linked to the land. This makes a building unique, and therefore an object of economical and juridical interest. In addition, it has social and cultural properties since it is useful in satisfying a number of human needs, both material and immaterial. In terms of the 'Cosmonomic Idea of Reality', the built environment, as a system or entity, is qualified by the physical modality. This is the specific aspect that guides and regulates the internal organisation or development of the system.

Although the built environment is characterised by the physical modality, it functions in all the other modal aspects, maintaining different relationships with them. For example, an urban district is usually formed by a number of houses, offices, banks, schools, roads and so forth (numerical modality), placed according to a particular layout (spatial modality). Within an urban district there is usually a constant movement of people, cars, bicycles, animals and goods (kinematics modality) which need energy in order to function (physical modality). People and other living creatures also need food, water, air to breath, houses for shelter and hospitals for health (biological modality). They display emotions and feelings in their relationships within a group (sensitive modality). Furthermore, people have an intrinsic logical dimension resulting in the discerning of entities (analytic modality). They build their houses on the basis of past experience and technological knowledge (historical modality) and they communicate with each other and with the outside environment through media (communicative modality). They have social intercourse (social modality) and often find their employment there (economic modality). The built environment can be beautiful and attractive both for the people who live in it and for tourists (aesthetic modality). A group of laws regulate the use of land and property (juridical modality) and often there is discussion on topics such as the environmental pollution caused by modern city life (ethical modality), but, in the end, there is usually a strong belief in science and technology as the solution to modern society's ecological problems (credal modality).

Table 6.2 classifies a number of issues related to the built environment according to the modalities. This list of issues can only be indicative. It cannot be exhaustive because of the complexity and richness of the urban environment.

The above description has made use of the 15 modalities of Dooyoweerd's theory for revealing the complexity of an urban environment as a system and its multi-dimensional meaning. However, if we want to understand the modal aspects more fully we need to isolate each aspect in our mind so that we can get at its individual natures and distinguish each aspect, making it irreducible to the others (Kalsbeek, 1975).

The 15 modalities for understanding sustainable development in the built environment

In this section, all the 15 modal aspects are outlined with specific attention to the 'role' that each of them plays within the context of sustainable development in the built environment. It should be emphasised that the modal order provides a particular position for each aspect. The modal aspects are so constituted that the earlier aspects serve as a foundation for the later. This order is not reversible within the 'Cosmonomic Idea of Reality'.

This order of 15 modal aspects is suggested as an approach that provides decision-makers with a framework with which to classify relevant sustainable development issues in an urban design or planning situation. The names of the modalities given below relate to Table 6.1.

Table 6.2 Examples of sustainable development aspects within each modality for the built environment.

Modalities	Issues of the built environment
Numerical	Population (human), amount of various resources available, number of species and their population levels, census statistical office, information.
Spatial	Layout, shape, building footprint, location, proximity, terrain shape – flat, mountainous, etc., neighbourhood area, urban area, district area, etc.
Kinematics	Infrastructures, roads, motorway, railways, cycling roads, pedestrian streets, car parking, transport and mobility, wildlife movement, mobility, accessibility.
Physical	Energy for human activity, energy for biotic activity, physical environment, structure of ground on which to build, building materials, components, buildings, districts, settlements.
Biological	Food, shelter, housing, air and air quality, water and water quality, hygiene, green areas, pollution, soil quality, biodiversity, habitat diversity and quality, resilience of ecosystem (ability to recover from imbalances), health and health services, hospitals, gyms.
Sensitive	Feelings engendered by living there, feeling of well-being, comfort, fitness, noise, security, safety, privacy, provision of peaceful surroundings, e.g., motorway noise that makes birdsong inaudible, counselling services, asylums, housing for domestic animals.
Analytical	Clarity with which issues are aired in the community, letting people clearly know facts and issues, quality of analysis for planning and evaluation, diversity, functional mix, knowledge, tendency to understand rather than react to issues, schools, universities, education services, research.
Historical	Encouraging creativity in the community, innovation, heritage, history of the community and area, technology employed, museums, archives, built heritage.
Communicative	Ease of communication in the community, quality of communication (e.g. truthfulness), lingual networking, symbols, information provision, monuments, signs, advertising, the media.
Social	Social relationships and interaction, recreational places, social climate, cohesion, plurality, competitiveness, collaboration, authority structure, social register, clubs and societies.
Economic	Use of land, use and replacement of renewable resources, use of non-renewable resources, recycling schemes, attitude to finance, efficiency, financial institutions, offices, banks, stock markets, industrial plants, employment.
Aesthetic	Beauty, visual amenity and landscape, architecture and design, architectural style decoration, social harmony, ecological harmony and balance, art galleries, theatres.
Juridical	Laws and law-making with regard to property, ownership, regulation and other policy instruments, contracts for building, rights, responsibilities, inequities, property-market interests, democracy, participation, tribunals, administrative offices, legal institutions, political structure.
Ethical	General demeanour of people towards each others, goodwill, neighbourliness, solidarity, sharing, equity, morality, health of the family, voluntary centres.
Credal	Loyalty to the community, general level of morale, shared vision of what we are (e.g. 'I shop, therefore I am', 'I am responsible to God'), aspirations (e.g. to car ownership), shared vision of the way to go (e.g. 'science–technology–economics will solve our problems'), religious institutions, churches, synagogues.

The numerical modality: numerical accounting

The numerical modality means a discrete quantity, awareness of how much there is of things, and it precedes all the following modalities. In fact it provides all the required quantification for an urban development. Some well-known examples in construction are: the number of hectares of ground on which a building is placed (spatial), the amount of resources required for the construction (physical) and the number of living creatures (sensitive) who occupy a building.

The spatial modality: spaces, shape and extension

The spatial modality refers to 'continuous extension'. It is one of the most fundamental modalities for this study since it qualifies spatial differentiation and all the following issues: building shape and layout, terrain shape, location, geographical position, proximity, area topology and form. It is the basis for the development of all the later aspects. For example, the accessibility to a site or to a building, which is recognised as a crucial factor for the quality of living, is characterised by the spatial modality but it is also qualified by the kinematics aspect (such as movement to a place or a site).

The kinematics modality: transport and mobility

The meaning of the kinematics aspect is movement. It characterises the movement of people and goods within an open or closed space, a city or a building. It qualifies mobility in towns and regions. Transport and mobility are crucial factors for the sustainable development of an urban context, both for their environmental ecological impacts and for their utility and quality-of-life features.

The physical modality: physical environment, mass and energy

The physical modality has its meaning in energy and mass. It qualifies different elements of our living environment, dealing *inter alia* with energy, water, air, soil, and natural materials and resources. Its core meaning qualifies physical (natural) elements, such as building materials and the ground on which to build, and also those natural barriers to the spatial development of regions, such as mountains and lakes, the oceans and so on. Artificial or man-made barriers, such as walls, bridges and other built infrastructures, are also qualified by the physical modality. Finally, the physical modality characterises all built (urban) environments, which are recognised as systems with a finite carrying capacity (Rees, 1992).

The biological modality: health, biodiversity and eco-protection

The biological modality has its core meaning in organic life. In terms of the built environment, it has been recognised that buildings have a major impact on the ecosystem as they are produced, consumed and continue to exist within the cycle of nature. This can be expressed by the concept of the *ecological footprint* (see Chapter 3) which is defined as the area of land required to produce biologically all the resources consumed by a community, and to assimilate its waste, indefinitely (Rees, 1992). It expresses the impact of construction on the natural environment, in biological terms. These can be associated within recurring impacts over the building's life, producing a remarkably large footprint. Unfortunately, an understanding and assessment of all the life-cycle impacts of a building is not an easy task. There is a need to know the types of information available and the problems that arise in assessing the existing situation, analysing past trends and projecting future ones.

Case studies and examples of sustainable development in planning have shown that both health and eco-protection or biodiversity are relevant issues in the development of an area. The consequences of building and construction activities influence the quality of air, the quality of water and the quality of the soil over a long time period, particularly in the case of an industrial plant. Biodiversity is not encouraged but penalised by the construction sector which has always removed land from the natural environment and from agricultural use for material extraction and the expansion of cities. Again, the waste derived from construction activities and other uses of land (industrial use or housing) can condition the biological functioning of the site and the urban complex. On the other hand, biological issues can provide direction, for example, in the importance of a 'green' design. A shape and form of building sensitive to environmental issues, as well as a good location in terms of reducing the pollution produced by a building, are key issues in sustainable development at the building level.

The sensitive modality: people's perceptions towards the environment

The biological modality anticipates a number of later modalities. For example, the presence of pollution and the lack of biodiversity of a site are able to influence the perception that people have towards the environment. The latter is an issue of the sensitive modality and it is crucial for sustainable development processes. The sensitive has its root in feeling, which is a quality belonging to everyday experience. Because feeling is irreducible, defining it is as difficult as defining the other meanings.

The feelings of comfort, safety and privacy or, say, the noise level all play a large role in the quality of living for human beings. If we did not feel safe in a place we would certainly not stay there long and would prefer to change our living environment. However, the feelings of privacy, security and comfort and the pleasure engendered by living there can make our lives more satisfactory and of higher quality.

Not only the biological issues but also the spatial and the physical characteristics of the built environment, such as the layout, shape and location of the building, also contribute to the quality of living. This means that the sensitive modality is able to encapsulate all the modalities preceding it.

The analytical modality: analysis and formal knowledge

Human feelings and perceptions are the basis for the logical process of analysis and discernment of the parts constituting a building. The sensitive is the base for developing analytical aspects.

The meaning of the analytical modality is logic and distinction. In planning and design, the analytical modality refers to analysis and formal knowledge. This usually helps decision-makers to recognise a good construction from a bad one and the quality of analysis used in the building design. In some cases the building can be viewed as a good example of design and it can act as an educational tool. Again, the shape, layout and form of the building play a strong role in providing information for this analytical function. This explains why the spatial and physical modalities are placed before the analytical in the modal order. But the latter is able to anticipate and provide information for other aspects, such as the historical modality. Education and the ability to rationalise and discriminate between elements are the foundation for developing a knowledge and a cultural background in construction. These are issues related to the historical modality whose core meaning is *formative power*.

The historical modality: creativity and cultural development

The historical modality qualifies creativity in design and the technology employed in construction. The expertise in construction usually comes from learning from good practice. Innovation in technology is made possible through research activities that make use of analysis. The relation between the historical modality and the analytical modality is particularly important here.

The historical modality represents the cultural and technological progress of human beings in achieving a better quality of living. The production of the built environment entails the use of natural materials and the consumption of energy, and impacts on local habitats. This modality governs the processes of modelling the physical materials and of assembling the components of a building and all the operations required for developing the construction plan. Therefore, it includes the spatial, kinematical, physical and analytical modalities. In planning and design for a human community this is reflected in creativity and cultural development, and it also refers to conservation strategies for the built heritage.

The communicative modality: communications and the media

The historical modality anticipates a number of modalities, and firstly the communicative. For instance, a new building (or renewal) can be regarded as an example of good practice or a laboratory for innovative technologies. In both cases it represents a way forward in scientific and cultural development. It represents a modification of the present environment that has been put in place in order to satisfy some community needs. It communicates symbols and messages to the community. This is an issue of the communicative modality whose significance is to provide information and meaning.

A building is usually able to inform people about the functions held within it. We can easily recognise a hospital as different from a station or from a bridge just by its external form and layout. Therefore, the communicative anticipates both the spatial and the physical but also the historical.

Often, a building such as a monument or a built cultural heritage or an example of modern architecture is able to communicate particular values to a community (credal) from an aesthetical viewpoint (aesthetic). In these examples, the communicative is the foundation for the higher modalities. Communication and the media are relevant factors in linking people together, facilitating participation in planning and the achievement of a common vision of sustainable development in the built environment. The communicative modality directly anticipates the meaning-nucleus of the social modality: a house or a site may provide a welcome message to its visitors. The building is usually a gathering place for people, such as a meeting point for friends in a bar or a club, but may also be an office or other building that encourages relationships with colleagues or other people.

The social modality: social climate and social cohesion

Social intercourse is the meaning-nucleus of the social modality. The size and form of the building, the biological quality of the internal and external environment, the accessibility of the building, the feeling of comfort, its design, the technology used and the messages provided by it – all these elements play a pertinent role in human attitudes towards social interaction and thereby condition it. The spatial, physical, sensitive, historical, analytical and communicative modalities precede the social modality in the framework and support it.

The economic modality: efficiency and economic appraisal

The use that a community makes of a building is connected to its economic value in the real-estate market. The social modality anticipates the economic modality. The link between the two modalities is very strong, as is also recognised by the utility theory of value for buildings (Forte & De Rossi, 1996).

A number of economic issues relate to construction activity and a number of decisions are taken with regard to the initial, limited amount of resources available to developers and builders for construction. Form, shape, layout and location are fundamental issues that determine the cost of a building. Physical and spatial resources also influence future economic decisions, as the life-cycle cost of a building demonstrates (Ferry *et al.*, 1999). The economic modality asks planners and designers to consider future costs for the design and development of buildings as it very often refers to an economic appraisal over the building life cycle.

The spatial, physical, sensitive, analytical and all the other earlier modalities are anticipated by the economic modality. Many economic decisions relating to buildings are determined by the environmental conditions of the site, the perception that people (e.g. developers, users, economic decision-makers) have of it, the analyses made for developing the building design, the technology available at the time, the information owned by the actors and finally the use made of the building.

In the literature, an existing interdependence that also encompasses social and cultural values is recognised between the economy and the environment (Costanza, 1991, 1993). On the one hand, environmental quality influences economic performance (e.g. a higher environmental quality could be reflected in a higher market value of buildings) and, on the other hand, the economy affects the environment (e.g. an industrial plant may provide pollution and stress the ecosystem). This influence is visible for both its positive effects, such as the improvement and regeneration of the built environment, and its negative effects, such as the damage that urban activities have caused, for example, to natural landscapes, to sites of historical, architectural or cultural interest and to local traditions and customs.

The economic modality precedes the softer modalities and reflects a key issue for sustainable development in the built environment. For example, the use that people make of a building has an impact on the harmony (aesthetic) of the urban complex. If the users of the building are functioning poorly in the economic aspect, by squandering physical resources or by inefficient handling of their domestic waste or by not caring about their gardens and their neighbourhood, the harmony of the whole urban area might be threatened and sustainability is low.

The aesthetic modality: visual appeal and architectural style

The concept of harmony between elements of a settlement or parts of the same building is the meaning-nucleus of the aesthetic modality. A number of factors occur to determine the harmony of a built system, such as the form, layout, location and distribution of the buildings; the quality of design; the use made of the built environment by the community; the cost paid and other economic choices that occur during planning, design and building. The aesthetic modality comes before all the more quantitative aspects in the modal order.

The particular architectural style and the decoration of a building possess an aesthetic meaning. The beauty of a building can be recognised not only by its inhabitants but also by neighbours and tourists. For example, a qualitatively high image of an urban area not only meets the requirements of the citizens but also attracts new investors, drawing in firms that intend to relocate and becoming a 'model' to be followed by other local administrations. Many effects of well-being are expressed only indirectly and may bear little relation to an increase in productivity or cost savings, such as the relationship of inhabitants to the urban context, the degree of social integration, safety, the presence of green areas and people's contribution to education and training.

The juridical modality: rights and responsibilities

The building can be in harmony with its surrounding or, alternatively, can be in contrast. These relationships between a building and its surrounding are usually regulated by technical and planning legislation. The latter is an issue of the juridical modality, which precedes the aesthetic aspect, specifically in the case of standards, codes of practice or norms regulating the development of the building in terms of architectural style, the colour of the facade and similar matters.

The meaning of the juridical modality is well explained through the concepts of rights and responsibilities. From a juridical point of view, a building belongs to a public or private owner within an administrative space, under the regulation of a local authority. The local administration governs and regulates the functioning of an urban complex through a complex body of laws. Regulations can also be found at different planning levels – local, regional and national. In the UK, for instance, the main planning legislation is the Town and Country Planning Act 1990 (amended and revised in 1991) and, in contrast to other Member States of the European Union, there are fewer provisions for planning at the national and regional levels. Spatial planning is largely the responsibility of local authorities, although central government retains considerable influence and control.

There are also several repercussions in terms of properties and use of land. In designing a building, urban and technical standards need to be taken into account. On the other hand, a new building can provide a modification to the actual property structure, and sellers and buyers are required to be formally registered.

The juridical modality follows and encapsulates not only the aesthetic modality but also the economic, social, sensitive and all the earlier aspects in the list. In particular, the relationships between the juridical and the biological modalities need to be emphasised in terms of sustainable urban development, for example, the environmental pollution caused by a building such as a factory or a waste disposal plant. In the juridical modality, the producers of pollution (the users or owners of the building) are responsible, in legal terms, for the negative service provided to the community. Consequently, in some countries they are required to pay a price or a particular tax for this pollution, according to the principle that 'pollutant (or user) pays' (Pearce & Turner, 1990). Unfortunately, it is not always easy to define the exact boundaries of a pollution source. The effects of pollution can often be felt very far away from the place or origin and this provides an obstacle to the application of the principle. Often the administrative boundaries (juridical) do not correspond to the natural (spatial and physical) ones.

The ethical modality: ethical issues

In its role of anticipating and supporting the ethical aspect, the juridical modality provides a fundamental contribution to our understanding of sustainable development in the built environment. The ethical modality refers to a particular attitude towards other entities, both living creatures and inanimate ones, which is governed by love and morality. In the context of this study, it specifically suggests that citizens (particularly building and land owners) go beyond mere duty in exercising ownership and responsibility and that those who live nearby should look beyond the traditional NIMBY ('not in my back yard') defensiveness.

The ethical modality precedes and encapsulates the meaning of all the earlier modalities. For example, we can think of the social conflicts arising from the decision to locate a waste disposal plant, an airport or a railway nearby. The spatial modality (in terms of location) and the biological modality are foundation dimensions of this modal aspect. However, other examples can be found in our everyday experience with regard to the wide repercussions that a legislative act (juridical) may have on the morale of a community.

Finally, the concept of equity – which is fundamental in a study of sustainable development – is an ethical issue, although the concept also holds an economic and juridical meaning when it is defined as a 'fair distribution of resources between members of the same community' (Voogd, 1995). It is based on humanitarian love for one's neighbour, love of nature and so forth or, in the words of the Brundtland Report (WCED, 1987): 'a respect for the needs of future generations'.

The credal modality: commitment, interest and vision

The ethical certainly anticipates the credal modality. It can often be observed that when the morale of a community is low for some reason, such as a political decision, an economic decline derived from an inefficient use of resources or a social problem (e.g. the presence of crime), people have no commitment towards their environment and no development is possible.

The meaning of the credal aspect is specifically faith. This is an essential part of the structure of human beings and not just a characteristic peculiar to Christian or other religions. The contents and the directions of faith differ among different people. For example, belief can be directed towards God or towards an idol or towards any other philosophy of life whether it be communism or materialism.

The built environment is, finally, a reflection of what we think it has to be. Urban form, the shape and layout of buildings and infrastructures, the design and the planning, the social attitude towards the environment, all the economic choices made and the aesthetical and ethical characteristics of our built environment are just a reflection of a simple but fundamental credal issue: *who we are and where we aim to go as individuals or as a community* (Lombardi & Basden, 1997).

Development of the multi-modal framework for decision-making

The development of the scientific procedure underpinning the framework is supported by the theory of Dooyeweerd described above. The 15 descriptions are suggested to provide decision-makers with a qualification system for classifying sustainable development issues in urban planning and design. A number of scientific criteria and specifications, followed by questions for examining sustainability, will guide the user in handling the evaluation of a planning or design proposal.

The limitations encountered in existing frameworks for decision-making (see Chapter 3) have suggested that the structure should be flexible and able to take into account various situations and planning and design problems. The structure should include criteria that are relevant to decision-making and at the same time are easily checked by users, providing information about the sustainability of an urban development.

This framework should be able to facilitate collaboration among stakeholders, aiding consultation and communication between the formal decision-makers (planners, designers and urban authorities who devise strategies and policies for the cities), and any members of the general public who may participate in this decision-making process (stakeholders and concerned citizens). In other words, it should possess a user-friendly terminology.

To illustrate the use of the framework, some example questions have been developed for an urban district that is being redeveloped. These questions will help decision-makers (planners or stakeholders) to examine each sustainable development aspect and to provide evidence that the aspect has been addressed in a planning situation.

This cannot be an exhaustive list of questions because of the complexity of the subject but it provides a prompt which may support and guide evaluation in planning. It is also worth noting again that the evaluation is not limited to technical factors but also includes non-technical aspects as it follows the checklist illustrated in Table 5.1. Each of them will represent a level of information that may be relevant for the stakeholders.

A final point is that the evaluation perspective adopted in the development of these questions is related to the so-called *ex ante* evaluation of potential alternatives. In this evaluation perspective, the aim of the framework is to aid choice by decision-takers and stakeholders in the decision-making process. Clearly this example may be one in a series. By changing questions and assessment techniques, the checklist of modalities remains the same and can be assumed as the basis for an *ex post* (retrospective) evaluation or a *monitoring*. In *ex post* and *monitoring*, both of which imply a different view of the planning and management process, the framework may be a useful guide for understanding the changes produced by a policy or a programme and for judging the degree of achievement of a planning process. The flexibility of the framework will be further discussed in Chapter 7.

The following provides a short illustration of the questions which will allow us to examine sustainable development, encompassing all the issues that might lead to a harmonic environment.

Key questions for examining sustainable development within each modality

As sustainable development is a process that includes also non-technical aspects, such as socio-economic and cultural factors (see Chapter 1), the process can only be assessed by a robust theoretical framework able to provide structure and support for this complex evaluation exercise. The authors have adopted the modal order based upon the philosophy of Dooyeweerd and illustrated in the early part of this chapter.

Starting from the top of the modal order, the following are potentially key questions related to each modality redefined in the context of sustainable development, as introduced in Table 5.1. These example questions are indicative of the issues that need to be addressed and aid the person making the assessment to consider all the key issues (and the moral imperatives).

Credal modality: commitment, interest and vision

❏ Is the political situation stable?
❏ Does the scheme meet the requirements of regional–national plans?
❏ Will finance be available for environmental protection and for how long?
❏ What commitment has each stakeholder made to the scheme?

Ethical modality: ethical issues

❏ Does the development scheme provide the same opportunities or improvements for people in the future as in the present?
❏ Does the development scheme reduce social inequalities? Does it support the action of voluntary groups?
❏ Does the scheme provide protection to the biosphere, ecosystem and animal species?
❏ Have all the stakeholders been involved in the development of the scheme?

Juridical modality: rights and responsibilities

❏ Have the rights and the responsibilities of all developers, land and building owners and users been accounted for in the long term?
❏ Does the scheme identify those who benefit and those who pay for the development? Does it include some possibilities for the reimbursement of damage and payment for the rights received?
❏ To what degree can people change their environment either directly or through elected representatives?
❏ Has a strategic environmental assessment (SEA) been undertaken (see Chapter 5)? Is there compliance with the technical–planning standards related to the protection of the environment?
❏ What citizens groups are entitled to participate in the decision process?

Aesthetical modality: visual appeal and architectural style

❏ Does the development scheme improve the artistic character and significance of buildings and settlement in the short and long term?

❏ Does the condition of the built environment enhance the visual appeal?

❏ Are the planned interventions aesthetically satisfying to all the stakeholders?

❏ Is the development in harmony with the context, the surroundings and the ecosystem? Does the scheme improve the visual appeal of natural settings?

Economical modality: efficiency and economic appraisal

❏ Has a long-term financial appraisal been undertaken?

❏ What is the financial distribution to the stakeholders?

❏ Has employment of the local labour force in construction been considered?

❏ Is there an efficient environmental management system? Are there exhaustive city-wide recycling programmes from which the development could benefit?

❏ How many of the stakeholders have committed themselves to the financial appraisal?

Social modality: social climate and social cohesion

❏ Does the plan enhance and sustain social interaction in the long term?

❏ Does it consider the impact of the development on the social climate in the long term?

❏ Does the plan favour cooperation and association between individuals and institutions? Does it improve the accessibility to social utilities for all the members of the community?

❏ Does the plan consider the impacts of tourism on the cultural and natural settings?

❏ Have social clubs, voluntary groups and cultural associations been involved in the development of the scheme?

Communicative modality: communications and the media

❏ Is a monitoring system for the area available?

❏ Will the communicative infrastructures be improved in the present and the future?

❏ Is a long-term programme for urban signs available?

- ❏ Does the plan improve the accessibility to communication facilities for all citizens, including the poor and disadvantaged?
- ❏ Does the plan include environmental audits? Is environmentally orientated advertising available for the area?
- ❏ Is information on the development scheme available to all stakeholders? Are all relevant citizen groups able to take part in the discussion, argument and evaluation in planning? Does everyone understand the language used?

Historical modality: creativity and cultural development

- ❏ Does the urban plan include a restoration programme to preserve the cultural heritage of the area?
- ❏ Is the innovation based on local practice?
- ❏ Does the plan improve the living standards of the poor and disadvantaged and their cultural aspirations?
- ❏ Are the technologies employed environmentally friendly?
- ❏ Does the city have a well-established consultation process? Has consultation been successfully undertaken in relation to the proposal?

Analytical modality: analysis and formal knowledge

- ❏ Has scientific analysis been applied to the problem including consideration of the long-term perspective? Does the funding provided support the proposed solution in the long term?
- ❏ Is an educational scheme available for citizens?
- ❏ Is an educational programme relating to the environment available for the community?
- ❏ Has the developed analysis been accessed and agreed by most of the stakeholders?

Sensitive modality: people's perceptions towards the environment

- ❏ Is a long-term security scheme available for the area?
- ❏ Does the plan address the issues of crime and vandalism in the area and surroundings? Will every stakeholder feel comfort and confidence in the design for safety within the surroundings? Is the viewpoint of children taken into consideration?
- ❏ Does the plan solve the problems of noise in the area? Does it take into account the visual impact?
- ❏ Are the viewpoints of all stakeholders, including those who have no voice, taken into consideration? Have groups representing the rights of children been active in decision-making?

Biological modality: health, biodiversity and eco-protection

❏ What is the carrying capacity of the area? Does the development scheme for the area take into account the maintenance of available capital of non-renewable resources in the long term?

❏ Is every stakeholder able to enjoy an appropriate quality of air, water and land in the developing area? Do they feel happy with the presence of green areas, hygiene, health and health services, hospitals, gyms, etc.?

❏ Is there an environmental-planning scheme available for the area? Does the plan improve air, water and soil quality in the area? Does it increase or improve health services?

❏ Are the community groups active on environmental issues? Have all stakeholders taken part in the development of the environmental-planning scheme?

Physical modality: physical environment, mass and energy

❏ Is an energy-saving scheme that takes into account the long-term perspective available?

❏ Is there an environmental-planning scheme available for the area?

❏ Does the development scheme for the area take into account the maintenance of non-renewable resources in the long term?

❏ Have local environmental action groups been involved in the development of the scheme?

Kinematics modality: transport and mobility

❏ Does the development scheme for the area improve the mobility in and out of the area for the long-term future?

❏ Is every stakeholder able to move easily using public transport? Are transport facilities available to all stakeholders?

❏ Is the transport-planning scheme environmentally friendly? Will it improve the air quality?

❏ Have all stakeholders taken part in the development of the transport-planning scheme?

Spatial modality: space, shape and extension

❏ Is the development sufficiently flexible to take into account future development schemes for the area? Will the urban form be stable through time?

❏ Is the urban density appropriate for every stakeholder?

Table 6.3 The proposed framework for sustainable development decision-making.

Goal	First-level aspects	Second-level aspects	Multi-modal aspects	Built environment and planning aspects
Sustainable development	Physical environmental capital	Urban and infrastructural development	Numerical	Numerical accounting
			Spatial	Space, shape and extension (e.g. urban density)
			Kinematic	Transport and mobility (e.g. infrastructure level)
		Environmental and physical quality	Physical	Physical environment (e.g. environmental quality level)
			Biological	Health and ecological protection or biodiversity (e.g. greenery)
			Sensitive	Perceptions of people towards the environment
	Human cultural capital	Education and scientific development	Analytical	Analysis and formal knowledge (e.g. university reputation)
			Formative	Creativity and cultural development
			Communicative	Communication and the media (e.g. information and communication technology [ICT] level)
		Social and economical development	Social	Social climate, social relationships and social cohesion
			Economic	Efficiency and economic appraisal (e.g. gross national product [GNP])
			Aesthetical	Visual appeal and architectural style (e.g. cultural heritage)
	Financial institutional capital	Governance	Juridical	Rights and responsibilities (e.g. legal framework)
			Ethical	Ethical issues (equity)
			Credal	Commitment, interest and vision

❏ Is the new urban density and form environmentally friendly?
❏ Have all stakeholders taken part in the development of shape and layout of buildings and settings?

Numerical modality: numerical accounting

❏ How long is the development process?
❏ How much redistribution of wealth is contained within the scheme?
❏ How much, in terms of natural and non-renewable resources, does the development cost?
❏ How many stakeholders have taken part in the decision-making?

It should be stressed again that these questions are merely examples and will vary from scheme to scheme. However, the basic framework remains the same. This provides the opportunity to 'think global' through the modalities, and yet to 'act local'. Even this limited list of questions illustrates the massive complexity in understanding and evaluating sustainable development.

Synthesis of results

A major problem faced in decision-making for sustainable development is the massive amount of information which can confuse decision-makers rather than help them to find a suitable solution. To overcome this problem, the 15 modalities and planning aspects have been regrouped into two more aggregated sets of dimensions of sustainable development as illustrated in Table 6.3.

The first set of sustainable development dimensions corresponds to the three major clusters of sustainable development ('first-level aspects' in Table 6.3), also defined as three different types of 'capital' (see Chapter 3), which are related to the physical environment, the human environment and the institutional environment (as suggested by Lombardi & Nijkamp, 2000; Nijkamp, 2007), in accordance with the EU definition of sustainable urban development (see *EC Report*, February 2002).

The second set of issues are the five classes of urban policies ('second-level aspects' in Table 6.3), that is, urban and infrastructure development, environmental and physical quality, education and scientific development, social and economical development, and governance, which reflect the main strategic areas where interventions can be made in the urban environment (Lombardi & Stanghellini, 2008).

This structure is intended to provide a synthesis of the results obtained from an evaluation process by incrementally aggregating the numerous aspects and evaluation issues into a smaller class of well-known key sustainable development dimensions. These are illustrated further in the case studies in Chapter 7.

Summary

Decision-making for sustainable development, particularly in the field of planning or design, requires a framework that is able to structure the problem. This enables us to understand the implications that the (re) development may have for the existing context.

This chapter has shown a new conceptual framework for understanding sustainable development in urban planning and design for the built environment. The framework developed in this study is based on a simplified version of the philosophical theory of the 'Cosmonomic Idea of Reality'. This is useful, not only because it recognises different levels of information but also because it suggests an integration of the key aspects to provide a continuum for harmony and decision-making.

Considering the multi-aspect nature of sustainability at the local level, all the 15 aspects of reality – from the numerical to the credal – are important for the true long-term sustainability of any built environment and its community (Lombardi & Basden, 1997). We can now revisit the definition of *Sustainable Development*, already provided in Chapter 1, by saying that, in the light of Dooyeweerd, 'this is a process which comes from a balancing between the multiple aspects of an urban system and it depends on specific relationships between these aspects, such as the functioning and the dependency' (see Appendix A).

The proposed framework aims at guiding designers and planners, official public developers and decision-makers through the process of understanding and evaluating sustainable development in planning and design on the basis of a new holistic structure that acts as a prompt and a checklist. For this reason, the framework has been recently adopted by the World Congress of Architecture 2008 at the International Workshop on urban transformation which explored the redevelopment of Basse di Stura in Turin which was a complex landfill site requiring a large number of different issues to be addressed. In addition, it has been suggested by Nijkamp (2007) as a promising approach for selecting sustainable development indicators.

The evaluation framework involves all of the following:

❏ A *technical assessment* of the construction under development with regard to dimension, space, functions, accessibility, etc.
❏ An ecologically orientated assessment of the project (a 'green design') illustrating the *environmental compatibility* of this development within the existing context.
❏ An understanding of the *historical and cultural significance* of the planning asset and of its *social desirability*.
❏ An analysis of the *financial and economic feasibility*.

❑ A check of the *visual appeal* of this new (re)development and of its *flexibility or adaptability* which may allow it to meet some future user needs.

❑ An assessment of the *institutional sustainability* of the project, based on an analysis of the juridical and procedural issues.

❑ An understanding of what *interest or concern* there is in the local agenda of the city and in its strategic plan.

Problems arise in decision-making for sustainable development: for example, the amount of information required for an evaluation is time-consuming and costly; the variety of vocabulary employed and required by each assessment method confuses the dialogue between stakeholders; the elements of uncertainty included in the available data make prediction difficult; and compromise is difficult because of the lack of an agreed structure.

The framework, as it has been developed, does not overcome all of these problems directly but it does provide new opportunities for collaboration between disciplines, experts and people; it adds new dimensions that were traditionally not covered in the evaluation (e.g. aesthetics); and it links all the knowledge and the special contributions of technique and science within the same structure, providing order, continuity and integration without falling into reductionism or lack of transparency. Finally, the framework helps decision-makers to understand, explain and communicate the complexity of the problem to all stakeholders and to assess progress towards sustainable development. Thus it can also act as a learning tool, addressing current demands for higher education in the field of planning.

In Chapter 7, four case studies provide an illustration of this structure at different planning levels, demonstrating the power of the framework as a tool for decision-making.

The Framework as a Structuring Tool: Case Studies

This chapter aims to show the robustness, relevance, comprehensiveness and flexibility of the proposed multi-modal framework for decision-making through some case study applications. Four real-world examples are provided which are related to various planning/design contexts and different operative levels. These are intended to demonstrate that this framework is able to make the key issues within a decision-making process explicit and transparent in the context of sustainable development and that it is able to cover a wide range of issues that are rarely addressed by current methods.

It is worth re-emphasising that technical information and scientific knowledge related to sustainability in the built environment are, at present, very limited. Moreover, experience in the field of sustainability in planning and the built environment is restricted to some good 'local' examples or case studies whose applicability cannot always be generalised (Selman, 1996; Cooper & Palmer, 1999).

Research on sustainability is still experimental and still very fragmented since it requires joint effort, collaboration and continuous implementation and monitoring, involving many different disciplines and many different people working together over a long period of time. A further major constraint is the lack of a comprehensive database on sustainable development, making it difficult to apply. Current debates on sustainable development tend to focus on statistical indicators and classification systems as a structure for organising the information required in decision-making but currently few of these

---

Evaluating Sustainable Development in the Built Environment, Second Edition
By Peter S. Brandon and Patrizia Lombardi   © 2011 Peter S. Brandon and Patrizia Lombardi

are available or operational (Mitchell, 1996; Bentivegna *et al.*, 2002; Deakin *et al.*, 2002a).

It is in response to the above that this book has been undertaken. The book has adopted a new theoretical base to address the need, with the support of the theory of the 'Cosmonomic Idea of Reality', suggesting a framework for the evaluation of sustainability in planning (see Chapter 6). This process has required understanding, investigation and information. It has also required testing and reviewing. However, the limited amount of information available at present on many of the issues in the framework means that future practical applications of the proposed multi-modal framework will be required to test it to the full. A continuous implementation and adaptation of the structure in each planning situation and decision-making process is necessary to encourage users to adopt it as a fully operative tool for the evaluation of sustainability.

As the information on which the proposed multi-modal structure relies is still in a state of change, it follows that applications can only focus on the theoretical structure underlying it. This structure encapsulates 15 modal aspects and the three clusters of sustainability aspects of physical environment, human environment and the institutional environment, illustrated in Table 6.3.

In this chapter four case studies are provided, based around the comprehensiveness of the framework to aid the decision-making process for sustainable development. These case studies try to address the following key questions:

❏ Is the proposed structure *flexible* enough to be able to produce meaningful results in different planning situations?
❏ Is it *transparent* enough to produce clear advice for decision-making within each modality?
❏ Do the framework components *help decision-making*, leading to an improvement in understanding, monitoring and learning about sustainability?

The first example provides evidence for the comprehensiveness of the modalities for the long-term planning of a situation by applying the modality approach to a decision-making problem that has been tackled previously by a traditional provisional (*ex ante*) evaluation method. Thus, it is possible to compare the new approach with the one undertaken previously in order to see whether there is an improvement. In this example, it is shown that the multi-modal structure is able to render all the factors underlying the decision-making explicit, pinpointing the limitations of the traditional method used in the case study. In turn, this helps to illustrate that the structure is comprehensive and able to address the identified problems sufficiently. The second example is based on a real-world case study in planning redevelopment problems; it highlights the benefits of the framework as a structuring approach in connection to the adoption of multi-criteria evaluation methods (Lombardi, 2009). The third case study proposes a retrospective (*ex post*) analysis of a decision-making process, adopting the multi-modal framework as a tool for detecting the stakeholders' views of the problem. The fourth deals with sustainability indicators, structuring the 'Social reporting' (or stakeholder reporting) of the City of Modena (Italy) by means of the suggested multi-modal framework. All four examples illustrate the relevance of the 15 structure components.

All the four case studies are related to different planning situations in order to show the flexibility of the proposed structure to different contexts and its potential for generalisation, that is, its replicability. As already stated, planning and design are multi-aspect activities and generally pose a variety of different problems that challenge decision-makers. For the purposes of illustration, the following major current planning/management problems for sustainability have been selected: management of technological systems at the infrastructure level, urban regeneration at the district level and strategic planning at the city level.

In the first case study, an example is used to show how multi-criteria methods (see Chapter 5 for an illustration of these methods) are able to tackle the problem of selecting a new waste treatment for the city of Turin, demonstrating that a number of aspects – which are important for true long-term sustainability – are left uncovered.

In the second case study, the modelling of the complex decision problems related to an urban redevelopment scheme is based on the multi-modal framework. The scheme is part of an Integrated Local Development Programme (ILDP) which includes the city Agenda 21 strategic objectives.

In the third case study, the multi-modal framework is used as a retrospective evaluation tool for prompting understanding and learning about sustainability. A multi-stakeholder decision-making problem that deals with the crucial sustainability problem of regenerating an ex-industrial area is illustrated (Curwell & Lombardi, 1999).

Finally, the fourth case study required rigorous fieldwork and three stages of development relating to social reporting in a city. The first stage concerned a deep understanding of the problem involved. The second stage applied the framework to the context within the city and this implied a structured collection of information. The third stage is the analysis of the results (Lombardi & Stanghellini, 2008).

All four case studies are based on previous applications of some traditional methodologies and are documented in Lombardi and Zorzi (1993), Lombardi and Marella (1997) and Comune di Modena (2004) respectively. Detailed background information can be found within these publications and it is not possible to replicate the detail here.

Case study 1: selection of a municipal waste treatment system

This example deals with a major ecological issue of concern for sustainable development: the problem of municipal waste. This generally consists of organic substances, paper, metals, textiles, glass, synthetic materials and small quantities of a large variety of toxic substances. Municipal waste is generally collected in most European cities, although in deteriorating neighbourhoods, removal systems do not always work adequately because of a lack of public funding.

In Europe, between 150 and 600 kg of municipal waste is produced per person each year. On average, each European produces more than 500 kg of waste per annum or 1.5 kg of waste each day. Estimates provided by the OECD for western Europe indicate an increase in the production of municipal waste at the rate of 3% per annum between 1985 and 1990 (OECD, 1994; CER, 1996). In addition, a major shift is occurring in the composition of municipal waste, with an increase in plastics and packaging materials.

A large proportion of municipal waste from cities is taken to landfills. Tipping, which is the most common method of disposing of urban wastes in landfills in Europe, is not always controlled. An alternative system for disposing of municipal waste is an incinerator. In western Europe it is used, on average, for 20% of produced waste. Incineration of municipal waste causes a reduction of up to 30% in the weight of the initial quantities of treated waste and can be designed to recoup the energy content of the waste. At the same time, this can cause notorious problems of air pollution, and harmful and toxic waste products. In addition, it is very costly and extremely difficult to manage (Stanner & Bourdeau, 1995).

Efforts are now undertaken in many European cities to set an example of good practice by recycling, with the aim of reducing the unnecessary import of materials as well as the volume of waste that leaves the city (EEA, 1995).

The present case study concerns the problem of selecting a new municipality waste treatment system for the city of Turin. At the moment, a public company called AMIAT manages the municipal waste through a system of controlled burial. Although the system is still operational, the problem of finding new technical solutions for the future will remain after the closing of the current system.

The disposal of urban waste by means of a new landfill raises the problem of finding suitable new sites with suitable hydrogeological characteristics, so that this will not add to underground water or soil pollution. In addition, the landscape can be blighted by unsightly views and smells during the life cycle of the tip and a considerable increase in dust, rats, insects and fire hazards may occur. These

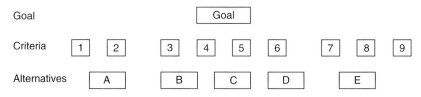

Figure 7.1   The hierarchical model structure.

Table 7.1   The goal, criteria and alternatives adopted in this evaluation.

Goal
Identification of a technical solution for waste disposal in Turin

Criteria
(1) Safeguarding the atmosphere   (2) Safeguarding the water supply   (3) Safeguarding the soil   (4) Protection of the landscape   (5) Protection of public health (maximum hygiene)   (6) Minimisation of danger (maximum safety)   (7) Maximisation of cost/revenue ratio   (8) Maximum life of plant   (9) Ease of operation

Alternatives
(A) Controlled burial   (B) Incineration   (C) Mixed recovery and controlled burial   (D) Mixed recovery and incineration   (E) Mixed recovery, incineration and controlled burial

problems are at the root of the social conflicts that are usually generated in decisions of this kind.

In the case study developed by Lombardi and Zorzi (1993), three main systems of municipal disposing – controlled burial, incineration and recovery/selection – were analysed (as alternative solutions) and an environmental impact analysis was developed for decision-making. In this application a number of environmental factors and socio-economical issues were taken into consideration (as evaluation criteria). These included: air, water, soil, landscape, public hygiene, technological risk, economic analysis, life cycle of the system and ease of operation.

The complete hierarchy used, with the goal at the top and the alternative solutions at the bottom, is illustrated in Fig. 7.1 and Table 7.1.

An assessment of the significance of the impact of each alternative solution, in terms of reversibility and duration in time, was also developed by creating a nine-point measurement scale. This impact analysis formed the basis of the application of three different multi-criteria analysis methods (MCA), in order to devise a single preference index for each alternative system of disposing of urban waste (see Chapter 5).

The reason why Lombardi & Zorzi (1993) used three different MCA methods (when one is generally considered sufficient for this problem) was to avoid the well-known problem of 'method uncertainty' (Voogd, 1983), which states that the results of an MCA application are fettered by the mathematical structure on which the method is based. Therefore, a comparison of the results obtained by different methods may be of advantage for the decision.

The application of the MCA methods devised a final ranking of alternative options which placed a mixed waste treatment system (mixed recovery and incineration) at the top, as best, and traditional systems (controlled burial and incineration) at the bottom.

This result is dependent upon both the subjective selection of the evaluation criteria used and their weighting vector (this has been identified as an additional 'uncertainty' of this method (Voogd, 1983)). The criteria and their weights were agreed on by experts within a consultative process that did not consider the views of non-experts and in fact only technical factors were considered in the analysis.

The MCA methods used in this application were the following: Concordance–Discordance Analysis – Electre II (Roy, 1985), Analytical Hierarchy Process (Saaty, 1980) and Regime Method (Hinloopen *et al.*, 1983). A short illustration of the multi-criteria analysis is given in Chapter 5.

An application of the multi-modal framework shows a number of problems in terms of threats to sustainable development, particularly with regard to the aspects not included in the above analysis. In particular, it shows the lack of commitment due to the absence of community non-expert participation in the evaluation (see Table 7.2).

Although some major environmental-technological and social-economical impacts have been taken into consideration in the assessment, the lack of elements related to users' perceptions and to social or ethical factors may have influenced the output, leading to a strictly 'expert-orientated' decision. For instance, the concern for non-renewable resources such as landscape, air quality, water quality and soil quality, and the attention paid to both public hygiene and hazardous materials (safety) are important in relation to the health of people and the value systems prevalent within a community. The chosen decision-making process did not consider these aspects.

In the literature, MCA methods are often considered useful tools for consultation with experts and the general public. However, practical examples of experience in this field are not easily accessible or available.

Table 7.2 Critique of the MCA application based on the proposed multi-modal framework. (Source: Lombardi, 2009.)

Modalities	Major concerns regarding sustainability
Numerical accounting	A cardinal scale with decimal indices was used by experts to compare the alternatives with the criteria and assign the relative importance to the evaluation criteria. Reduction in the analysis is sometimes dangerous in analysing sustainable development processes.
Space, shape and extension	The assessment did not take into consideration spatial location of a waste treatment system. The only spatial concern was 'safeguarding the soil in terms of land occupation' as one of the evaluation criteria.
Transport and mobility	Not considered in the above decision-making.
Physical environment, mass and energy	Considered the landscape on one hand and the impacts on the human system from hazardous materials on the other.
Health, biodiversity and ecological protection	A number of environmental criteria were used in this evaluation, such as: safeguarding the atmosphere, safeguarding both the surface and the underground water supply, protection of public health in terms of maximisation of hygiene.
Perceptions of people toward the environment	Not considered in the above decision-making.
Analysis and formal knowledge	The criterion used to compare the relative strengths of alternative waste treatment systems was related to the analytical level 'easy to operate'.
Creativity and cultural development	Two different criteria were used at this level, i.e., minimisation of danger (for technological risks) and maximum life of a plant. Both are important for the sustainability principle of futurity.
Communication and the media	Not considered in the above decision-making.
Social climate, social relationships and social cohesion	Not considered in the above decision-making.
Efficiency and economic appraisal	One evaluation criterion refers to the 'maximisation of cost/revenue ratio derived from economic analysis'.
Visual appeal of buildings and settings and architectural style	The visual impact of alternative waste treatment systems is not considered as such but in terms of protection of the landscape.
Rights and responsibilities	The regulatory framework considered was limited to technical issues and had no reference to political and legal structures.
Ethical issues	Not considered in the above decision-making.
Commitment, interest and vision	Not considered in the above decision-making.

Note: The proposed definitions of the modalities have been used here to aid clarity.

In many contexts, only a few sporadic and mainly theoretical experiments are available and the results of these are not very satisfactory (Archibugi, 2002). MCA requires an explanation of the individual preferences of each decision-maker in an explicit manner. The decision-makers require *a priori* agreement on the criteria to be included and the weights to be assigned, avoiding interrelations between them (Zeppetella, 1997). This is not always possible or easy to carry out, and therefore discussions and negotiations cannot take place.

The suggested multi-modal framework illustrated in Table 6.3 is able to guide the decision-makers in the selection of the most suitable criteria for the evaluation. The new hierarchical structure of criteria and sub-criteria suggested for evaluating the five selected alternative solutions is illustrated in Table 7.3.

Compared with the original hierarchy of elements shown in Table 7.1, this list is more comprehensive as it incorporates all the relevant sustainable development issues for decision-making (including user's perception and social or ethical factors). It also places the previous criteria (*in italic*) inside each appropriate group of sustainable development modalities.

Case study 2: evaluation of sustainable redevelopment scenarios for an urban area

This example, taken from Lombardi (2009), is based on a real-world case study in planning redevelopment problems. It shows how the framework can be adopted for supporting the identification of both the evaluation criteria and the structuring of the model in complex planning/design decision-making problems. Finally, it highlights the benefits of the framework as a structuring approach in connection with the adoption of multi-criteria evaluation methods (MCA).

As was illustrated in Chapter 5, by taking into account different points of view and a weighting of the criteria to be used in the evaluation of alternative options, MCA methods usually provide the possibility to realise a meaningful and pluralistic evaluation of planning proposals, synthesising all the contributions of the different experts and the points of view of the actors involved (stakeholders and decision-makers).

Because of these features, the MCA approach is often applied to urban planning and design for evaluating alternative options, assessing their impacts on all built and natural environments and the institutional, socio-economical context (Munda, 2005). For instance, in Italy, a number of regulations and laws on public works and environmental evaluation suggest the use of MCA for assessing alternative design/planning options at an initial stage of development.

However, the large number of MCA methods currently available and the lack of specific hints on the 'best' or preferred method to be

Table 7.3 The new list of criteria and sub-criteria identified on the base of the multi-modal framework. (Source: Lombardi, 2009.)

Goal	Modalities	Criteria	Specification of criteria and sub-criteria
Sustainable development	Numerical accounting	Urban and infrastructure development	Considers quantitative issues such as population density, the location and extension of the waste disposal and the issue of transportation.
	Space, shape and extension		
	Transport and mobility		
	Physical environment	Environmental and physical quality	Includes the following sub-criteria: ▫ Safeguarding the atmosphere ▫ Safeguarding the water supply ▫ Safeguarding the soil ▫ Protection of the landscape ▫ Protection of public health (maximum hygiene)
	Health and ecological protection or biodiversity		
	Perceptions of people towards the environment		
	Analysis and formal knowledge	Education and scientific development	Takes into account the technological development in this field and the issue of good communications for sustainable functioning of the waste disposal, including the sub-criterion: ▫ Ease of operation
	Creativity and cultural development		
	Communication and the media		
	Social climate, social relationships and social cohesion	Social and economical development	Includes the following sub-criteria: ▫ Minimisation of danger (maximum safety) ▫ Maximisation of cost/revenue ratio ▫ Maximum life of plant ▫ Visual appeal of the site
	Efficiency and economic appraisal (e.g. GNP)		
	Visual appeal and architectural style		
	Rights and responsibilities	Governance	Includes rights and responsibilities, the participation of people in decision-making, the ethical issues and the vision of a sustainable development.
	Ethical issues		
	Commitment, interest and vision		

used for a specific design or planning problem, do create difficulties in practice (Kazmierczak *et al.*, 2007). An additional complication in the adoption of MCA methods in planning and design is the rigid hierarchical structure underlying most of these methods which does not sufficiently reflect the interdependences among aspects recognised in decision-making problems related to sustainable urban development (Kohler, 2002; Brandon & Lombardi, 2005).

This case study does not specifically deal with the problem of selecting the appropriate method for the right problem (see Lombardi, 1997), but it shows the application of a new promising MCA method, named Analytic Network Process (ANP), an advanced version of the Analytic Hierarchy Process (AHP) (Saaty, 1996), which seems able to better tackle and reflect the complexity of a decision-making problem without reducing it to a hierarchy structure but allowing and involving interaction and dependence among the elements (see Chapter 5). The modelling of the decision problem is based on the multi-modal framework illustrated in Chapter 6, which seems to be able to handle the multiplicity of the issues embodied in the concept of urban sustainability, guiding the selection of appropriate evaluation criteria.

The problem

This case study is related to an urban redevelopment scheme for an urban area, located in a small Italian town (about 50 000 inhabitants), in the metropolitan area of Turin.

The scheme is part of the Integrated Local Development Programme (ILDP) of the city which aims at valorising the urban area having a number of Agenda 21 strategic objectives as follows: environmental and urban quality, including promotion of environmental awareness, regeneration actions, existing resources' and cultural heritage enhancement; sustainable mobility; social cohesion, including economic development, human capital and local welfare. These complex and multiple issues of the ILDP are considered of great importance for the sustainable development of the urban area by the Local Municipality (Città di Collegno, 2005).

The area also includes historical buildings with a total floor surface of about 2000 m^2. An additional area with buildings and green space of about 1100 m^2 is linked to the historical one, providing opportunities for hosting a mixture of urban functions (Città di Collegno, 2006). Therefore, the problem was how to select the most suitable reuse scheme for the area, which is able to take all the above strategic issues and requirements into account, in an appropriate manner.

The design team has developed a number of preliminary studies aiming at identifying the level of environmental and physical damage of the buildings. These studies have highlighted the bad current physical conditions of all (floors, roofs, walls) structural elements. On the basis of the results obtained from the above studies, the Municipality and the design team have developed a number of different scenarios for the regeneration of the area, which can be synthesised into the following four alternative hypotheses of urban reuse:

A. 'Do nothing'.
    This solution means there will be no consequences from new constructions or reuse, but, at the same time, this could lead to an urban decay, particularly serious in the field of cultural heritage.
B. Business services.
    This solution aims to provide support to small and medium companies and is encouraged by recent regional strategic development directives.
C. Cultural and leisure centre.
    This scenario involves a mix of urban services and activities related to leisure, fitness and a museum, which is also able to give an investment return.
D. 'City of Health'.
    This solution is linked to the region's decision to concentrate hospitals and health structures in an area close to the one under study, in order to serve the whole of Turin's metropolitan area. This decision would have influenced the use of the buildings.

The model structuring approach

For evaluating the most preferable scenario, the consultant team of planners experimented with a new MCA approach, the ANP described in Chapter 5.

The identification of the evaluation criteria and their interrelation in the network structure was realised by using the multi-modal framework. The list of modal aspects listed in Table 6.3 and their meaning have guided the identification of both the clusters of the ANP model and the most suitable criteria for the assessment of the alternative scenarios. For instance, the following questions have been asked: 'To what extent does the proposal consider biodiversity?' which is an issue of the Biological aspect in the Physical–Environmental cluster; 'To what extent does it consider innovation and creativity?' which is an issue of the Formative aspect in the Human–Cultural cluster and again 'To what extent does it provide a shared vision of the future?' which is the top-level Credal/Vision aspect placed in the Institutional–Economic cluster. The above are only few examples of the list of questions developed by the consultant team on the base of the multi-modal framework; the full list is available in Città di Collegno (2006: 25–30).

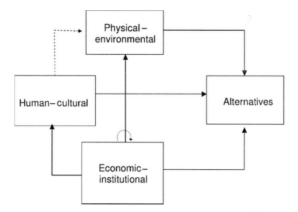

Figure 7.2 The final network model. (Source: Lombardi, 2009. Reproduced by permission of The Institution of Civil Engineers.)

What is important to highlight is that this taxonomy of aspects has allowed the design team to avoid missing relevant issues and/or the inclusion of redundant aspects which would have affected the scientific validity of the analysis.

The final network model is shown in Fig. 7.2. This is formed by four clusters: Alternatives, physical–environmental, human–cultural and economic–institutional.

The cluster of alternatives encompasses the four urban scenarios (A, B, C, D) described above. The three clusters of evaluation criteria include the basic heterogeneous elements constituting the strategic objectives underlying the local development programme, that is, the environmental and physical aspects of urban quality; the social and cultural issues connected to human capital and social cohesion; the economic and institutional promotion and awareness of sustainable regeneration actions.

In addition, the multi-modal framework has supported the structuring of the model. Here, the network structure and the links among clusters and nodes are built on the base of the dependency among the 15 modal aspects.

According to the multi-modal framework, there is a dependency between the aspects. The Vision (Credal) is placed on the top of the hierarchy and it is connected with all the modal aspects below in the list. This top aspect is included in the Economic–Institutional cluster which, in turn, is linked to the others. As a consequence of these links, there is a 'loop' in the cluster of the Economic/Institutional aspects, because the nodes included in this cluster (economic, aesthetical, juridical, ethical) are connected and assessed with reference to the vision (the top aspect in this hierarchy). In Fig. 7.2, the above-described characteristic of the model is represented by a rounded arrow on the Economic–Institutional cluster.

In addition, both the Physical–Environmental and the Human–Cultural clusters are dependent on the Economic–Institutional one because all the nodes of the network (the modal aspects) are connected to the Vision aspect. This interrelation among clusters is represented in Fig. 7.2 by an arrow which connects the Economic–Institutional cluster with both the Human–Cultural and the Physical–Environmental clusters. Finally, although the multi-modal framework reveals a dependency between the Physical–Environmental cluster and the Human–Cultural one, there is no need to show a connection in the scheme (see sketched line in the figure) because both are automatically linked by being dependant upon the same node (the vision aspect) in the Economic–Institutional cluster.

This model network is consistent with both the internationally recognised 'triple-bottom-line' definition of sustainable development provided by international organisations (e.g. OECD, 2003b, 2008; United Nations, 2007) and Maureen Hart's approach (1999) which nests the three dimensions of sustainability as concentric circles – economy within society, and both economy and society within the environment. In fact, economy is a part of, only exists within, and was invented by, the human realm. Thus, it is appropriately nested within the society which, in turns, is supported by the environment.

Finally, in the model, all the three clusters of aspects are connected to the cluster of the alternatives (see Fig. 7.2). On the base of this link, an evaluation of the impact of the four transformation scenarios against the identified sustainability criteria can be also developed.

Results and conclusive remarks

The application of an ANP requires pairwise comparison and relative weight estimation, as in the standard AHP. The determination of relative weights is based on pairwise comparison of decision elements (Saaty, 1980, 1996). These give a basis to the decision-makers to reveal their preference by comparing two elements. Pairwise comparisons of the elements at each level are conducted with respect to their relative importance towards control criteria or clusters.

In this case study, each node of the clusters has been assessed with regard to the node placed at the top of the model, that is, the vision (credal modal aspect). For instance, it has been asked: 'what element is more important between the Physical aspect and the Spatial aspect with regard to the vision of the local community, and how much?'.

Both experts and public representatives involved in this participative evaluation process, had the opportunity to express their judgement, measured on a nine-point scale, on all the relevant decision-making issues. These values have been then reported in pair-comparison matrices, such as the one illustrated in Table 7.4. Here one can see that the Physical aspect has been strongly preferred (5) to the Spatial and the

Table 7.4 Example of pairwise matrix related to the physical/environmental elements. (Source: Lombardi, 2009. Reproduced by permission of The Institution of Civil Engineers.)

	Numerical	**Spatial**	**Kinematics**	**Physical**	**Biological**
Numerical	1	5	2	1/5	1/7
Spatial	1/5	1	1/3	1/5	1/7
Kinematics	1/2	3	1	1/5	1/6
Physical	5	5	5	1	1/2
Biological	7	7	6	2	1

Note: Each pairwise matrix is squared and reciprocal; the diagonal is composed by units. Users have to complete just a half of the matrix because the rest is done automatically by reciprocal values.

reciprocal number (1/5) is assigned to the Spatial in comparison to the Physical. In addition, each alternative vision has been assessed with regard to each node of the three clusters of modalities, and their impacts have been measured and recorded. If expert opinions are different or conflicting, the method suggests a need for compromise though discussion and an intermediate pairwise weight can be selected in the nine-point scale.

This assessment process has been developed for all the elements in the clusters and, subsequently, a supermatrix of paired comparisons and its normalisation by cluster, has been established in accordance to the ANP procedure (Saaty, 1996). This application has been supported by some specialist software (see http://www.superdecisions.com/).

At the end of the process, the global priorities of the network elements, including the alternatives is finally derived, as illustrated in Fig. 7.3. This shows that the cultural and leisure centre is the urban scenario that, compared with the others, is able to better meet all the sustainability criteria, obtaining the highest percentage (38%). The second best choice is the 'Business Services' scenario (22%), while the 'Do nothing' alternative (15%) and the 'City of Health' (14%) are the worst alternatives. These results are in line with the transformation strategies of the city which are reflected in the high priorities given to the followings aspects:

❏ *Social aspect*: The city aims to create 'social attraction points' in order to increase citizens' 'sense of belonging' to their urban environment and to prevent the emigration of population.
❏ *Biological aspect*: The city wishes to preserve the environmental quality of the urban area.
❏ *Credal aspect*: The vision is to reflect the local community's expectations which are assumed as the main objective of this assessment process.

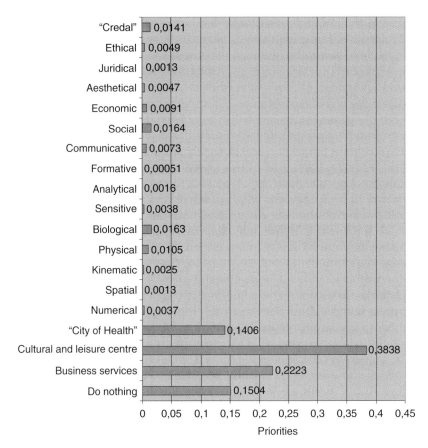

Figure 7.3 Final priorities of evaluation criteria and alternatives. (Source: Lombardi, 2009. Reproduced by permission of The Institution of Civil Engineers.)

One of the benefits of the multi-modal framework approach highlighted by this case study is that it explicitly recognises that sustainable development of an urban area is a multi-aspect issue and acknowledges the interdependences between environmental, social and economic systems. Compared with the traditional BOCR structure of an ANP model, this does not force the analysis towards a hierarchical classification of positive (benefit) and negative (cost) issues. On the contrary, it allows a meaningful and holistic impact evaluation of alternative scenarios against all relevant sustainability aspects in an integrated manner.

In conclusion, the recognised benefits of this approach are twofold. It helps experts, like planners, socio and political actors and other stakeholders to consider all relevant aspects of a planning decision so that none is ignored, and a final decision can be achieved (Lombardi &

Basden, 1997). This benefit has been already highlighted in the previous case studies reported in this chapter. A second important advantage of this approach, as highlighted in this case study, is that it provides a clear understanding of the interconnections between the relevant aspects of a planning decision, so that it is possible to recognise the main 'cause–effect' of an action. For instance, preservation of the environmental quality of the urban area (Biological aspect) is dependent on the 'sense of belonging' that citizens have towards their urban environment. The latter is an issue of the Sensitive aspect which, in turn, is connected to the Social problem of emigration of population, an issue that the Municipality wishes to prevent. Unfortunately, this is linked to the Aesthetical aspect ('it is not a nice place to live') which, in turn, creates disaffection and a neglect attitude in the population (Ethical aspect), asking for a new 'vision' of the place (Credal aspect).

Case study 3: 'multi-stakeholder' urban regeneration decision-making

In decision-making processes related to public and private sectors, conflict often occurs when competing interests who value land in different ways, such as house-builders and amenity societies, seek to promote or prevent development of the same site. During the planning process many public and private interests have to be considered, for example, healthy environmental conditions for living and working, social and cultural needs of the citizens, the demand for home-ownership and social equality, mobility and conservation.

In general, urban planning laws protect the individual corporation or citizen against disadvantages and encourage equal opportunities and competition in the real-estate market and urban development. However, in practice there are many problems, especially those of communication, between public and private decision-makers who often do not cooperate. There are often lengthy negotiations without any result. In particular, there are few shared values concerning the development of the urban area, nor is there agreement about measures to promote development (Kaib, 1994; Koster, 1994). If the preferences of certain groups are in conflict, it is usually necessary to know the comparative 'strengths' of the interests, generally expressed in terms of costs and benefits, in order to increase the information available to assist in the resolution of conflicts through the decision-making process (Lichfield *et al.*, 1975; Lichfield, 1996).

In this case study, the multi-modal framework has been used as a guide for analysing the various stakeholder decision-making processes that took place in relation to the redevelopment of an ex-industrial area in Muggia (Trieste). The methodology involved a study of the decision-making problems related to the area, an understanding of the objectives and strategies of the different actors and a detailed analysis of the project in spatial and economic terms. The analyses required investigation, collection of information and interviews with the key actors.

The case study refers to the long decision-making process involved in the regeneration of the area. This involved four different stakeholders:

❑ The local authority of Muggia.
❑ The private industrial owner of the area.
❑ The local authority of Aquilinia (a small village developed by the employers during the firm's year of activity, under the jurisdiction of Muggia).
❑ The local authority of Trieste, the biggest town adjacent to the area, which as regional capital holds territorial jurisdiction over Muggia.

The opportunity to understand a redevelopment of the area arose at the beginning of the nineties thanks to the Italian law n.179/92 on urban regeneration which facilitates public–private partnership by providing national funding to cover the cost of the reclaimed land (D.M.LL.PP, 1994).

The local authorities and an industrial firm started a number of time-consuming negotiations in order to reach an agreement. The main conflicts related to the new land uses to be included in the area. Muggia and Aquilinia sought residential and tourist areas, and Trieste aimed at developing its territorial influence by including public services for its harbour and fruit market; the private owner was interested in making the highest profit. Large differences in the interests of all these actors made it very difficult to achieve a solution. A simple financial appraisal had been applied but this method was not able to assist in the resolution of the conflict.

After years of discussion and a long process of design, it was possible to reconcile the interests of all the actors in a single project. This final project included residential and tourist areas, commercial areas and public services, providing a synthesis of the numerous negotiations undertaken by the actors.

A retrospective analysis of the above decision-making process was undertaken, using the multi-modal framework (Lombardi & Marella, 1997). This analysis was useful in that it recognised the major areas of integration between the actors, the nature of the conflicts and their dependence on the interests of each actor, and the relationships between the design factors and other factors that could have led to an earlier resolution of the above conflicts.

An outline of the differences is provided in Table 7.5. In particular, the analysis showed that there are reasons of a different nature

Table 7.5 A retrospective analysis of the decision-making process on the basis of the modal aspects. (Source: Adapted from Lombardi & Marella, 1997.)

Aspects	Decision-makers (stakeholders)			
	Land owner	Aquilinia	Muggia	Trieste
Numerical accounting	516 000 volume	321 000 volume	321 000 volume	352 000 volume
Space, shape and extension	Building layout according to landscape	Building layout according to landscape	Building layout according to landscape	Building layout according to landscape
Transport and mobility	To improve accessibility: building a new motorway	To solve urban traffic: building a railway, a motorway and a pedestrian street	To improve connection with Trieste: building a new motorway	To improve connection with Muggia: building a new motorway
Physical environment	Not addressed	Reduce energy use of traffic	Reduce energy use of traffic	Recycling of building materials
Health, biodiversity and ecological protection	Attention to reclaimed land	Attention to reclaimed land	Attention to reclaimed land and water quality	Attention to reclaimed land and water quality
Perceptions of people, welfare	Not addressed	To improve security	Not addressed	Not addressed
Analysis and formal knowledge	Suggested land uses from the analysis: shopping mall; business district; hotel; residence	Suggested land uses from the analysis: business district; residence	Suggested land uses from the analysis: business district; hotel; residence	Suggested land uses from the analysis: public services; harbour services; residence
Creativity and cultural development	Not addressed	To break with previous activity	Not addressed	To develop public service and residential areas

Continues

Table 7.5 *Contd.*

Aspects	Decision-makers (stakeholders)			
	Land owner	Aquilinia	Muggia	Trieste
Communications and the media	To include signs and advertising for commercial activity	Not addressed	Not addressed	Not addressed
Social climate, social relations, social cohesion	Not addressed	To improve social interaction, e.g., design an urban square	Not addressed	Not addressed
Efficiency and economic appraisal	To use public funding, minimising private resources	Frugality in the use of the land	To use national funding for building local infrastructures	Recycling schemes for building harbour wharves
Visual appeal and architectural style	To improve visual impact and to harmonise landscape	Harmony within the landscape	To improve visual impact, to harmonise accessibility	Not addressed
Rights and responsibilities	To reduce own responsibilities in construction	To move property rights from private to public sector	To increase responsibilities of private owner in construction	Not addressed
Ethical issues	Not addressed	To improve health of families	Not addressed	Not addressed
Commitment, interest and vision	To increase own profit and improve 'image' for company marketing reasons	To improve well-being of its citizens and increase young population	To improve tourism, increasing areas for recreational activities	To expand its territorial influence and increase areas for new services

underlying the interests of each actor (see the credal modality: 'commitment, interest and vision'), but there are also strong integrations of interest among the actors (concerning the issues of 'transport and mobility', 'health, biodiversity and ecological protection' and 'visual appeal of buildings and settings'). The major conflicts arose in dealing with issues related to the 'efficiency and economic appraisal' and 'rights and responsibilities' and these have led the stakeholders to end up with different results from the ones they wanted, both in the amount of construction and in their proposed design, particularly with regard to land use and the allocation of resources (see 'numerical accounting' and 'analysis and formal knowledge'). For example, the purpose of the land owner was to use public resources (efficiency and economic appraisal) to improve his marketing image (commitment, interest and vision) and to reduce his responsibility in construction (rights and responsibilities). This would result in a design scheme with a greater amount of construction (numerical accounting) and a 'highest and best use' of the land identified in a shopping centre (analysis and formal knowledge). However, the same land owner agreed with the other stakeholders regarding accessibility of the site (transport and mobility), the land reclamation (health, biodiversity and ecological protection) and the harmonisation of the redevelopment with the landscape (visual appeal of buildings and settings).

This retrospective analysis of the conflict in this 'typical' (at least for the Italian context) decision-making process suggested that the multi-modal structure provides a useful theoretical foundation for the comprehension of a planning (and design) process in the context of the sustainability of our built environment. The analysis also suggests that the structure may assist in the resolution of conflicts between actors involved in a planning process. It makes a number of critical factors that underlie a decision-making process explicit, stimulating thought and 'opening up' the field to problems that were not previously evident.

An application of this structure at an early stage of decision-making (as a proactive evaluation tool) would have helped to explain the relationships between the actors, showing the aspects that qualify the interests of each stakeholder. This, in turn, would have revealed those aspects that are in opposition and this might have guided the stakeholders towards a different result in planning. Finally, it would have helped decision-makers to recognise the areas where negotiation was needed.

In planning, particularly at the strategic level, there is a great demand for, but also a lack of, systematic methods that are able to help (Bentivegna, 1997). It may be that the proposed framework can improve this situation.

Case study 4: social reporting of Modena City strategic plan

This case study deals with the sustainability reporting of Modena, which has recently been developed in the context of the strategic planning process of the city (Comune di Modena, 2004).

In planning, traditional tools have largely lost their original meaning in predicting the future assets of a town. There is a clear understanding that, on the one hand, local development takes into account a bigger spatial scale with many more stakeholders. On the other hand, globalisation and transnational integration processes have increased the role of cities inside the socio-economical and territorial development of countries (Mazzola & Maggioni, 2001).

The role of strategic planning is to build incrementally a shared vision of the future development of a city through networking and multi-disciplinary effort (Archibugi, 2002). The main differences from traditional physical planning, for example, the City Master Plan, are the inclusion of uncertainty and discontinuity in the decision-making process, the networking of actors and competitiveness, global vision and direction for future urban development (Ciciotti & Perulli, 1998).

According to Bryson (1988) the main steps of a strategic planning process are:

(1) Framing of the issues.
(2) Networking of the stakeholders.
(3) Evaluation of the actions undertaken.

The framing and networking activities aim at:

❑ Exploring the decision-making problem.
❑ Identifying the strategic issues for the development of the vision of the future.
❑ Analysing the relationships between the issues and the actors involved.
❑ Recognising the partnerships and strategies of the stakeholders.

Strategic planning implies taking a holistic view of the context in which the action is performed. It requires retrospective and monitoring evaluation approaches as learning tools for transparent, inclusive decision-making (Ciciotti et al., 2001; Pugliese & Spaziante, 2003).

The model of *participatory democracy* postulates that policy-making takes place in continuous interaction with citizens and aims to build up the capacity of individuals to exercise greater control over decisions (Davidson, 1998; Davoudi, 1999). It originates from a generally accepted definition of strategic planning as 'the process which aims at building a shared vision

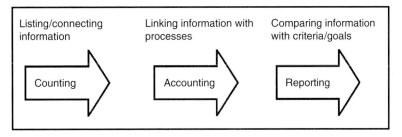

Figure 7.4 The evolution of the concept of social reporting. (Source: Adapted from CLEAR Project, 2001.)

of the future development of a community or a town' (Bryson, 1988). The stakeholders in this shared vision are all individuals who have specific interests regarding the future development and who have the opportunity to influence decision-making and all those contributing to the building of value. It also includes all concerned citizens (Lichfield, 1999).

The 'social reporting' is a retrospective evaluation process based on a system of performance indicators of economical, social and environmental nature (thus the term 'triple-bottom-line approach'). The aim is to evaluate the actions (decisions, projects, investments, etc.) undertaken by a local authority in the past in order to improve future decisions and eventually correct current mistakes (Hinna, 2002).

Key issues of social reporting

The key issues of social reporting are:

- ❑ It is a marketing and managerial tool for local governance, derived from the private sector with an ethical underpinning (e.g. eco-audit).
- ❑ It has evolved from a 'one bottom line' to a 'triple bottom line' approach: economical, social, environmental.
- ❑ It is based on *ex post* evaluation and *monitoring*.
- ❑ It includes both tangible and intangible effects of the actions undertaken by the local authority.

The concept of social reporting has evolved during the past few decades from a simple act of counting, that is, of listing information of a financial nature (one bottom line), to a more sophisticated tool which links this information to the underlying process of actions (i.e. the accounting), and finally with the 'Social reporting', comparing the required information with appropriate criteria or goals, in order to evaluate and produce evidence to the local community of the consequences of those actions (see Fig. 7.4).

Table 7.6   The legal framework. (Source: Adapted from Hinna (ed.), 2002.)

Italy		EU
Private sector	**Public sector**	**European Union**
Battelle Institute, Geneva, 1975 Legge Draghi, 1998 GBS-Task-group Guidelines, 2001	L. 142/1990 Digs 77/1995 Digs 267/2000 (TUEL)	EMAS, 1993 for eco-audit Network for Building Social Responsibility in Europe, www.ebnsc.org Green Book, 2001, www.europa.eu.int/comm/off/green/index_it.htm Corporate Social responsibility, 2002

The evolution of social reporting has been reflected in the legal framework of both Europe and the Member States, including Italy and the UK. Table 7.6 illustrates this framework.

Current reporting on environmental issues (e.g. in the context of local Agenda 21) faces a number of problems related to sustainability indicators developed with the aim of identifying current urban problems in order to assist local administration decision-making processes.

Chapter 4 has already discussed the main problems associated with the current lists of indicators. Previous studies (see Lombardi & Basden, 1997; Lombardi, 1998b, 1999) have also shown that they do not put the same weight on all the sustainability aspects recognised in the literature, but mainly emphasise the issues of 'environmental sustainability' and specifically the threats to the natural environment arising from issues such as mobility, transportation and decisions related to economic appraisal. The extensive literature available in this area has confirmed this observation. In turn, this also reveals a general imbalance in the decision-making process, due to an overemphasis on certain issues rather than others (Lombardi & Basden, 1997). The lists of sustainability indicators developed by international organisations such as the United Nations and OECD show a lack of harmonious distribution among the aspects related to an urban system. This is seen as a problem of imbalance, with more emphasis on certain issues than on others, leading to unsustainable decisions (see Lombardi & Basden, 1997; Lombardi, 1998a,b).

More specific criticisms of social reporting are related to the availability of the information required. The reporting activity is strongly related to contingent aspects, political elections or administrative and marketing reasons. The data are often stored in different statistical databases that are difficult to access, manipulate and compare. The lack of an available structured database is due mainly to the fact that social reporting is not an obligatory tool. On the contrary, it is undertaken at the end of an administration process and is not linked to the forward programming stage. A major problem is the selection of the 'right' indicator which is best able to represent the urban situation.

In this case study, the selection of indicators was developed on the basis of a number of criteria largely chosen from the principal international organisations on sustainability, such as the United Nations. These were chosen because they appeared to relate to local needs, data was available and easy to update, they were scientifically sound at both national and international levels and they were relatively simple and easy to communicate. The social reporting process of the City of Modena was developed using a number of steps (see Comune di Modena, 2004; Lombardi & Stanghellini, 2008):

(1)   An identification of the main actions and programmes undertaken by the local authority during the first administrative stage of the major provisional programme and its additional administrative documentation (i.e. the Italian local 'Programma elettorale' and 'Relazioni previsionali e programmatiche').

(2)   A taxonomy analysis of the actions and programmes, which are grouped in five strategic axes, or macro-programmes (packages of programmes containing groups of projects), as follows:

(a)   Strategic axe n.1: *Innovation*. This deals with economic development and technological and infrastructure endowment.

(b)   Strategic axe n.2: *Urban quality*. This deals with environmental and physical quality, parks and greenery, waste management, energy consumption, transport and mobility, and urban regeneration.

(c)   Strategic axe n.3: *Sociality*. This deals with social integration, crime, sport, culture, tourism and citizens' rights.

(d)   Strategic axe n.4: *Welfare*. This deals with education and sanitary policies (hospitals, nurseries, etc.).

(e)   Strategic axe n.5: *Administration*. This deals with an improvement in public services supplied to citizens.

(3)   The selection of a number of performance indicators for each action, related to four specific measures of:

(a)   *Efficiency*: This deals with the managerial capacity of the local administration by measuring the number of projects undertaken compared with those planned, and their degree of realisation.

(b)   *Economics*: This measures the minimisation of the financial resources used for the development of the projects.

(c)   *Efficacy*: This measures the goal achievement of each project.

(d)   *Effects on the community*: This measures the benefits of each project to socio-economic sectors and to the community.

(4)   A measurement of each performance indicator in terms of percentage of decrease or increase in the period of analysis (1996–2003).

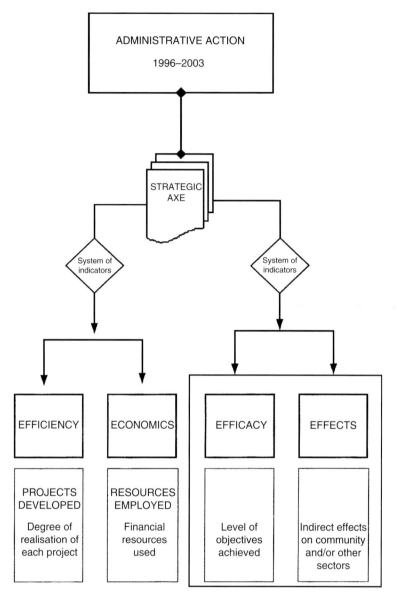

Figure 7.5   A graphical representation of the model used for each strategic axis of the social reporting of the City of Modena.

Figure 7.5 provides a graphical illustration of this model (named the '4-*E* model').

This system of performance indicators provides a rich picture of the results obtained by the local administration during the years of activity, by measuring the achievement of each target declared in the Administrative Political Programme. However, it does not provide a final synthesis of the results obtained or a judgement on the sustainability of the local authority's action. The large number of indicators and measures may confuse the decision-makers who generally want an easy measure to illustrate the sustainability of these actions. The aim of the multi-modal framework is to achieve a comprehensive and holistic view of the results.

Table 7.7 shows the re-classification of the strategic axes (and consequent actions and indicators) by using the multi-modal framework illustrated in Table 6.3. This forces the identification of a limited number of 'sound' indicators which refer to the modalities. It provides a systematic and logical design for the performance indicators to be used in the social reporting, which is comprehensive but which avoids an overload of unprocessed information. At the same time, it drives all the different measures and actions towards a restricted number of sustainable development criteria.

As illustrated in Chapter 6, the framework articulates the concept of sustainable development by using three different levels of criteria which are interlinked.

The third level of criteria is represented by the 15 modalities. The second level of criteria incorporates the five classes of urban policies:

❑ Urban and infrastructure development.
❑ Environmental and physical quality.
❑ Education and scientific development.
❑ Social and economical development.
❑ Governance

These are reflected in the strategic axes of urban quality, welfare, sociality, innovation and administration. They are linked to the first level of sustainable development aspects named physical environment capital, human cultural capital and financial institutional capital, which in turn encapsulate the concept of sustainable development (see Chapter 3).

The key role played by an information base in decision-making within the context of sustainable development should be re-emphasised. An overflow of data may hinder a decision because it is difficult for stakeholders and decision-takers to distil the correct and appropriate information to be used in the decision-making process. The benefit of the proposed framework is to allow this selection, emphasising those indicators and/or criteria that are meaningful to citizens and stakeholders for sustainable development.

Summary and conclusion

This chapter has illustrated the application of the multi-modal framework to four case studies related to different planning contexts. In these examples, the structure has assisted in making the relevant issues of a

Table 7.7 Structuring the social reporting of Modena City according to the multi-modal framework.

Goal	Second-level aspects	Strategic axes and public policies	Modalities	Examples of indicators	Decrease/increase value (1996/2003*)
Sustainable development	Urban and infrastructural development	AXE N.2: URBAN QUALITY	Numerical accounting		
			Space, shape and extension	Total built-up area	+6.3%
			Transport and mobility	Length of cycle-roads	+50%
			Physical environment	Energy consumption (gas)	+5.1
	Environmental and physical quality	AXE N.2: URBAN QUALITY AXE N.4: WELFARE	Health and ecological protection or biodiversity	Presence of green areas	+38.4%
			Perceptions of people towards the environment	Available rooms in nurseries	+5.6%
	Education and scientific development	AXE N.1: INNOVATION AXE N.4: WELFARE	Analysis and formal knowledge	Number of registrations at university	+2.7
			Creativity and cultural development	Unemployment rate of young people	-8.8%
			Communication and the media	ICT endowment	Not found
	Social and economical development	AXE N.3: SOCIALITY	Social climate, social relationships and social cohesion	Crime rate	-4.8%
			Efficiency and economic appraisal (e.g. GNP)	Number of enterprises	+21.1%
			Visual appeal and architectural style	Number of museum visitors	+18.2%
	Governance	AXE N.5: ADMINISTRATION	Rights and responsibilities	Simplifying administrative actions	-38.7%
			Ethical issues	Number of people participating in voluntary activities	Not found
			Commitment, interest and vision	Population voting in the administrative elections	Not found

Note: *The value of some indicators refers to a different year due to a lack of data availability.

decision-making process explicit and transparent in the context of sustainability. It is able to cover a wider range of issues which are rarely addressed by current methods.

The four case studies have also shown that a great many aspects of urban sustainability for decision-making can meaningfully be checked for completeness, consistency, duplication and internal logic by deploying the three classes of sustainable urban development and the 15 constituents (including the five main groups of urban policy actions) from the proposed structure (see also Nijkamp, 2007).

Within the extraordinary variety of planning contexts and evaluation perspectives (both retrospective and predictive), the framework provides a flexible guide that is able to identify the critical factors for sustainability and the decision-making problem, 'opening up' the field to key issues that were not previously evident. It also suggests that it is able to aid the analysis of different stakeholders' perspectives, providing useful insights for the resolution of conflicts.

As the planning process is itself a dynamic one that can change over time, the findings of the above applications support the view that the multi-modal framework can be used in different contexts, for different stakeholders and multi-objective problems. However, this framework was never intended to be in itself an alternative method for evaluation in planning and design. Rather it is proposed as a structure for all: supporting applications of multi-criteria analysis by helping the identification of a list of relevant evaluation criteria (Case study 1); for structuring the decision-making problems highlighting interrelations and links among decision issues (Case study 2); for illustrating different stakeholders' views (Case study 3) and for synthesising the results of a quantitative analysis based on statistical indicators (Case study 4), widening the horizon of current practice and opening up new boundaries and directions for research work in this field.

Future, practical applications are required to test the validity of this approach in real decision-making to see whether it increases the likelihood of greater sustainable development in urban districts and cities. An example of implementation of the deficit of sustainable construction in urban areas and the strategies to overcome this deficit by using the multi-modal approach can be found in the work undertaken by Han Vandevyvere in Flanders, the northern part of Belgium, at the Department of Architecture, Urbanism and Planning of the Catholic University of Leuven (K.U.Leuven) (Vandevyvere, 2009; Vandevyvere & Neuckermans, 2009).

This is an evolutionary process which will develop in time but the structure should remain stable as the techniques and content emerge.

Towards Management Systems and Protocols

At the heart of the sustainable development agenda is the question of management. If we take the broad definition of management as being '… the act of controlling, directing affairs to succeed, coping …' (*New Webster's Dictionary*, 1992), these are issues that are at the centre of the sustainable development agenda. We need to *control* in order to *avoid* the perceived calamities that might ensue if we do not intervene and control in some way. We need to *direct affairs* in order to take positive action that will address the agenda identified as necessary to improve the position of future generations and we need to act to *cope* with what is perceived to be a worsening environmental and social disorder.

The paradox is, of course, that it is the management actions of human beings that have resulted in the present unsatisfactory situation and is the reason why it is now thought necessary to encourage an agenda entitled 'sustainable development'. Throughout human history, mankind has found it necessary to take decisions that he or she believed would enhance his or her status and position within nature. Humans strove to be *in control* of nature and, in so doing, many forgot that in fact they were part of the natural environment and part of its delicate balance. Now that we have come so far with one set of objectives, which were about controlling nature, is it possible to find a new paradigm which seeks to re-establish the position of humans *within* nature? In essence this was the debate within the 2002 Johannesburg conference of the United Nations and to which we referred in the spectrum of views on sustainable development in Chapter 1. The world is full of examples where humans have attempted to change things for the

Evaluating Sustainable Development in the Built Environment, Second Edition
By Peter S. Brandon and Patrizia Lombardi © 2011 Peter S. Brandon and Patrizia Lombardi

better, only to find that in a comparatively short period the results of their actions have resulted in another problem in another area which was not foreseen at the time. All technologies have the power to provide positive advantages but, if used improperly, they can often lead to disastrous consequences. This is a warning to all of us seeking to find 'solutions' to the sustainability problem.

In past centuries, the population of the world, the level of technological sophistication and the geographical impact were all of a smaller order and, while some damage was done, it could be corrected in time and often by natural means. Now we have a different situation where, in some instances such as global warming, it requires a massive effort by all nations to solve the problem. Pollution does not recognise national boundaries, nor does it recognise human jurisdictions, nor does it have respect for culture or religion. Human development contributes to both the physical environment and also the behavioural consequences of the life in that environment. It can be beneficial or it can be harmful. The problem is that it is not always possible to tell, at the time of making the decision to develop, what the impact will be. Apart from war situations, there are very few instances where it could be said that humans have undertaken development to deliberately harm the planet or indeed its human population. It is true that sometimes decisions have been made recklessly and without regard for the consequences, often with an economic motive in mind, but, by and large, decisions were made to 'improve things'. If improvement was the aim, why do we have the problems we now face?

It is impossible to be exhaustive about the reasons why a breakdown has occurred but it must be partly due to the changing nature of the human world; see Table 8.1, for example.

There is little doubt that the changes brought about by technology have made managing towards a sustainable environment much more difficult. This is coupled with a shift towards democratic processes whereby the political machines have to respond to the voice of the people. The result is a much more complex world where the institutions and mechanisms of governance can be found in a variety of different locations, where it is often the short term that is being addressed instead of the long term, and where the impacts of technologies are difficult to gauge in a holistic manner.

So how do we intervene in such an environment? It appears an impossible task. Is it realistic to expect governments to unite around a common set of principles? Can managers across the world agree on what constitutes sustainable development within their context? Can we expect a common filter on all decision-making in the future that engages with the sustainable development debate? It is unlikely.

If not we must, at least for the foreseeable future, consider what is possible at this point in time and what the conditions are that encourage good management. It would be fair to say that few would claim to

Table 8.1   The changing nature of the human world.

Past generations	Current generations
Human settlements were bounded largely by people's ability to travel and the natural resources available.	Human settlements are engaged across the planet and wealth is the constraint not technology.
Technological development was to enhance human labour and its impact was limited to the individual or to small communities.	Technological development has moved to the wider community and global level and its impact is beyond national boundaries.
Management control was in the hands of the few.	Management control is exercised by a plethora of agencies.
Financial power was localised and within the control of the local community.	Financial power exists within a vast number of institutions, many of which are multi-national and global.
Regulation was exercised locally within the cultural context of the community.	Regulation is now exercised nationally and internationally and it reflects the demands of those with power at this level.

have solved the problem of managing development in such a way that it is sustainable. This is not surprising since the concept of sustainability has not been adopted until comparatively recently. Many philosophers and writers have made statements over the centuries which demonstrate that wise men have understood the problem, but it was only in the latter part of the twentieth century that this became a major agenda item for the world. Good husbandry for the locality has become good stewardship for the world.

In some ways this gives us the clue for advancement because there are links between the two. The global agenda depends on a multitude of decisions at the local level. The disposal of refrigerators, the choice of energy for housing, the method of manufacturing building products and the planning framework for a local authority are all examples of the billions of small decisions that contribute to sustainable development. Thus the maxim *think global, act local* has become a motto for many within the field.

It is not difficult to see that although this may be a useful call to improve the situation, it is extremely difficult to implement in practice. A decision in one area has an impact in another which may lead to an unsustainable development. Examples abound. The method of insulating a building may save energy at the local level but the extraction process for the raw materials may require more energy than it saves and may deplete the earth of a valuable resource or at least increase its cost in a market situation. The regeneration of one urban area may lead to the decline of adjacent areas as people move to take advantage of the improvement and another community is deprived of its economic resource to maintain or improve its standards. The shift to out-of-town shopping centres can lead to deprivation in the traditional city centres, and so it goes on.

How can 'management', whatever that might be and by whoever it might be implemented, deal with such complexity? I think most people would say that at one level it cannot. We have not yet developed the tools or systems that allow us to address the issues and certainly not in a way that is understandable and actionable by all stakeholders concerned with decision-making in the built environment, or indeed elsewhere. Even if we were in favour of a totalitarian regime, which could control all inputs and outputs from the process, we do not know enough about the interrelationships that exist between the various impacts of millions of decisions to *know* what the outcome would be. In fact we are not yet sure what the destination might be, if there is such a thing. Over time these relationships will change and consequently the decisions will need to respond accordingly. What is considered to be sensible now might well appear stupid to a future generation.

In a democratic society, where the will of the people determines policy, much depends on the knowledge and commitment of the people to the objective of sustainable development. This requires a high standard of education coupled with a willingness to make sacrifices now in order to allow future generations to have choice in their own futures, equal to what we enjoy now (the need for education is enlarged upon in Chapter 9). All the constraints that politicians work with in such societies come clearly to the fore. Will this result in good economic performance, allowing the current population to achieve its present aspirations? Will it attend to the health needs of this generation? Will it resolve current difficulties in society before the next election? These are some of the major issues that will probably decide whether the politician is elected in the next round of voting. A short-term approach related to voters' inclinations at a single point in time does not sit well with the long-term view required for sustainable development. In other key professions, such as property developers, the motivation may well be an even shorter term than the politicians and depend on meeting the bottom-line requirements of the shareholders or investors.

This could be considered a very pessimistic scenario, and indeed would be if we thought we had to resolve everything right now. However, the nature of the management process must be to learn as we progress. This suggests that whatever system is developed must have clear and structured feedback mechanisms to allow continual review and improvement. The important question is 'Who manages?' in order that feedback can be systematically established in such a way that there is corporate learning at all levels.

Who manages?

A simple answer to the question of who manages sustainable development would be *'Everyone'*. At least everyone has a contribution to make. On environmental issues, for example, the way each household purchases its products and disposes of waste is a management responsibility within the home. The local authority usually has responsibility for waste disposal and recycling of waste material under the auspices of a central government that provides legislation and directives as to what to do. The companies that produce the products manage the wrapping and promotion, and transport companies deliver the products in a particular way. The list is endless but it illustrates the complexity of the management process and the complex ownership issue within the problem. In broad terms, the management of sustainable development can be categorised as follows:

❏ *Government*: The government has the responsibility of providing a legislative and regulatory framework within which management can operate. In addition, as a large client for many activities within most countries, it has a management responsibility to encourage and implement sustainable development within those activities and to educate the public about such issues. It is also the mechanism whereby global initiatives between nations, such as Agenda 21, are realised.
❏ *Local authorities*: These authorities have the responsibility of working out government policy within the context of their own jurisdiction. They too determine policy and work out their policies through actions in areas such as transport, policing, waste disposal, infrastructure works and so on. At the urban level they are the managers who set the framework within which all others have to operate.
❏ *Organisations and firms*: These institutions have to comply with what government and local authorities demand but they can also manage their organisations to be sensitive to sustainable development, and indeed many firms have their own policy on such issues which is available for public scrutiny. It can be complex, particularly when the organisation is a multi-national company operating across the world. The sensitivities and requirements of a country such as India or China may be quite different from those in the West.
❏ *Individuals*: All of us have some responsibility for managing our lives and we do this within the context provided by government and local authorities and within the constraints of those who provide goods and services for us. While we can change these 'controllers' through the election processes and through purchasing power, this is usually a long-term affair and we have to adapt accordingly.

While the above appears as a hierarchy it is really much more complex as between the levels there is interaction which changes according to the decision-making process that is adopted. It is also almost impossible to opt out from the system as many small communities who consider themselves self-sufficient have suggested they might do. They find themselves dependent at some level on others or controlled in some way, and their freedom to act is curtailed. This might be the provision of utilities (water, energy or waste disposal) or access through transport, or the supply chain for food or other commodities, or it may be that they suffer from the bad behaviour of adjacent communities, say pollution, for which they have to take action. There are also the remaining freedoms to act which individuals can exercise at will, whether within the law or outside it, and these individual acts will have a bearing on sustainable development. In a free society it is not possible to control every aspect of human behaviour. For example, communities with high crime rates can find their position unsustainable through the actions of individuals outside the legal and regulatory framework.

The planning framework

Whatever management system is implemented for sustainable development, it has to respond to and contribute to the regulatory framework within which it must operate. One of the primary frameworks, at least for the built environment, must be that of the planning process. This is the process by which government, at all levels, exercises influence and power as to what is allowed or encouraged to be built. Usually this is defined within a process that has legal enforcement. However, there might also be a number of less formal constituents which are advisory and might be taken on board by a planning authority when it uses its discretionary powers. This can make the sources for management decision-making quite varied and complex unless these are made explicit. It also varies from region to region of each country and from country to country, making it impossible to generalise about such issues. In fact there is a growing realisation of the interdependence between countries and between communities within those countries, which means that no country can act alone – it therefore becomes a global problem.

An international project called SUSPLAN, funded by European Union Framework Funds, involving three local government and university partnerships across Denmark, the Netherlands and the UK looked at how attitudes to sustainable development impact on urban and rural planning. One study produced a useful map of the way in which the concept of sustainable development was integrated into the planning process in the UK (Porter, 2000) as shown in Fig. 8.1. It can be seen that the local authority at the centre of the map is responding to directives and enabling planning through a variety of instruments. It

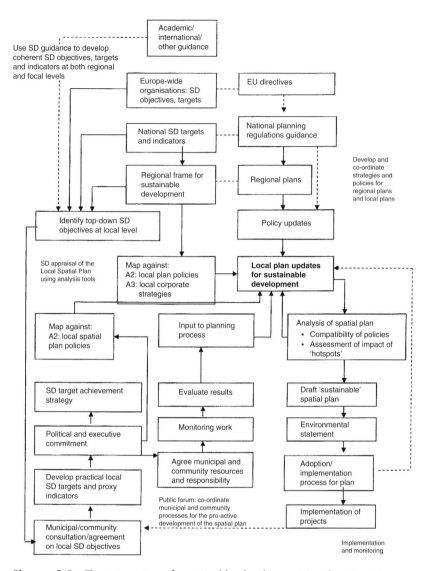

Figure 8.1 The integration of sustainable development in planning. (Source: Porter, G. (2000), in Mawhinney, M. (2002) *Sustainable Development. Understanding the Green Debates.* Blackwell Publishing Ltd, Oxford.)

responds to European, national and regional objectives and targets and initiates a complex process and system that engages sustainable development issues alongside the conventional planning criteria. In an ideal world the two would be synonymous since part of the object of planning must be the sustainability, in its widest interpretation, of the community that it serves.

In a very real sense the planning authority is managing the process of sustainable development through its planning processes. This is fine at the strategic level but at some point the more detailed aspects of sustainable development have to be owned by those who operate and develop within the framework that has been instigated. Again, regulation and legal enforcement can be used as an instrument to make sure that firms, organisations and individuals comply with what is thought to be needed in order to achieve the current view of what is sustainable. These tend to be minimum conditions as there is a sensitivity about individual freedoms in most democratic societies. To achieve major improvements may require much more stringent discipline by all concerned and this in turn may need a greater focus on education. It is interesting to note that the Club of Rome, which did so much to bring the plight of the earth's dwindling non-renewable resources to our attention in the 1970s, is now making education a major policy driver.

The nature of the education will vary and will have to take place at many different levels from the education of the policy-makers to the education of the child, and from the education of the corporation to the education of the household. This is a long-term task and for some areas of sustainable development, where the damage to the environment is both critical and irreversible, we may not be able to wait that long.

The knowledge that needs to be imparted is evolving and emerging slowly. There is not a comprehensive body of knowledge, in an easily digestible form, which can be put before all the various stakeholders for them to implement. Indeed, in many areas there is a debate to be had as to what is sustainable and which issue takes precedence over another. This is part of the process and requires feedback and continuous learning as our knowledge is enhanced.

Management in a learning organisation

We have suggested in this book that sustainable development is a process rather than a destination. In other words, it can never be said that we have arrived at 'sustainable development' but we can say that we are striving to improve the environment within which humans live and that we are seeking to leave that environment in a better position for future generations. We are aiming not to close down their options. This is important because it means that we have to keep the trends in sustainable development under constant review and match them with our improved understanding of what is required for sustainable development. Any management system that we set up must therefore have systematic feedback as part of the process.

Pete Senge, in *The Fifth Discipline* (Senge, 1990), makes the case that the organisations that will survive in the longer term will be those that are *learning organisations*. He defines such organisations as:

'… organisations where people continually expand their capacity to create the results they truly desire, where new and expansive patterns of thinking are nurtured, where collective aspiration is set free and where people are continually learning how to learn together'.

It would not be pushing the definition too far to say that these are the attributes of a society that wishes to take sustainable development seriously within the context of what we understand sustainable development to be. Even the definition is likely to change with time as we learn together about what sustainable development means to the current generation. Senge goes on to provide some 'thinking tools' for achieving this desirable state of affairs where we learn, provide feedback and implement, and this becomes the normal way of operating for the organisation.

In most cases it is necessary to do this activity in a systematic way. The complexity of the interrelationships and the wide spectrum of stakeholder involvement means that anything else would be ad hoc and would eventually lead to chaos. Even today we can often see conflicts between regulatory bodies in terms of the legislation they bring forward. One piece of legislation, although well intentioned, can have the opposite effect to what was intended within another field. We need a holistic approach in which the *learning* can be shared for mutual benefit. Until quite recently the technology required to share such complex knowledge has not been available. Now, with the advent of the internet and the concept of *knowledge grids* arriving in the near future, there is the opportunity to tap in and gain the knowledge we need quickly and, we hope, reliably. This suggests that we can move more quickly towards an understanding of what is needed, and an assessment of what the impact of our management decisions might be, fairly soon. It will not happen overnight but in time the diversity of knowledge will be available to those who want to know and it will be structured in a way that will allow people to incorporate it within their decision-making processes. Not only this, but it will be possible for the results of those decisions to be collected and fed back into the system to enhance the knowledge that will be there. In this sense it will be organic and constantly reviewing itself for the benefit of its users.

At one level this sounds useful but, like most technologies, it has the potential for harm as well as good. The way information is handled and presented affects the messages that are given. It will be based on the values of those who create the systems and, by their nature, the systems will be designed to be used frequently by the many. If they do not evolve quickly they can create a fossilised view of knowledge and an oppressive tool which will dominate thinking and not allow the expansive patterns of thinking encouraged by Senge. Even outside the wrong hands this can be dangerous but a tool of this nature in the hands of a malevolent dictator could be disastrous.

The building of such systems is also exceedingly complex and will be a learning process in its own right. It is most unlikely that a definitive system can be produced which will match the advances in communication technologies and be able to create its own brain-like tendencies to deal with these problems. In fact, modelling such a system on the human brain may impart the limitations of the human brain to the machine. On the other hand, not modelling it on the brain may create problems for the human mind in comprehending what the machine is doing. These may seem fanciful scenarios but in the time frame of, say, three generations, our grandchildren may not find it so remote or so speculative. It looks as if information technology as we know it today will be an issue in sustainable development within the fairly near future (see Chapter 9).

If we accept that the process is key and that we need to systemise it in some way to make it understandable and comprehensive, we have to consider what tools might be available. These tools have to be flexible and to be adaptable over long periods of time. They have to be forward-looking to ascertain what *might* happen in the future and prepare the ground for various possibilities. Conventional management systems are unlikely to fulfil this combination of requirements. One possibility might be *soft systems methodologies*.

Soft system methodology

The concept of soft system methodology was developed by Peter Checkland and Jim Scholes (Checkland & Scholes, 1999) to combat some of the limitations they had perceived in traditional systems engineering. Although trained as systems engineers, they found that real-world management situations were always too complicated for the straightforward application of the systems engineering approach. They said that

> '... they had to accept that in the complexity of human affairs the unequivocal pursuit of objectives which can be taken as given is very much the occasional special case: it is certainly not the norm'.
>
> (Checkland & Scholes, 1999)

In other words, the likelihood is that we will find conflicts within the operation of objectives, an inability to decide on the most appropriate objectives and consequently will have difficulty in meeting those objectives. Sustainable development has, at the moment at least, great difficulty in setting out objectives and creating harmony within the various conflicting objectives of those who participate as stakeholders over very extensive periods of time. It does not lend itself to hard systems thinking.

The initiators of soft systems identified four key thoughts which led them to develop their new approach. They suggested that all human activity was *purposeful and meaningful* to the person undertaking it. This led to the idea of modelling purposeful 'human activity systems' as a set of linked activities which together could exhibit the emergent property of purposefulness and they developed models to handle this concept.

Secondly, they realised that as you begin to develop such models several *interpretations* of any declared purpose are possible. There are a huge number of human activity models that can be built in any complex human problem and a choice has to be made between the models as to which ones are relevant. It is therefore necessary to focus on which ones are useful and which ones reflect the perspective from which the results will be built and viewed. This perspective needs to be made explicit.

Thirdly, as they moved away from an obvious problem that required a solution they moved towards the idea of a *problem situation* instead. They used the handful of models that might be produced of human activity as a source of questions to be asked of the real situation rather than as a representation of that situation.

The final shift was to argue that the learning that came out from the models of purposeful activity could provide an entry into work in information systems.

In a book of this nature it is not possible to argue the full case or to present the methodology, but the Checkland book quoted will provide the necessary knowledge in this respect. The approach is based on action learning and research where participation becomes an essential aspect of the process. It moves away from an argument about systems to a systemic approach. The methodology is systems-thinking-based but recast in a different form. Systemicity is shifted from modelling the world to the *process of enquiry* into the world. The system is no longer a part of the world which is to be engineered or optimised: the system is *the process of enquiry itself.* This allows reflection upon action taken, and this becomes analysable.

Such an approach may well be the appropriate one for the management of sustainable development over the longer term. It allows us to build a model, in fact several models, which we can use to enquire about the process of sustainable development and from which we can learn. It deals with the issue of purpose which underlies the need for addressing sustainable development and it provides tools for improving our understanding by reflection. The potential has not yet been harnessed because we are still in the early days of exploring the approach but there seems to be strong potential for aiding us in the decision-making process. Eventually it may be able to capture hard knowledge within tools such as knowledge-based systems and other information systems in such a way that they do not become inflexible and oppressive, but that is some way off. Information is needed for the exploratory models, but its encapsulation into knowledge arises from the reflection and perspectives given by humans and for the moment these are best dealt with through human experience.

Wicked problems

It is worth reflecting on the nature of the problems we are dealing with in sustainable development. They belong to a class of problems which have been described in the planning literature (Rittel & Webber, 1973) as 'wicked problems'.

Rittel and Webber suggested that the problems that planners face are inherently different from the problems that scientists and engineers deal with, which they consider are mainly 'tame', that is, they are clearly defined problems with a clear mission and clear indicators for when the problem has been solved. Some of the differences they suggest are as follows:

❏ There is no definitive problem formulation; instead 'the formulation of a wicked problem' *is* the problem.
❏ There are no criteria to indicate when a solution has been found and the eventual solution is decided through reasons external to the problem such as time or cost constraints.
❏ Solutions to wicked problems are value-based, that is, they are not true or false, but good or bad.
❏ There is no way of testing and fully appreciating the consequences of a solution as the full scope of its repercussions cannot be traced.
❏ There is no opportunity for trial and error; every solution has an immediate and irreversible impact on the system.
❏ There is no fixed number or set of permissible solutions to a wicked problem; they tend to be unique and, therefore, there are few replicable solutions.
❏ Wicked problems are nested across levels in the sense that every problem can be considered a symptom of a problem at a different level.
❏ The usual rules of science to formulate and test a hypothesis cannot be applied and the explanation of a discrepancy, and hence the proposed resolution of the problem, is mainly determined by the 'world view' of the analyst.
❏ Unlike a scientist whose hypothesis can often be refuted without major consequence, the planners cannot afford to be wrong as the solutions to his or her problem have direct and irreversible impacts.

There are clear parallels here with problem solving in the area of sustainable development. The vastness and complexity of the variables under consideration coupled with their interdependence and the changing nature of the domain over time make a conventional 'solution' (i.e. one which solves the problem) impossible to achieve.

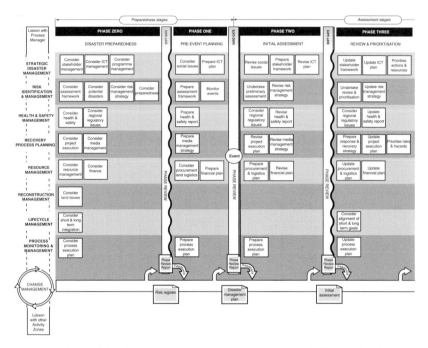

Figure 8.2 High level Disaster Management Process Protocol. (Copyright: Fleming, Lee, Kagioglou, University of Salford, RICS, 2009.)

To tackle such problems it may be appropriate to start with transparency and awareness and we need models to allow us to do this, but remember models, by their very nature, are simplifications of the world they represent and in complex systems will fail at some point.

Process protocols

It is one thing to create systems, whether for enquiry or not, and another to articulate the process of what, when and where decisions have to be made. Developers, local authorities and individuals are having to make decisions at this point in time and these cannot be delayed until all the knowledge is available. They have a goal to achieve and for them it is a 'destination', not a 'process'. Those who wish to engage in sustainable development require guidance as to when the principles of sustainable development should be included in the decision-making they are undertaking. This requires a protocol, that is, a framework of rules which can be followed to achieve, as far as possible, the desired objective. We have already stated that it may be difficult to identify the objective but in some cases, where the goals are clear, such a protocol can be delivered.

If we observe the construction of a building we know we have to deliver accommodation of the type required by the client (and to some

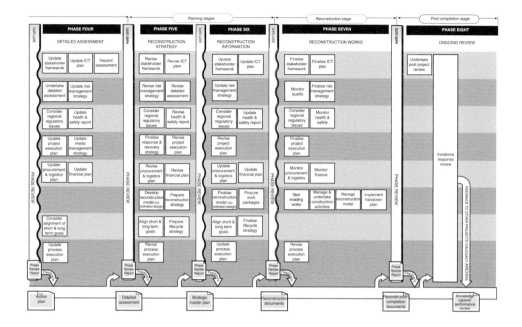

extent the stakeholders) within budget, of the right quality and within a certain period of time. Usually there is not much flexibility. We also know that there are activities that have to be enacted to get the building we require. We have to ascertain the client's requirements, draw up plans, tender for the construction and then build the building. It is not quite that easy, but nevertheless a process can be established which in some part can be considered generic. Researchers at the University of Salford, UK, have been exploring such a protocol for some time (Cooper *et al.*, 2004). The result is a map of the activities in a construction project which can be used to assist in determining what decisions are to be made, at what time and by whom. Each activity can be driven down to further levels of detail to reveal the information required and its complexity. Figure 8.2 demonstrates this for another application, the processes involved in dealing with disaster management.

Upon this process can be overlaid other factors such as risk management (Ceric, 2003). Risk management is driven by many of the processes below each high-level activity. Another might well be sustainable development and the incorporation of the Sustainable Material Advice and Resource Tool (SMART) within the Process Protocol generic model as described by Gilkinson (Gilkinson *et al.*, 2002). This enables the process owners within the project life cycle to be prompted to consider a particular issue at the appropriate time in the decision-making process.

One aspect of creating a sustainable development is to deal with any crisis that might appear during the lifetime of a community or development. The University of Salford, working with the Royal Institution of Chartered Surveyors, has developed a Disaster Management Process Protocol (Fleming *et al.*, 2009) which provides a blueprint for the processes and knowledge required in the rebuilding of a community infrastructure after a major disaster (see Fig. 8.2). In the wake of such a disaster, after the humanitarian effort has been completed there is usually a very confused situation in which knowledge and people are all over the place and nobody quite knows what is going on and who is doing what. The Protocol brings a map of processes and a level of communication to the problem which all participants can adopt and which eventually brings order and stability. Initially after, for example, a Tsunami, there may be difficulty in mapping the terrain to see what needs to be done. The ownership boundaries need to be established again because boundary markers may be washed away. The organisation of a responsive workforce needs to be established and government or local authority positions on the planning of work need to be agreed. This sounds simple but in fact chaos often reigns. Knowledge is reaching the management team almost randomly, communications are broken, financial support is slow to arrive but there is an urgent need to restore essential services and so it goes on. Without some sort of map is almost impossible to know where to place the new emerging knowledge, what actions need to be taken and what resources are required.

It could be argued that such a disaster is a microcosm of the nature of sustainable development. There is a wealth of emerging information on what makes various aspects of development sustainable but it is difficult to pull together into a coherent strategy, no matter what level is being considered. Evidence for this can be found in the difficulties nations find in gaining agreement, for example, on climate change and, at the other end of the spectrum, the difficulty an individual finds in changing a lifestyle which is consistent with sustainability principles. It may be that by identifying the processes that are needed we may be able to find ways of building a coherent strategy at every level. We may also be able to unite the various levels in order to produce a coherent and coordinated approach.

A feature of the Process Protocol is the concept of *hard* and *soft* gates. Hard gates are those where the decision-maker must have the information and must make a decision before he or she moves on to the next phase. These are mandatory and must be adhered to. Soft gates, on the other hand, allow some permeability if information is not available in order that the process can progress. Such a protocol could well be an advantage in decision-making with regard to sustainable development and within any built environment process as it would force managers to consider and decide on a course of action at each hard gate. At each soft gate the sustainability issue would also be raised, creating awareness of sustainable development throughout the process. This does not mean that a good decision will be made but, by pointing to key issues and possibly suggesting suitable techniques to evaluate or aid decision-making, it increases the probability of a satisfactory solution being found. Of course, as in any other situation, all such decisions are based on the information provided and the skills of managers in using it.

It may well be possible to extend the concept into the urban planning process but then further complexity will arise due to the multiple phasing of the regeneration and renewal of a large number of properties and the infrastructure. Other techniques may be more appropriate in these circumstances. Nevertheless, a conceptual approach to ascertaining and evaluating sustainable development has been developed through a study by the City of Vancouver described later, but first we need to identify why the city is so important in the evaluation task.

A possible approach

We have already raised the question in this chapter of who establishes policy and we have suggested the role of the various arms of government, but at what level can it be implemented? This raises the whole question of long-term strategies for sustainable development. Who *does* own the problem of developing strategies for action and who can implement them?

This is an interesting question which we raised previously. Figure 8.3 shows where we might see decisions being made with some examples. It demonstrates where we can expect responsibility to lie. However, in terms of *policy* it is the top four layers that have most impact and the bottom three where this policy *is implemented*. In fact the 'city' is at the pivotal point between policy and implementation as it both makes and implements policy.

This is made clear in Fig. 8.4 where it can be seen that the city plays a very significant role at the interface between policy and enabling action. While we need to act in each layer of the triangle, a useful focus for sustainable development in the first instant could well be the city and its environs. This would combine policy with action and is likely to have the greatest impact.

If cities do provide this useful interface, it is worth considering 'how' cities might address a long-term policy and action agenda. There are very few examples of where this is happening at the present time. Most cities have to consider relatively short-term perspectives on the future because of a number of factors which impact upon their decision-makers. A major factor for the politicians might be the length of time until the next election. However, there are some useful role models of which the Vancouver study is probably one of the best because it integrates all the knowledge of sustainable development into a coherent plan with the interrelationships shown and with a plan of action which has a wide 'buy-in' from a large number of stakeholders.

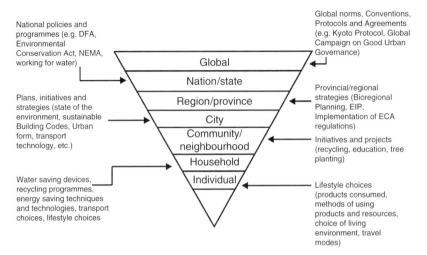

Figure 8.3 The sustainability complex. (Source: Mathew Cullinan, MCA Planners, South Africa, 2003.)

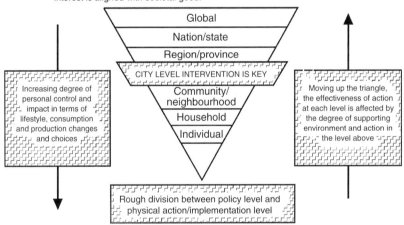

Figure 8.4 What is the significance of the city? (Source: Mathew Cullinan, MCA Planners, South Africa, 2003.)

The Vancouver study

One of the most interesting challenges presented in recent years was the International Gas Union competition to determine a sustainable city in 100 years' time. It was set appropriately in the millennium year of 2000 and nine cities were invited to compete. The winner was

Vancouver in Canada and it is worth looking at the approach that was taken and why it impressed the judges. It is not usual for a city to look as far ahead as 100 years and it requires an approach that can engage as many stakeholders as possible.

What the Vancouver study showed was that once the timescale moved beyond 20 years or so, the 'baggage' of the present is left behind. People become much more open about what they think is really needed for a sustainable future, and begin to build a consensus. This allows strategies to develop which can be translated into policy and into pro- grammes of long-term action. One hundred years, or approximately three generations, is probably the maximum sensible time to expect cities to plan ahead but even then it must be recognised that any plan will need to be kept under review and updated at regular intervals. None of us can forecast too far into the future but we can put in place systems that will act as reference points which can be modified as our knowledge increases and as we see events unfolding.

'CitiesPLUS' (PLUS standing for Planning for Long-term Urban Sustainability) was the term used by the Vancouver study and was undertaken over a period of 18 months with around 500 people, repre- senting major stakeholders, involved. These people spent that period in 'thinking, dreaming, talking, drawing, assessing and most impor- tantly, committing themselves to a process and plan'. This is an extraor- dinary achievement in the time and one of which many other cities would be envious. The full plan can be obtained from Sheltair Group Inc., 1100-111 Dunsmuir Street, Vancouver BC, V6B 6A3 (web site: www.sheltair.com) and the authors are indebted to the members of Sheltair for their assistance in providing this résumé. The brief descrip- tion that follows cannot do justice to the considerable amount of work and thought put into the full report. The report does provide an outline plan for the Greater Vancouver Region but, more importantly for the rest of the world, it provides a suggested process which could be adopted by many even if the plan itself addresses the needs of Vancouver. It did this by focusing on three main stages.

Stage one: defining the context

The first stage of the process was to identify the context for the 'vision' of what forces might be acting upon the city over the specified period. These included the following:

❑ *Technological transformations*: Including movement of informa- tion, improvement in machine energy efficiency, economies of scope rather than economies of scale, progressive lightening of structures/components, progressive miniaturisation, discontinu- ity in manufacturing technique and transition from carbon to hydrogen content fuels.

❏ *Climate change*: Which for Vancouver included an expected temperature increase of 3°C–4°C, average precipitation increase of 5%–20% in winter and average precipitation decrease of up to 20% in summer.
❏ *Demographic change*: Which demographers are suggesting could peak at 9 billion globally and then decrease to 6 billion in 2100. For Vancouver lower fertility rates and increased longevity will result in a proportionately smaller working population, causing labour shortages and higher dependency rates within the first two decades of the twenty-first century and suggesting the encouragement of further immigration.
❏ *Resource scarcity*: The accompanying disturbance of the global marketplace may lead to Vancouver facing food shortages, increased demand on water supply, land shortages around the city and timber loss through deforestation and disease, and to non-renewable energy sources being affected.
❏ *Globalisation*: Will dissolve national and cultural boundaries and may result in a new economy based on emerging technologies with a 'world city' at its centre and hinterland cities at the perimeter.
❏ *Worldview shifts*: Away from the view that nature was to be exploited to one where our physical and spiritual connections to the biosphere are rediscovered and we respect the ecological limits of our planet.

The report goes on to look at the specific forces related to the context for Vancouver which included its place, people, economy and infrastructure.

The report then describes three challenges that arise from these studies:

❏ Firstly, the need for a move from urban planning viewing cities as a series of discrete components, to finding common solutions which would cut across urban planning disciplines and jurisdictions. In other words, a holistic rather than a reductionist model.
❏ Secondly, the challenge of how to deal with the uncertainty inherent in planning 100 years ahead.
❏ Thirdly, the challenge of how to think globally while acting locally. The team rejected any view that there was a correct development pathway generic to all situations and decided that they must find local solutions to local problems.

Stage two: developing the long-term plan

Having set out the context, the team then moved to developing the long-term plan. This adopted the following three phases:

❏ *Phase one – envisioning our future*: This involved defining Vancouver region as 'one system' where the people, the place, the infrastructure and governance are in constant interaction; identifying core themes underlying the vision ('sustainability, resilience and liveability' were chosen); determining the constraints to be faced; building on assets and past successes as the 'seeds of sustainability'; and determining one broad vision and then specific visions and end-state goals for each of the individual components of the urban system.

❏ *Phase two – exploring the options*: Forecasting techniques were used to determine the impact of the forces shaping the next century and then measurable 100-year targets were set for each component of the urban system together with an assessment of their current status to determine the critical path towards achievement. The magnitude of change required to achieve the critical path was evaluated and where it was possible to achieve the target earlier (the preferred path) the 'solution space' was established. Then best practices were found and used to suggest the best path, and backcasting methods were used to develop staged scenarios for getting into the solution space.

❏ *Phase three – implementing the plan*: A long-term plan of 100 years involves great uncertainty so the team focused on finding integrated strategies that would guide implementation plans (rather than the traditional reductionist approach). They identified eight catalyst strategies to stimulate movement in the right direction and used an integrated design workshop to visualise the transformation. Finally, they identified a series of implementation measures that could be taken in the short run using a suite of policy tools to set the wheels of change in motion and then they defined key roles for a broad range of actors.

The above description is inadequate for the amount of thinking and preparation that went into the effort. To determine such a plan for a city region is a daunting task and it is also extremely ambitious. It is to the credit of the team that they managed to provide such a high-level proposal in the time available.

Stage three: the legacy of the endowment

The legacies of cities include the long-term plan for the city/region along with a transferable process and networks of people. Without this legacy the exercise would be almost worthless. There must be 'follow through' and this requires current and future generations to 'buy in' to the process and own its operation. This means that there must be a network of people able and willing to work together to achieve the aims of the plan who are also willing to educate and inform future members of the network about the whole process, not only of planning but of implementation. There needs to be an agenda to which all stakeholders can subscribe in such a way that it affects their present-day decision-making and their future priorities.

In the case of Greater Vancouver, the long-term plan sparked a process of integrated comprehensive planning. All urban components were examined or re-examined and then transformed in accordance with a shared set of visions, goals, targets, scenarios and strategies. It engaged a broad cross section of actors in a collaborative process based on significant communication and trust-building. It was and is an interesting experiment and it will be interesting to see whether it can stand the test of time. Already some problems are emerging. In particular, it will be interesting to see whether shared values can be maintained when some of the global changes mentioned earlier place pressure on the system.

The networks have played a key role in this exercise and the Vancouver team has established networks at different scales. There was the regional network in the first instance and then this was extended to a national network engaging other cities and organisations. Initially an international network was established bringing together over 30 like-minded cities willing to share experiences, tools and talents. There is still considerable interest in the approach and a number of other cities worldwide have engaged with or adopted the process. This provides an opportunity for sharing of emerging knowledge.

The conclusions of the Vancouver study

The process of undertaking the study seems to have given unexpected 'added value' to the issue of sustainable development as viewed from the city level. It allowed the Vancouver team to forge new partnerships, to clarify and galvanise a commitment to sustainability and to establish new and extensive networks for the future. The team's conclusions are appropriate for a book of this nature and they include the following:

❑ Forecasting scenarios emphasised that major change was needed if the region was to remain liveable and secure. Backcasting scenarios showed that it was possible to 'close the loop' over the century ahead and reduce the ecological footprint to become a region that lives comfortably within the carrying capacity of its resource base.

❑ Sustainable development is both a goal and a process and they achieved useful results whenever they combined a clear understanding of the goal with participatory processes involving government, private and civil sectors.

❑ The 100-year time horizon enabled all parties to look beyond immediate preoccupations and vested interests, discover powerful unifying ideas and consider responsibilities to future generations.

❑ Integration is the key to sustainable development. It requires determination to focus simultaneously on all dimensions, that is, social, economic, environmental; short-, medium- and long-term; from the local to the global levels.

❑   The future of a particular city is intimately connected with the well-being of other cities. The flows of materials, resources, finance and information have impacts well beyond the city under examination. Responsible planning involves dialogue and alignment with the interests of other urban and rural areas.

❑   Planning a large urban region is much more complex than planning for a neighbourhood or city. The challenge is to find common ground and move beyond abstract generalisations.

❑   The adaptive management framework and integrated design process provides a transferable model for long-term planning.

❑   It is important to create opportunities for big thoughts that can produce big plans. Taking the long view and imagining one urban system has changed the way the participants see their city/region and the way they see themselves.

❑   Competition with others brought out the best. As Ron Clark, President and CEO of SaskEnergy, said of the Vancouver study:

'The Process generated informed choices. It is not about seeing the future, and it's certainly not about guaranteeing an outcome, but it is about defining a rich and intellectually robust and defensible process. Win, lose or draw, we've already gained immensely'.

There is much in this case study from which all cities can learn and in investigating such approaches it may be possible to develop generic and yet flexible methodologies which will allow comparisons and evaluations to be made across national and international boundaries. In turn this will allow the body of knowledge regarding sustainable development to build into a robust source of information which will benefit countries and communities around the world.

Follow through on the Vancouver study

Now that a decade has passed it is possible to reflect on the CitiesPLUS study and examine the problems and the successes of the approach. The study was a formal collaboration, owned by many, but with the regional government playing a key role as a secretariat, participant and sponsor. Leaders within that government provided leadership, embraced sustainability principles and became thoroughly involved with the exercise. The senior people within the Greater Vancouver region established a parallel internal process called the 'Sustainable Region Initiative' which is still ongoing and which adopted the same planning framework which had been established for the CitiesPlus project. However, just as the CitiesPlus study came to an end and was poised to establish a clear set of new directions for the region, a local election produced a whole new regional board and, as is typical, felt no commitment or excitement around the CitiesPlus idea. It fell to the 'not invented here syndrome' and as a new board they felt they had to do something different. There followed a period of around 2 years when the study and its proposals were largely ignored. It illustrates the fact that while local government seems the most appropriate promoter and leader in long-term planning (as they have the greatest credibility and have the mandate that best fits), they have also become volatile and short term in their thinking as a consequence of the election cycles. This complaint can be repeated around the world and is a major negative force in implementing sustainable development which demands a long-term view.

However, it would be wrong to see CitiesPLUS as a failure for Vancouver. It just took longer to establish. The ideas and processes behind it have developed a force of their own. Even the language invented by the team (end-state goals, catalyst projects, pathways that combine forecasting and backcasting, resilience by design, etc.) have become a part of the local planning culture. CitiesPLUS helped new ideas achieve currency and helped the leaders throughout the bureaucracy become familiar and comfortable with new approaches. The people who have recently completed the exciting new Regional Growth Strategy for the region were intimately involved with CitiesPlus and continue to present the slides and ideas to visiting groups and integrated the ideas into their latest plans. The excellent Eco-Density initiative for the City of Vancouver was crafted with the help of the staff of Sheltair (who played a major part in the developing CitiesPLUS, led by Sebastian Moffatt) and by a mayor who valued the study and so it goes on. The thinking behind the study permeates the thinking of the region even though it may not be implemented under the CitiesPLUS name.

Perhaps the most interesting and exciting aspect, however, is the influence the study is having on cities outside the Vancouver region. Sometimes a distant view can provide insights which establish its true worth. A few examples might illustrate:

❏ Within Canada, presentations were made to many other cities on CitiesPLUS during and after the study and to seven federal departments, and subsequently CitiesPLUS became the new approach to progressive planning. It was the one that all participants decided to promote. It was adopted completely by the University of British Columbia Centre for Sustainable Design and it became the specific model for defining the Integrated Community Sustainability Plans which are now occurring across Canada. Other cities are building upon the CitiesPLUS model in many respects and with impressive results, for example, Imagine Calgary www.imaginecalgary.ca

❏ In Auckland, New Zealand, the regional government investigated the use of long-term planning tools and compared 26 examples worldwide, narrowing down to a short list of six for further intensive study and chose CitiesPLUS as their model. They were then given instruction and have implemented and improved on the model. It now looks as if other New Zealand regions and authorities might follow.

❏ CitiesPLUS played a significant part in the World Urban Forum in 2006 and the idea for networking emerged from the collaboration. It launched an international network of cities engaged in long-term planning, known as the PLUS 30 network, in concert with the World Urban Forum, which involves many cities worldwide in regular meetings and demonstration projects.

❏ Sebastian Moffatt, the leader of the CitiesPLUS initiative, has built on his team's experience in developing methods and tools (forecasting, influence diagrams, scenario planning, collaborative processes, urban metabolism, foresight workshops, etc.) with support from the International Gas Union and collaboration with five of the cities who participated in the original competition in developing a consensus approach to long-term planning for cities. China and the Netherlands have produced books on the consensus approach and several large projects have been awarded to universities in these and other countries. The information on this work can be accessed through www.bridgingtothefuture.org

As with many successful ideas and with such a complicated subject, it takes years and possibly decades for the concepts to filter through, be taken up by the leaders of the day, and exposed and tested for public consumption and implementation. The large team behind CitiesPLUS should be congratulated for what they have achieved in a relatively short space of time.

Resilience

One of the topics which has arisen out of one aspect of the sustainability agenda has been resilience. When something occurs which has made a community or area unsustainable then how do we make it function sufficiently for the period until the problem can be resolved after the external pressure has abated? This largely applies to major disasters such as floods, fires, earthquakes and the like but might also include attacks on major communication networks due to hacking and other major technical malfunctions. As climate change accelerates we are seeing more unusual events, which cannot be easily forecasted yet have the potential to wreck any long-term planning with regard to sustainable development. James Lovelock (Lovelock, 2009) suggests that as sea levels rise and climates across the globe make living impossible, we might be left with what he called 'lifeboat islands'. These are islands where the climate and living was conducive to human life, to which the population of the world might retreat (or at least those who are able to do so through economic and social circumstances). Such a scenario would create major problems for many countries in the world and sustainability planning would be almost pointless. Already the government of the low-lying Maldives in the Indian Ocean has been reported as seeking to purchase other territories with higher ground to which its population can flee should sea levels rise as predicted. This is an extreme situation but quite possible for the Maldives within the space of one working lifetime! For most, these disasters are spasmodic and temporary. In the UK, for example, the incidence of flooding seems to be increasing and while some communities are vulnerable it is not at the moment a permanent catastrophe for the majority. Consequently, it is being suggested that perhaps houses within flood plains should be so designed that they are not permanently or expensively harmed by a flood. This might mean, for example, that electrical points are placed high on the walls of the ground floor, hard tile floors are used which can easily be washed through after the flood and the water can be allowed to flow through without too much impediment. Once the flood has gone then the function of the house or other building can resume its normal use as soon as possible.

Resilience theory has been around for several decades but has had a renaissance in the last two as sustainability issues have risen to the top of the world agenda. Carl Folke *et al.* prepared a scientific background paper on resilience for the World Summit on Sustainable Development in 2002 (Folke *et al.*, 2002). The Resilience Alliance (www.resalliance. org) define resilience as applied to integrated systems of people and nature as (a) the amount of disturbance a system can absorb and still remain within the same state or domain of attraction, (b) the degree to which the system is capable of self-organisation (versus lack of organisation, or organisation forced by external factors) and (c) the degree to which the system can build and increase the capacity for learning and adaptation.

Since sustainable development would be considered by many as being about creating and maintaining our options for prosperous social and economic development, there is an obvious link between resilience and the sustainability agenda. If we can use our ability to design to create systems that respond to adversity and remedy the situation quickly then the chances of complete failure begins to diminish. If we can retain function through adversity then we have a better chance of enabling a comeback from any situation, at least within certain parameters.

Folke *et al.* suggested a different approach to just using technology or economics or even social adjustments to solve sustainable development problems. They quite rightly pointed out that these combine and are interrelated when attempting to address their complexity. They felt that efforts should be made to create synergies between them and they looked to adaptive capacity to mitigate and perhaps solve the problem.

Adaptive capacity is the ability of a socioecological system to cope with novel solutions without losing options for the future. Systems with high adaptive capacity are able to reconfigure themselves without significant declines in crucial functions in relation to primary productivity, hydrological cycles, social relations and economic prosperity. They identified four critical factors that reflect the characteristics needed for adaptive capacity which interact across temporal and spatial scales and that seem to be required for dealing with natural resource dynamics during periods of change and reorganisation. These are:

❏ Learning to live with change and uncertainty.
❏ Nurturing diversity for resilience.
❏ Combining different types of knowledge for learning.
❏ Creating opportunity for self-organisation towards social-ecological sustainability.

They go on to explore and clarify the human–nature relationship and what to sustain and why. They considered timescales to be important, as something can be resilient at one point in time because of technical innovation but then be a contributor to unstable conditions later on, for example, the iron axe helped clear forest for agriculture and more food but much later on the clearing led to soil infertility and even the reduction of the absorption of CO_2 emissions and the resilience of the land and other systems was eroded. It seems that every day such breakdown of the resilience of systems is brought to our attention and they vary from depletion of fishstocks by overfishing, pollution affecting coral reefs, contaminated land from chemical poisoning, and sickness of humans by transfer of diseases from one part of the world to another where there is no immunity.

Resilience is a perspective on sustainable development which appears to reinforce the world view of humankind being part of, rather than dominating, nature. However, it can also be used to examine the growing impact of technology on humans as a species. As machines begin to develop intelligence and knowledge which may not always be transparent then does this make humans more vulnerable as a species? If we talk about sustainable development being a movement which attempts to maintain the human species then perhaps its survival may be more threatened by the technology it itself has created. How resilient are we to that change? The potential for such change is not so far away.

The development of this thinking to decision-making and management means that adaptive management systems need to be created which can absorb and respond to change. We cannot make the assumption that we have 'solved the problem' for ever and a day. It must be a virtuous cycle of feedback and improvement which can rise to the challenge of the new circumstances. It is interesting to hear politicians speak and seem to assume that the world is predictable and any problem can be solved. The media plays its part by chastising them if they change their mind and therefore a kind of paralysis takes place in which the real world is ignored and a mechanical predictable world is advanced. To address the problem of sustainable development from the point of view of resilience there must be flexibility, learning systems and an understanding of interdependence which we have postulated on many occasions through this book.

Education and Research

This book has attempted to provide an introduction and overview of the key issues with regard to evaluating sustainability. It is, as was stated earlier, just a beginning. Each chapter could be expanded into a book in its own right. The subject is evolving fast and new insights and techniques are being developed all the time. It would be unwise to assume that the subject will reach stability for some time to come. In this it is not unlike many other disciplines. In their early stages, when they are identified as a new area of study, there is an exploratory process, which is also evolutionary in nature. In this period the subject gains definition and methodologies which establish it as a bona fide area of study worthy of formal recognition in universities and in policy-making.

Some of this development has already taken place with regard to sustainable development and it is now found in many educational and research institutions as part of the academic content not only for environmental courses but across the spectrum. In government too it is found as part of the policy-making units of a large number of ministries, particularly where the government has signed one of the many sustainability protocols. However, it would also be true to say that often these policies are not carried through in practice, and only time will discover whether there is true intent. The fact that they exist must give encouragement to all who believe that this is a significant subject for future development and worthy of substantial research.

These shifts in thinking and content recognise the all-embracing nature of the subject and the fact that sustainable development permeates and affects all our lives. Perhaps, also, the recognition of the subject as *sustainability science* is also a milestone, although it still has some way to go. The Sustainability Science Program at Harvard University's Centre for International Development seeks to:

'Advance basic understanding of the dynamics of human-environment systems; to facilitate the design, implementation and evaluation of practical interventions that promote sustainability in particular places and contexts; and to improve linkages between relevant research and innovation communities on the one hand and relevant policy and management communities on the other'.

Kieffer *et al.* (2003) give a more broad-based definition as:

'The cultivation, integration and application of knowledge about earth systems gained especially from the holistic and historical sciences such as geology, ecology, climatology, oceanography co-ordinated with knowledge about human relationships gained from the social sciences and humanities, in order to evaluate, mitigate, and minimize the consequences, regionally and worldwide, of human impacts on planetary systems and on societies across the globe and into the future – that is, in order that humans can be knowledgeable earth stewards'.

This definition gives a very wide remit for the subject and reflects much of the discussion in the earlier chapters of this book.
Reitan (2005) noted that the new paradigm:

'Must encompass different magnitudes of scales (of time, space, and function), multiple balance (dynamics), multiple actors (interests and multiple failures (systemic faults)'.

Mjwara (2008), Director General of the Department of Science and Technology in South Africa, in his introduction to the book *Sustainability Science* (Burns & Weaver, 2008), says that sustainable development in South and Southern Africa poses challenges to our traditional approaches to research. The complex interactions between society and our life-supporting systems require a coordinated response that goes beyond the boundary of single disciplines, that cuts across our separate research institutions and that transcends the current gap that exists between knowledge producers and knowledge users. Du Plessis (2009) in a powerful study in the same book addresses the complexity by postulating a conceptual framework for understanding socioecological systems and it is this kind of study which will help all those engaged in sustainable development to build the body of science required to address the key questions we face.

We recognise that these are extremely complex issues and in a book such as this it is sometimes easy to give the impression that all is solved and that all we need to do is apply the knowledge and techniques and we will have dealt with the sustainable development issues. It is not true. There is even still a debate among some academics as to whether environmental sustainability as currently perceived (only part of the full sustainability agenda) is appropriate, although they are in a very small minority.

The agenda becomes much more complex when we face the issues raised by those aspects related to sustainable communities. The world congresses, such as those identified in Chapter 1, have taken this concept of sustainable development and made it high priority, but the tools and policies needed to understand and exercise sustainable communities are not well established. When we address communities, we are dealing with all aspects of human social and political behaviour and their impact on development. If this is coupled with environmental factors, the whole of humankind's relationship with its environment and with one another and all living species is brought into play.

It is a vast canvas on which to research and herein lies its potential downfall. There is a danger that its spectrum is too wide to be meaningful or to manage. Management must be at the root of the study of sustainable development. It is assumed that if something is going wrong we can intervene and do something about it, that is, manage it! Our experience in the past has shown that, when humans do intervene, the full impact is often not addressed and while a problem is solved in one area another is created elsewhere. The reductionist view which deals with a highly focused sub-area of the total problem has developed because we as human beings find it difficult to handle all the interrelationships at once. This approach has taken us far in many topics, particularly in the physical sciences, but it can be found wanting in the social sciences, mainly because of all the interdependencies between the players and between the players and the multitude of variables.

We do not know what will happen in the future that may enable us to explore issues at a global level. It is difficult, even in something more straightforward like economic or financial investment forecasting, to know what will happen next (e.g. the credit crunch of 2008/2009). The models used are based on previous experience, and who knows what new features are on the horizon? The number of interrelationships is so huge that it only needs a small change from previous experience for us to find that a domino effect has been created and a totally new paradigm with which the model cannot cope. Models are by nature simplifications of the real world and are myopic. If they were perfect, those in the know would all be millionaires as we could presumably play the stock exchange to our advantage. This does not happen.

In some ways this can be depressing and can send rather negative vibrations around the world. How do we take this very important matter forward? What is there that may help us? This book has tried to lay down some parameters within which we can work. It has outlined the key areas for investigation. It has provided a comprehensive structure which goes beyond mere lists of indicators to approach the subject. It has provided a list of the more common techniques that can be applied to measure events and enable informed decision-making (even though it recognises their shortcomings) and it has suggested ways in which management may address the issue. Each of these matters requires substantial further investigation and there are many researchers across the world who are undertaking such studies. Is this enough?

Of course, these studies are of benefit and will contribute significantly to what might evolve in the future. Scenario planning will also help 'try out', albeit in a limited way, what the future might be like. Foresight studies may help prepare for or influence the future and all models of all types may warn us of future impending problems. There are some technologies that will influence us in a way that we will not have seen before. It could be argued that a zero carbon energy policy might change many things. The types of energy source would change, creating a whole new infrastructure of manufacture and delivery. Fuel cell technology, thought to offer enormous potential, is still in its comparative infancy and we do not know whether it will be applicable beyond the local environment. Using existing technologies, the Three Gorges Dam in China is a new infrastructure designed to supply a large proportion of China's future energy need as the country continues with its economic growth. Developing hydroelectric power is relatively 'green'. However, up to 2 million people have been 'displaced' in order for the dam to be built, creating a reservoir 450 miles long. For those who are dependent on them, these technologies will have a major impact on the way they behave and their built environment. They may make them more or less vulnerable in the future, which in turn may instigate social behaviour related to self-protection. Will another country use the vulnerability of the dam, for example, to attack or place pressure on the country and its policies? The 'community' may well change its behaviour to make it less sustainable in the long term from the perspective of most sustainability models.

Perhaps the biggest unknown is the influence of information technology on the way we behave. We have never faced such an information explosion before. We do not know how we will react in the long term and we do not know what the increased connectivity between humans, and between humans and machines, will do to what humans expect from the built environment. At the moment there is some evidence that those engaged in providing information technologies and their content are binding themselves together in conclaves around the world such as Seattle or Dubai. This is counter-intuitive as most predictions have suggested that geography is no longer a barrier for work, but here we see the big players apparently reaping major benefits from being geographically close to each other while encouraging the rest of us to work apart! This may be a temporary situation, but who knows?

So what are the trends in information technology that may have an impact on sustainable development? Broadly they are as follows:

❏ *Convergence*: The concept of convergence is at two levels. At one level the technologies themselves are converging together through digital processes so that they can interact in a way that has not happened before. Television, audio, telephone, camera, music can now be transmitted and received by a single source machine. It allows all media to be incorporated together. The second is convergence of content. The internet even as currently operated has few boundaries and knowledge is passed seamlessly around the world. Those who own the distribution of such knowledge may find themselves in a strong strategic position. It is a way of influencing values, sometimes intentionally and sometimes not. All knowledge has a filter which is provided by the authors or disseminators and this can be for good or ill. It provides bias which in the normal course of events is subject to debate and criticism. This provides checks and balances. But what happens when a piece of knowledge is used repeatedly for convenience and expediency? It can establish a 'conventional wisdom' in which thinking can be fossilised and an oppressive tool can emerge. The benefits then depend on the benign or malign nature of the knowledge. The new technologies are designed to be repeated to aid the less informed. Who will provide the checks to take on the large-scale providers? For those opposed to a particular filter on knowledge it represents a threat which can lead to an undermining of their perceived value system and in extreme cases to acts of terror as the only way out.

❏ *Connectivity*: Alongside convergence we need connections to be made so that we can realise the potential of sharing these different media. The last decade has seen a massive increase in the penetration of computers per head of population in the developed world coupled with access to a wide variety of devices to transmit and receive the information. Mobile phones are now pivotal points for the exchange of music, knowledge, visuals, games and many other things, in addition to the use for which they were originally developed. We are now moving towards 'knowledge grids' where computers act together and become more powerful and their knowledge more accessible. This opens avenues for sharing information in ways we have never seen before. These machines can also act as the repositories for data collected by sensors and it may be that the kind of knowledge capture required for complex domains such as sustainable development becomes available without the enormous expense of manual labour.

❏ *Culture*: As technology becomes more user-friendly and education on how to use it becomes more widespread, the patterns of behaviour among human beings will adapt to the new environment. The computer games industry has changed the nature of leisure time, the internet has changed the way students access knowledge as well as having led to the development of online shopping. These are all indicators of behaviour change and it is difficult to know where these developments will end. Will there be a reaction to them reversing current extrapolations or will they continue to a point where an outside observer might see the human race as an interconnected whole, entirely interdependent and able to be manipulated at will? Extreme scenarios these may be, but it could happen. What is clear is that at the moment the way we live our lives has changed dramatically in one generation.

❏ *Creativity*: For many years computers have been seen as machines that constrain creativity. The rules which have to be obeyed to operate them have been seen as limiting what can be done. This is changing, and increasingly, as the technology mimics the real world and the degrees of freedom we experience in the real world become available in the virtual environment. In fact they may well go further because the things at which human beings are not good may well be the things at which machines excel, and the combination could lead to real breakthroughs in creativity. The boundaries may well disappear and already technologists are talking about enhancing human performance by 'jacking in' the machine to the brain. At present it is to enhance the brain where there is impairment, but in the future it could be used for overcoming natural human constraints and providing life enhancement. It could be the next recreational drug if not used wisely!

❏ *Content*: It is the content of these knowledge networks that is critical to their take-up and the way they are used, and what actions follow from this increase in knowledge. The knowledge has the power to bind people together by dispelling ignorance and allowing free communication. On the other hand, it has the power to divide and reinforce prejudice. It remains to be seen what this will do to make communities more sustainable. Will they come together or will they fight? Already tensions can be seen between communities where there is strong religious belief that divides them. Does one group's value system, as conveyed by the technology, lead to the undermining of the other? Is it a tool for harmonisation or dissent? It is likely to be both, but which will prevail at a particular point in time we just do not know.

❏ *Collaborative working*: Despite the clustering of those engaged in IT in certain parts of the world, there is also a development in collaborative working across normal geographic boundaries. Aeroplanes are designed and constructed with design and sub-assembly plants thousands of miles apart. Supply chains for industry are linked through the internet, and can act online and monitor easily the performance of their teams. Many firms encourage their personnel to work at home for part of the week to avoid paying for large buildings and to assist performance. What does this do for the concept of a sustainable community? Does it enrich or destroy?

The above list gives an indication of some of the issues related to perhaps the biggest technological driver the world has ever seen. Its effect is being debated throughout the world and arguments will continue for many years to come. It is possible to paint a very positive scenario in which information technology may well be a player in providing a solution to many of the sustainable development problems. We may be able to avoid people travelling as much, we may be able to break down ignorance and improve understanding, we may be able to engage the Third World and assist in the education it needs but can ill afford. On the other hand, the technology can be seen as an oppressive tool by which the poor are excluded, human beings are manipulated, privacy is jeopardised and values drop to the lowest common denominator.

From this perspective the future is in our hands, or at least in the hands of those who control the technology. It is here that governments have a part to play. If we wish to have a benign technology that will help sustainable development, what aspects should we be encouraging? This is a key question for all future governments and every individual.

However, it is not only the technology which will play a role. Those institutions which have the responsibility for communicating the prevailing culture together with its knowledge have an obligation to address this issue from both a moral stance and from the fact that the culture now demands it. Step forward the universities, schools and learning institutions and all those which provide the basis of knowledge for our society to operate efficiently and effectively. They have the biggest responsibility of all for if they do not prepare the minds of those who learn then whatever governments or markets may encourage there will be no fertile ground on which the seeds of policy can mature.

The authors of this book had the privilege in April 2009 to assist in the drafting of the Torino Declaration on Education and Research for Sustainable and Responsible Development. This Declaration was signed by the representatives of all the Universities in the G8, G20 and most of the developing countries committing themselves to encourage the understanding and application of sustainable development across their whole spectrum of work from course content to the way in which they themselves conduct their behaviour as organisations and institutions. The resultant Declaration was then brought to the attention of the following Heads of State meeting in July 2009. It was built on the previous 2008 meeting in Sapporo, Japan where the Heads of the Universities throughout the world acknowledged the important role that education and research play in informing, promoting and implementing sustainable and responsible development. They recognised that sustainability cannot be achieved by merely engaging natural sciences but 'must also engage life sciences, social sciences and humanities. The interdependence and interaction among economics, ethics, energy policy and ecology (the 4 'E's) is one critical example which needs to be explored'.

It is worth noting the key elements of the 2009 declaration text to which the Rectors committed themselves and which was structured according to their *principles and engagement* with regard to education and research policies (G8 University Summit, 2009). A summary of the main elements is as follows:

Section 1: The Principles

1. *New models of social and economic development consistent with sustainability principles*

The argument here was that existing models fail to reflect the wider well-being of all members of the human race and the infrastructure which needs to be sustained to allow development which does not damage the opportunities for future generations. It is not just economic but social issues which need to be addressed.

2. *Ethical approaches to sustainable development*

Here the Rectors encouraged commitment to approaches to sustainable development which fully engage ethical considerations such as trust, distributional fairness, cultural diversity and intergenerational perspectives within their own institutions. Externally, they believed that universities should encourage engagement of the broader community to promote ethical, balanced, responsible and fair global policies for sustainable development.

3. *New approaches to energy policy*

Under this principle, universities agreed to provide expertise and impetus towards the rational use of natural resources and the proactive development of a transition to alternative energy sources away from carbon fuels. However, it is recognised that with the current understanding of science it would be difficult to shift entirely to alternative energy sources within a short time span. Interim arrangements are required and many would advocate nuclear energy as a stopgap despite the known problems with disposal of nuclear waste. Others would disagree. Novel solutions are emerging such as artificial trees and artificial leaves for absorption of CO_2 emissions. Surely many others will follow.

The universities also encouraged the development of energy saving techniques and here there is scope for advancement from known research. Many governments are implementing incentives for such techniques but sometimes the embedded energy is forgotten in the drive to cut energy use for the individual or corporate consumer.

4.   *Focus on sustainable ecosystems*

Here the representatives agreed that they should encourage an additional focus on generating and disseminating knowledge, practice and lifestyles relating to sustainable ecosystems with more emphasis on the interdependence between the environment and human activities. They argued that universities should encourage systems which are resilient and can survive major disturbance whether natural or man-made. The object of this principle is to aid society and policy-makers to understand the impact of their activities and to enable informed decision-making.

Section 2: Engagements
Having established the principles, the university representatives agreed that strategies need to be developed and employed to implement the agenda proposed in Section 1. This recognises that aspiration without action will not lead to the changes that are sought. It also recognises, hence the heading 'engagement', that universities cannot do this alone and that their knowledge base is a tremendous asset to those who seek to improve the human need for sustainable development. The issues identified were as follows:

1.   *Broad, global engagement to promote awareness of sustainability issues*

Here the universities recognise their responsibility to communicate their knowledge in both the developed and developing world. In particular they state that they should be providing leadership, advocacy and guidance to policy-makers, industry, the community and individuals, which will foster the awareness and understanding of the interdependence among the different regions of the globe. They also say that they should play their part in educating the next generation of leaders in fields relevant to sustainable development and suggest that *all* students should be exposed to the issues connected with sustainable development and encouraged to be involved in the creation of a sustainable and responsible society in the spirit of global citizenship.

2.   *Restructuring of education and research to incorporate and integrate cutting-edge knowledge*

They argue that a sustainable society requires the latest knowledge restructured to reverse past tendencies towards mono-disciplinary approaches and fragmentation in education and research and to foster an integrated holistic approach to decision-making and problem-solving, requiring a shift from disciplinary to systems thinking.

3. *Governance for strategic development*

In this section they argue for universities to provide policy-makers with high-level education and research results so that they develop policy based on the latest knowledge. They should also advocate sound governance based on participative, multi-scale, polycentric approaches to policy-making and administration, regulation and law. They consider that efforts should be made toward the establishment of a new ethical foundation of sustainability and in addition proper communication channels between universities and policy-makers should be established so that governments can respond effectively to the results of research and new knowledge.

4. *Networking of networks*

At their 2008 summit the universities had suggested that a network of networks be established aiming to link various discipline-specific research networks already in place. This was to avoid knowledge silos being created and an aggravation of the lack of interdisciplinary working. They also called for the establishment of *an Education and Research Virtual Centre on Sustainable and Responsible Development* as an integrated yet autonomous virtual research centre to pursue the principles identified.

Section 3: Recommendations to the G8 Leaders
The above principles and engagements were then enshrined in a series of actions which the universities agreed to undertake through 'living laboratories' as an institutional and organisational response to the above. These actions included forming partnerships with the private and other sectors to transfer knowledge and commercialise new technologies which help sustainable development.

These were followed by suggested actions for governments (bearing in mind that the declaration went forward to the 2009 Head of States' meeting) and these included sharing of good governance and policy-making, encouraging developing countries to participate and the creation of a sustainable economy with the universities acting in partnership to provide scientific approaches to public policy. Finally, they suggested actions which both government and universities could take together including awareness, developing ethical behaviour, holistic thinking and the increase in research within this area.

A Caveat
A heavy caveat must be placed on such a declaration. Firstly, it can only be an aspiration as there is no sanction or incentive that can be

applied beyond a kind of obligation which generally has no legal force. The exception is perhaps CO_2 emissions. Secondly, there is no resource of any substance which can be put behind such an aspiration at the present time except that provided for by nation states or philanthropic funding agencies. Despite its importance the global agreement to address sustainable development is likely to take many years (although issues such as climate change are in the process of being agreed) and even then it is unlikely that a global source of funding will be established. Thirdly, the fragmentation of the funding base will mean that cooperative work across nations will be difficult to achieve in a coordinated way. Knowledge is likely to emerge piecemeal.

These are however not insurmountable problems. In most subjects, whether it be science, engineering or medicine, for example, knowledge has always emerged according to routes more related to serendipity. The difference might be that sustainable development is something which the whole global community has to own and act upon and the motivation of the market to make money may not be the most appropriate driving force for such an initiative. Nevertheless, the green economy is being sold by governments to their peoples as a means of gaining economic advantage and more recently a way of providing an economic driver to allow countries to emerge from a serious recession. There is little doubt that the markets are responding to the challenge but the problem might be that there will be winners and losers and it is likely that it will the poorer nations who will suffer, despite the fact that very often their lifestyles are more conducive to sustainable development. Herein lies a moral imperative for all of us, to ensure that the well-being of so many of humankind is foremost in our minds as we tackle probably the greatest threat so far that has existed to the survival of the human species.

A research agenda

This book has provided an overview of the current state of knowledge with regard to the evaluation of sustainable development. It cannot be exhaustive as the potential spectrum of activity that falls under the heading of sustainable development is enormous. Evaluation methods in practically every aspect of social, economic, political and technological behaviour can be brought to bear on the subject. It is practically impossible for a single individual to have the knowledge and skills required to undertake such exercises in a complete way. It has to be a corporate effort and projects such as the Vancouver study in Chapter 8 provide pointers to the way this can be handled. We are in the middle of an action learning process whereby we all bring our knowledge gained formally and informally to the issue and we endeavour to find an improvement in the way we can evaluate and manage sustainable development.

In this book we have tried to provide an outline of the scale of the task that has to be faced but at the same time we have tried to suggest ways in which this can be addressed. At the root is a structure which is robust and which can be used for all such studies. The Dooyeweerd structure (see Chapter 6) is the closest we have found to answering some of the questions we have posed about integrating information and providing meaning to the subject. Sustainable development can 'mean all things to all people' but by providing a strong theoretical structure it gives the opportunity to rigorously address the subject and establish 'building blocks' of knowledge. However, it does not answer questions about process and this is where the Vancouver study may provide assistance. The process adopted by the Vancouver team echoes some of the issues raised by Dooyeweerd in terms of a holistic approach and goes on to establish how this might be implemented.

It would be true to say that there are no right or wrong answers to methods and processes of evaluation. More standardised approaches would have advantages in terms of knowledge-building and making comparisons. However, meeting the needs of today without jeopardising the opportunities for future generations to meet their own needs means that a flexible and adaptive system is required. Whether this can be done within a framework to which all can bring their understanding and sets of values is not yet proven. The following is a suggested research agenda (one of many, we are sure) which could help in understanding this complex issue:

❏ Develop, test and assess a framework for addressing sustainable development in which various value systems can be represented in such a way that it does not produce a prescribed solution. Dooyeweerd's 'Theory of the Cosmos' as adapted by Lombardi and Brandon (see Chapter 6) might be a good starting point for such a study.

❏ Test the above framework across international boundaries and develop an adaptive, generic process which can form the basis of international comparison and policy-making, always realising that new technologies and events will occur which may change the processes and evaluations involved.

❏ Place evaluation methods within the framework and investigate how these might act together to aid the achievement of consensus on action. The evaluation methods should not dominate the result but merely be aids to educating stakeholders as to the implications of their actions. Where there is a shortfall in evaluation methods, new approaches should be sought.

❏ Provide a manual that gives guidance to all concerned with the subject at various levels (e.g. building, district, city, region) and provides a coherent and robust approach to a holistic approach to the evaluation of sustainable development.

It would be simplistic in the extreme to believe that the issues raised in this book can be dealt with through a new framework but it is a good starting point to bring all parties to a common understanding. It has to be underpinned by a massive development of theory and indeed philosophy so we begin to understand more deeply why we behave collaboratively in the way that we do. Areas of study such as complexity theory, chaos theory and consilience (the unity of knowledge) must be brought to bear on this important problem together with the powerful techniques of engineering and science and the social sciences. It is a challenging and fascinating agenda which will ensure the survival and growth of sustainability science. In short it demands a new world view which transforms the way we think and behave.

As Albert Einstein has said, 'Our problem is that we are trying to find solutions from within the same thinking, the same tools, and the same worldview that caused the problems in the first place'. He also went on to say that 'Imagination is more important than information'. If there is a problem which is crying out for imagination then it is sustainability and it is the role of all of us to encourage such imaginings.

In conclusion

The reader will no doubt be aware of the complexity of the subject now if he or she were not before. The authors have attempted to give an overview that provides pointers to the future based on their experience and the literature in the field. It is not possible to cover in every detail the requirements of a full system for sustainable development, and indeed no such system exists. Those engaged in sustainable development are acting rather like the learning organisation suggested by Peter Senge (Senge, 1990) in *The Fifth Discipline*. He starts his book by saying:

'From an early age, we are taught to break apart problems, to fragment the world. This apparently makes complex tasks and subjects more manageable, but we pay a hidden, enormous price. We can no longer see the consequences of our actions; we lose our intrinsic sense of connection to a larger whole. When we try to see the "big picture" we try to reassemble the fragments in our minds, to list and organise the pieces. But, as physicist David Bohm says, the task is futile – similar to trying to re-assemble the fragments of a broken mirror to see a true reflection. Thus, after a while we give up trying to see the whole altogether'.

He then goes on to say that:

'When we give up this illusion – we can build "learning organisations", organisations where people continually expand their capacity to create the results they truly desire, where new and expansive patterns of thinking are nurtured, where collective aspiration is set free, and where people are continually learning how to learn together'.

Sustainable development demands this corporate enlightenment and commitment. It also requires an acknowledgement that there is not one solution but many and that our understanding will emerge in an evolutionary way in a continual process of improvement over time.

At the start we said that this book was just a beginning, and so it is. There is still much to do and much to learn. We hope that the content provides further insight to the reader and encourages him or her to engage in the 'learning together' process for the benefit of all those who engage with the built environment… and that is practically all of us!

Appendix A: The Philosophy of the 'Cosmonomic Idea of Reality'

Note: The following text provides an outline summary of the very extensive philosophical underpinning of the 'Cosmonomic Idea of Reality'. It cannot be comprehensive but for those who wish to know more it may provide additional insight which will lead to further study of the subject. However, the reader should be warned that this is not an easy exercise to be undertaken.

The proposed framework is based on the 'Cosmonomic Idea of Reality' theory of Dooyeweerd (1955), which underlies the systemic approach named multi-modal system thinking (de Raadt, 1991, 1994, 1997). The multi-modal system thinking approach aims to make complex systems intelligible by escaping from the traditional Cartesian approach by means of comprehensive philosophical studies of multi-level perspectives.

Compared with previous system schools, such as the open system theory proposed by von Bertalanffy (1968) and later developed by Le Moigne (1994), the multi-modal system thinking approach maps systems according to two axes, a multi-modal one (vertical) and a systemic one (horizontal). Specifically, this approach is based on the 'Cosmonomic Idea' philosophy of Dooyeweerd and cybernetics as developed by Ashby (1956, 1976) and Beer (1967, 1981). Adapting and modifying these two foundations, multi-modal system thinking has shifted the focus of systems design and usage onto a number of levels of functioning (named *modalities*) in which systems operate, instead of being on the systems themselves.

Evaluating Sustainable Development in the Built Environment, Second Edition
By Peter S. Brandon and Patrizia Lombardi   © 2011 Peter S. Brandon and Patrizia Lombardi

Table A.1 Comparison between systemic schools of thinking.

Common ground	Systemic approach (Le Moigne)	Multi-modal system (de Raadt)
Both promote a reconception of science in a personal relation denying the objective, independent notion. Both consider the loop of information and organisation as fundamental in making social sciences intelligible as distinct from the traditional energetic notion of natural sciences. Both oppose the popular notion that social science is less exact or more fuzzy. Both try to find alternatives to the cybernetic paradigm, which is considered to be insufficient. Both admit that ultimately faith is the last criterion of choice, or the last station on a multi-modal stair.	Emphasis on the inadequacy of the analytical paradigm in understanding complexity. Constructivism makes how we construct knowledge intelligent. This is received neither through senses nor by way of communication but is actively built up by a cognisant subject. The function of cognition is adaptive and serves the subjects' organisation of the experimental world, not the discovery of an objective ontological reality. This does not tell us what kind of knowledge is constructed. It may fall into relativism.	Emphasis on the inadequacy of isolation of normative and determinative orders. The assumption is that there is an absolute truth and ordered reality independent of human beings. It escapes relativism by focusing on *a priori* knowledge, which is justified by faith. Our knowledge is limited. However, it uses the cybernetic paradigm as an attempt to make social systems intelligible.

(Source: Based on Eriksson, 1996.)

The main similarities and differences between the two systemic schools of Le Moigne and de Raadt are shown in Table A.1.

As said above, the groundwork of the multi-modal system thinking is the scientific methodology of Dutch philosopher Herman Dooyeweerd (1894–1975), known as the 'Cosmonomic Idea of Reality'. It is based on the fundamental notion that nothing, not even theoretical thought, is absolute: all is relative to the Creator God who, by the act of creation, gave everything meaning.

In the words of Basden (www.basden. demon.co.uk/Dooy/ summary.html):

'...the main motivation behind Dooyeweerd's work was to form a philosophical framework that did not make God-avoiding assumptions right from the start, and one that was self-consistent. He wanted it to account for the unity and diversity that we experience. Dooyeweerd was troubled by the fact that Biblical ideas do not seem to fit "comfortably" with most theoretical thinking, yet he was not satisfied with the explanation given by both secularists and fundamentalists that religion has nothing to do with this world of science, technology, business and, in particular, thinking'.

For a general description of Dooyeweerd's work see Clouser (1991) and Kalsbeek (1975), and for full theoretical treatment see Dooyeweerd (1955) and Hart (1984). The present illustration makes copious references to the expositions of de Raadt (1991, 1994, 1997) and Basden (unpublished, 1996, 2008).

The theory of the 'Cosmonomic Idea' acknowledges an external reality that is independent of the acting and knowing subject (hence the term 'Cosmonomic'). We are affected by it but also affect it and have views and desires concerning it. In particular, the theory claims there are two 'sides' to reality as we know it: a *law side* and an *entity side*.

The entity side concerns things, systems and, in fact, anything that does something: for example, a person, a flower, a house, a town, a government, a symphony. The law side concerns *modalities* in which entities operate: for example, physical, social, biotic, ethical, technical.

A modality can be defined as an irreducible area of the functioning of a system. It is characterised by a nucleus of meaning which provides it with an internal order named *sphere sovereignty* and has its own order, or set of laws, by which it is governed (hence the alternative name *law sphere* given by Dooyeweerd), for example, the laws of arithmetic, the laws of physics, the laws of aesthetics, the laws of ethics. These not only guide but also enable entities (people, animals, etc.) to function in a variety of ways.

The law and entity sides can be seen as orthogonal: an entity crosses several modalities. For instance, an entity such as a tree is characterised by a number of modalities, including the spatial (it occupies a limited space) and the physical (it is made of materials), up to the biological (it is alive!) but, compared with a person, it has a more limited range in which it actively functions. It is unable to learn or to speak, and it does not have social interactions or financial businesses. On the contrary, it can be used (as an object) for learning, can be given as a present to a friend, or can be sold or bought (see Fig. A.1).

In everyday living the entities stand to the fore, as it were, and the law side recedes into the background, but in science the law side comes to the fore while the entities recede. So when we analyse reality we should study the law side, not the behaviour of entities. It is the law side (i.e. the modalities) that expresses the fundamental *meaning*, and it is the law side that enables entities to 'exist'.

Modal laws – or orders – are fulfilled in two different ways. In the earlier (or lower or 'hard') modalities, such as numerical and spatial, and their equivalents in the scientific disciplines, mathematics and geometry, the orders, or set of laws, that govern these modalities are more determinative, that is, 'the law always exerts its own fulfilment'.

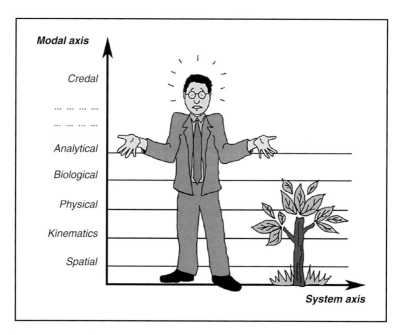

Figure A.1   Two-dimensional representation (modality/system axes) of entities (a man and a tree) crossing different modalities.

For example, within the physical modality the law of gravity is always obeyed; it is a law of spatial aspect that nothing can be both round and square. However, in the later (or higher or 'soft') modalities, such as the ethical and the juridical, the laws are more normative since their fulfilment is contingent on people's inclination to follow these laws and they cannot be described through the harder modalities' determinative rules.

The laws are unique and irreducible, differing from modality to modality, so that it is not possible to entirely understand the behaviour of one modality on the basis of the laws of another modality (sphere sovereignty). However, there are definite relationships between them which allow an entity to function in a coherent rather than fragmented manner. These relationships between modalities are of three kinds.

(1)   *Dependency*: The laws of later aspects depend on and require those of earlier ones. Thus, biotic laws require those of physics, which require those of movement, and so on. The philosophy of the 'Cosmonomic Idea' has not placed the 15 modalities in an arbitrary order and the earlier aspects serve as foundations for the later (Dooyeweerd calls this 'the cosmic order of time').

(2)   *Functioning*: An individual structure (entities and systems) functions in each aspect either as subject or object. While human beings

can act as subject in all aspects, animals have a more limited range
in which they can function as subject. A sheep might act as an economic object, for instance, but not an economic subject, that is, it
can be used as exchange but it cannot itself do an exchange. This
functioning individuality structure serves as an integration point
for the aspects.

(3) *Analogy*: Components of each aspect are mirrored or echoed in
others. Such an analogy is the basis for the symbolic representation
of knowledge on a computer. The correspondence between the
orders of different modalities allows one modality (named the
source) to be used as a metaphoric representation of another or
several other modalities (named *idioms*). For example, social scientists often express aspects of social behaviour (operating in the
social modality) in terms of quantitative measures (operating in
the numeric modality). They can then use the laws of mathematics
to manipulate aspects of behaviour in the social modality and
derive conclusions that have been difficult to arrive at without the
aid of these laws. In the words of de Raadt (1991), it is important
to note that '… these conclusions rest upon the laws of the numeric
modality and not on the basis of the social modality. Therefore,
while they may be mathematically valid, they need not be necessarily valid in the social sphere'.

Although every modality can be an 'idiom' for another, its effectiveness
as an idiom varies and the degree of correspondence declines as the
distance between one modality and another increases. For example,
the numeric modality is not a very suitable idiom for the juridical
modality and it would be better to use a closer modality such as the
ethical modality. In the words of de Raadt (1991), the softness of the
normative order is not due to any indefiniteness, but due to the lower
homomorphism that exists between the soft modalities and the logical
and numerical modalities (these latter being the idioms employed by
much of the hardest science) when compared with the homomorphism
that exists between the hard modalities themselves.

Dooyeweerd illustrates a 'working' list of 15 modalities whose
properties are exhibited by the objects of people's experience. These 15
aspects and their meaning-nuclei (in brackets) are as follows: numerical
(quantity); spatial (continuous extension); kinematics (movement);
physical (energy, mass); biological (life function); sensitive (senses, feeling); analytic (discerning of entities, logic); historical (formative power);
communicative (informatory, symbolic representation); social (social
intercourse, social exchange); economic (frugality, handling limited
resources); aesthetic (harmony, beauty); juridical (retribution, fairness,
rights); ethical (love, moral); and credal (faith, commitment, trustwor-
thiness). They were derived by taking every large-scale kind of property
that has been distinguished in the history of philosophy and science.

In identifying the modalities and their order, however, not all authors are in accord. Hart (1984) identifies only fourteen modalities, as she does not include aesthetic. In addition, she places the analytic modality between the historical and the communicative modalities. de Raadt (1997) adds two new aspects: epistemic (whose essence is wisdom) and operational (whose essence is production). These are placed, respectively, next to the communicative modality and the social modality. Kalsbeek (1975) discusses the meaningfulness of including kinematics within physical as part of it.

The framework developed in this study keeps the original number and order of the modalities given by Dooyeweerd as a consistent list for interpreting sustainable development processes of the built environment. The aim was not to rethink reality, but rather to provide a useful tool for aiding decision-making in planning.

References

Adams, W.M. (2006) The future of sustainability: Rethinking the environment and development in the twenty-first century. *Report of the IUCN Renowned Thinkers Meeting*, 29–31 January 2006. www.iucn.org (accessed 27 May 2006).

Alberti, M. (1996) Measuring urban sustainability. *Environmental Impact Assessment Review*, **16**, 381–424.

Alwaer, H. & Clements-Croom, D.J. (2009) Key performance indicators (KPIs) and priority setting in using the multi-attribute approach for assessing sustainable intelligent buildings. *Building and Environment*, **45**, 799–807.

Archibugi, F. (2002) *Introduzione alia pianificazione strategica in ambito pubblico.* Centro di Studi di Piani Economici, Rome.

Ashby, R. (1956) *Introduction to Cybernetics*. John Wiley & Sons Inc., New York.

Ashby, R. (1976) *An Introduction to Cybernetics*. Methuen, London.

Ashworth, A. & Langston, C.A. (2000) Whole of life assessment and the measurement of sustainability. In: *Cities and Sustainability: Sustaining our Cultural Heritage* (eds P.S. Brandon, P.L. Lombardi & P. Srinath), pp. 42–52. *Proceedings of the Millennium Conference*, University of Moratuwa, Sri Lanka.

ATEQUE (1994) *Identification of Actors Concerned with Environmental Quality of Buildings*. Technical Document No. l, December, Paris.

Basden, A. (1996) Towards an understanding of contextualized technology. In: *Proceedings of the International Conference of the Swedish Operations Research Society on Managing the Technological Society: The Next Century's Challenge to O.R.*, University of Lulea, Sweden, 1–3 October, pp. 17–32.

Basden, A. (2008) *Philosophical Frameworks for Understanding Information Systems*. IGI Publishing, New York.

Beer, S. (1967) *Decision and Control*. John Wiley & Sons, Chichester.

Beer, S. (1981) *Brain of the Firm*. John Wiley & Sons, Chichester.

Evaluating Sustainable Development in the Built Environment, Second Edition
By Peter S. Brandon and Patrizia Lombardi © 2011 Peter S. Brandon and Patrizia Lombardi

Bentivegna, V. (1997) Limitations in environmental evaluations. In: *Evaluation of the Built Environment for Sustainability* (eds P.S. Brandon, P. Lombardi & V. Bentivegna), pp. 25–38. E & FN Spon, London.

Bentivegna, V., Curwell, S., Deakin, M., Lombardi, P. & Nijkamp, P. (2002) A vision and methodology for integrated sustainable urban development: BEQUEST. *Building Research International*, **30**(2), 83–94.

BEQUEST (2001) *Final Report 2000–2001*, Contract N.ENV 4 CT/97/607, EC Environmental and Climate Programme (1994–1998) Research Theme 4: *Human Dimensions and Environmental Change*, University of Salford.

Bergh, J., Button, K., Nijkamp, P. & Pepping, G. (1997) *Meta-Analysis of Environmental Policies*. Kluwer, Dordrecht.

Bernstein, H. & Bowerbank, A. (2008) *Global Green Building Trends (SmartMarket Report)*. McGraw-Hill, New York.

von Bertalanffy, L. (1968) *General System Theory*. Braziller, New York.

Birkeland, J. (2005) Building assessment systems: Reversing environmental impacts. *Website Discussion Paper*, Vol. 1. http://www.naf.org.au/nafforum/birkeland-2.pdf (accessed 28 August 2008).

Bizarro, F. & Nijkamp, P. (1997) Integrated conservation of cultural built heritage. In: *Evaluation of the Built Environment for Sustainability* (eds P.S. Brandon, P.L. Lombardi & V. Bentivegna). E & FN Spon, London.

Bossel, H. (1998) *Earth at a Crossroads*. Cambridge University Press, Cambridge.

Boulding, E. (1978) The dynamics of imaging futures. *World Futures Society Bulletin*, **12**(8), 1–8.

Brand, S. (2000) *The Clock of the Long Now: Time and Responsibility: The Ideas Behind the World's Slowest Computer*. Basic Books, New York.

Brandon, P.S. (1992) *Quantity Surveying Techniques*. Blackwell Science, Oxford.

Brandon, P.S. (ed.) (1998) *Proceedings of the CIB World Congress, Symposium D: Managing Sustainability – Endurance Through Change*, Gavle, Sweden, 7–12 June 1998.

Brandon, P.S. & Lombardi, P. (2005) *Evaluating Sustainable Development in the Built Environment*. Blackwell Science, Oxford.

Brandon, P.S., Lombardi, P. & Bentivegna, V. (eds) (1997) *Evaluation of the Built Environment for Sustainability*. Chapman & Hall, London.

Breheny, M.J. (ed.) (1992) *Sustainable Development and Urban Form*. Pion Limited, London.

Brooks, C., Cheshire, A., Evans, A. & Stabler, M. (1997) The economic and social value of the conservation of historic buildings and areas. In: *Evaluation of the Built Environment for Sustainability* (eds P.S. Brandon, P.L. Lombardi & V. Bentivegna). E & FN Spon, London.

Brown, P.F. (1996) *Venice and Antiquity: The Venetian Sense of the Past*. Yale University Press, New Haven, CT.

Brugmann, J. (1999) Is there method in our measurement? The use of indicators in local sustainable development planning. In: *The Earthscan Reader in Sustainable Cities* (ed. D. Satterthwaite), pp. 394–407. Earthscan, London.

Bryson, J.M. (1988) *Strategic Planning for Public and Nonprofit Organizations*. Jossey Bass, San Francisco, CA.

Burns, M. & Weaver, A. (eds) (2008) *Exploring Sustainability Science: A Southern African Perspective*. Sun Press, Stellenbosch, South Africa.

Capello, R., Nijkamp, P. & Pepping, G. (1999) *Sustainable Cities and Energy Policies*. Springer-Verlag, Berlin.

CER – Ministero dei lavori pubblici (1996) *Rapporto sulle condizioni abitative in Italia*. Paper presented at *United Nations Conference on Human Settlement* (*Habitat II*), Istanbul, 3–14 June 1996.

Ceric, A. (2003) *A framework for process-driven risk management in construction projects*. PhD thesis, University of Salford, Salford.

Checkland, P. & Scholes, J. (1999) *Soft Systems Methodology in Action*. John Wiley & Sons Ltd, Chichester.

CIB – "Conseil International du Bâtiment" (International Council for Building). http://www.cibworld.nl/

Ciciotti, E. & Perulli, P. (eds) (1998) *La pianificazione strategica*. Daest, Venice.

Ciciotti, E., Dall'Ara, A. & Politi, M. (2001) Valutazione delle politiche territoriali e governance dello sviluppo locale: aspetti teorici e di metodo. In: *Crescita regionale ed urbana nel mercato globule. Modelli, politiche, processi di valutazione* (eds F. Mazzola & M.A. Maggioni). Angeli, Milan.

Città di Collegno (2005) Bando Regionale Programmi integrati per lo sviluppo locale, De Amicis – Certosa Reale Porta Ovest Dell'area Metropolitana, Relazione illustrativa, pp. 1–29. http://www.provincia.torino.it/sviluppolocale/pti/ for further details (accessed 24 July 2009).

Città di Collegno (2006) Studio di Fattibilità. Recupero e rifunzionalizzazione degli ex Laboratori dell'Ospedale Psichiatrico e alla riprogettazione degli spazi pubblici aperti della Certosa Reale, pp. 1–78. http://www.comune. collegno.to.it/aree-tematiche/territorio/programmi-complessi/pisl/ fattibilita2.pdf (accessed 24 July 2009).

CLEAR (2001) *City and Local Environment Accounting and Reporting*. Life Environment Programme.

Clouser, R.A. (1991) *The Myth of Religious Neutrality*. University of Notre Dame Press, London.

Cole, R. & Lorch, L. (eds) (2003) *Buildings, Culture & Environment*. Blackwell, Oxford.

Collins English Dictionary, 5th edn (2000). Harper Collins Publishers, Glasgow.

Comune di Modena (2004) *Un decennio di scelte. Bilancio Sociale di Mandate per un Piano Strategico della città*. Tracce, Modena.

Construction Research and Innovation Panel Report (1999) *Sustainable Construction: Future R & I Requirements – Analysis of Current Position*, 23 March.

Cooper, I. (1997) Environmental assessment methods for use at the building and city scale: Constructing bridges or identifying common ground. In: *Evaluation of the Built Environment for Sustainability* (eds P.S. Brandon, P. Lombardi & V. Bentivegna). E & FN Spon, London.

Cooper, I. (1999) Which focus for building assessment methods? *Building Research & Information*, **27**(4), 321–331.

Cooper, I. & Curwell, S. (1998) The implications of urban sustainability. *Building Research & Information*, **26**(1), 17–28.

Cooper, I. & Palmer, J. (1999) Il programma di ricerca sulle città sostenibili nel Regno Unito. *Urbanistica*, **112**, 83–87.

Cooper, R.G., Aouad, G., Lee, A., Wu, S., Kagioglou, M. & Fleming, A. (2004) *Process Management in Design and Construction*. Blackwell Publishing Ltd, Oxford.

Costanza, R. (ed.) (1991) *Ecological Economics*. Columbia University Press, New York.

Costanza, R. (1993) Ecological economic systems analysis: Order and chaos. In: *Economics and Ecology* (ed. E.B. Barbier), pp. 29–45. Chapman & Hall, London.

CRISP – Construction and City Related Sustainability Indicators. http://crisp. cstb.fr/default.htm

Curwell, S. & Lombardi, P. (1999) Riqualificazione urbana sostenibile. In: *Analisi e valutazione di programmi e progetti di sostenibilità urbana. Alcune esperienze* (ed. P. Lombardi). *Urbanistica*, **112**, 96–103 (English version 114–115), June 1999.

Curwell, S., Hamilton, A. & Cooper, I. (1998) The BEQUEST network: Towards sustainable urban development. *Building Research & Information*, **26**(1), 56–65.

Curwell, S., Yates, A., Howard, N., Bordass, B. & Doggart, J. (1999) The green building challenge in the UK. *Building Research & Information*, **27**(4/5), 286–293.

Curwell, S., Deakin, M. & Symes, M. (eds) (2005a) *Sustainable Urban Development: The Framework, Protocols and Environmental Assessment Methods*, Vol. 1. Routledge, Oxford.

Curwell, S., Deakin, M., Cooper, I., Paskaleva-Shapira, K., Ravetz J. & Babicki, D. (2005b) Citizens' expectations of information cities: Implications for urban planning and design. *Building Research & Information*, **33**(1), 55–66.

D.M.LL.PP (1994) *Programma di requalificazione urbana a valere sui finanziamenti di cui all'art.2 comma delta leggem, 179 del 17 febbraio 1992 s.m.i.*

Daly, H.E. & Cobb, J.B. (1989) *For the Common Good: Redirecting the Economy Towards the Community, the Environment and a Sustainable Future*. Beacon Press, Boston, MA.

Davidson, S. (1998) Spinning the wheel of empowerment. *Planning*, **1262** (3 April), 14–15.

Davoudi, S. (1999) sostenibilità: una nuova visione per il sistema britannico, di pianificazione. *Urbanistica*, **112**, 78–83.

Davoudi, S. (2000) Sustainability: A new vision for the British planning system. *Planning Perspectives*, **15**(2), 123–137.

Deakin, M. (1997) An economic evaluation and appraisal of the effects land use, building obsolescence and depreciation have on the environment of cities. In: *Evaluation of the Built Environment for Sustainability* (eds P.L. Brandon, P. Lombardi & V. Bentivenga). E & FN Spon, London.

Deakin, M. & Lombardi, P. (2005a) The directory of environmental assessment methods. In: *Sustainable Urban Development: The Framework, Protocols and Environmental Assessment Methods*, Vol. 1 (eds S. Curwell, M. Deakin & M. Symes), pp. 175–192. Routledge, Oxon.

Deakin, M. & Lombardi, P. (2005b) Assessing the sustainability of urban development. In: *Sustainable Urban Development: The Framework, Protocols and Environmental Assessment Methods*, Vol. 1 (eds S. Curwell, M. Deakin & M. Symes), pp. 193–208. Routledge, Oxon.

Deakin, M., Curwell, S. & Lombardi, P. (2001) BEQUEST: Sustainability assessment, the framework and directory of methods. *International Journal of Life Cycle Assessment*, **6**(6), 373–390.

Deakin, M., Curwell, S. & Lombardi, P. (2002a) Sustainable urban development: The framework and directory of assessment methods. *Journal of Environmental Assessment Policy and Management*, **4**(2), 171–197.

Deakin, M., Mitchell, G. & Lombardi, P. (2002b) Valutazione della sostenibilità: una verifica delle tecniche disponili. *Urbanistica*, **118**, 28–34 (English version 50–53).

Deakin, M., Mitchell, G., Nijkamp, P. & Vreeker, R. (eds) (2007) *Sustainable Urban Development the Environmental Assessment Methods*, Vol. 2. Routledge, Oxon.

Derickson, R.G. (2006) We're not dumb enough to survive as a species, but are we smart enough? In: *Proceedings of the 50th Annual Meeting of the ISSS*, Sonoma State University, Rohnert Park, CA, 9–14 June 2006. http://journals. isss.org/index.php/proceedings50th/article/viewFile/293/84   (accessed August 2009).

DETR (Department of the Environment, Transport and the Regions) (1998) *Sustainable Development: Opportunities for Change. Sustainable Construction.* Stationery Office, London.

Devuyst, D. (1999) Sustainability assessment: The application of a methodological framework. *Journal of Environmental Assessment Policy and Management*, **1**(4), 459–487.

Devuyst, D., Hens, L. & De Lannoy, W. (1999) *Sustainability Assessment at the Local Level*. Columbia University Press, New York.

Ding, G.K. (1999) MCDM and the assessment of sustainability in construction. In: *The Challenge of Change: Construction and Building for the New Millennium*, Vol. 1 (eds D. Baldry & L. Ruddock). RICS, University of Salford, Salford.

Donne, J. (1623) *Devotions Upon Emergent Occasions, Meditation XVII*. http:// en.wikisource.org/wiki/Meditation_XVII.

Dooyeweerd, H. (1955) *A New Critique of Theoretical Thought*, 4 vols. Presbyterian & Reformed Publishing Company, Philadelphia, PA.

Dooyeweerd, H. (1968) *In the Twilight of Western Thought*. Craig Press, Nutley, NJ.

Dooyeweerd, H. (1979) *Roots of Western culture: Pagan, Secular and Christian Options*. Wedge Publishing Company, Toronto.

Doughty, M.R.C. & Hammond, G.P. (2004) Sustainability and the built environment at and beyond the city scale. *Building and Environment*, **39**, 1223–1233.

Du Plessis, C. (2008) A conceptual framework for understanding social-ecological systems. In: *Exploring Sustainability Science – A Southern African Perspective* (eds M. Burns & A. Weaver), pp. 59–90. Sun Press, Stellenbosch, South Africa.

Du Plessis, C. (2009) *An approach to studying urban sustainability from within an ecological worldview*. PhD dissertation, School of the Built Environment, University of Salford, Salford.

Dupuit, J. (1933) De l'utilité et de la mesure. La Riforma Sociale, Turin.

EA (2003) *Integrated Appraisal Methods. Final Report*. EA, Bristol.

Ecological Building Criteria for Viikki, Aaltonen-Gabrielsson-Inkinen-Majurinen-Pennane-Wartiainen, Helsinki City Planning Department Publication 1998:6.

EEA (1995) Europe's environment – The Dobris Assessment. *State of the Environment Report No. 1*. European Environment Agency, Copenhagen, Denmark.

EEA (2007) Halting the loss of biodiversity by 2010: Proposal for a first set of indicators to monitor progress in Europe. *Technical Report, 11*. European Environment Agency, Copenhagen, Denmark.

Eriksson, D. (1996) System science: A guide for postmodernity? A proposition. In: *Proceedings of the International Conference of the Swedish Operations Research Society, Managing the Technological Society: The Next Century's Challenge to O.R.*, University of Lulea, Sweden, 1–3 October 1996, pp. 57–71.

European Commission (1990) *Green Paper on the Urban Environment*. Commission of the European Communities, COM (90) 218 CEC. Office of Publications of the European Commission, Luxembourg, Brussels, 27 June 1990.

European Commission (2005) Attitudes of European citizens towards the environment. *Special Eurobarometer* 217. Wave 62.1 – TNS Opinion & Social, April 2005. http://ec.europa.eu/public_opinion/archives/ebs/ebs_217_en.pdf (accessed December 2010).

Eurostat (2007a) *Analysis of National Sets of Indicators Used in the National Reform Programmes and Sustainable Development Strategies*. Office for Official Publications of the European Communities, Luxembourg.

Eurostat (2007b) *Measuring Progress towards a More Sustainable Europe. 2007 Monitoring Report of the EU Sustainable Development Strategy*. Office for Official Publications of the European Communities, Luxembourg.

Expert Group on the Urban Environment, EGUE (1994) *European Sustainable Cities. Consultation Draft for the European Conference on Sustainable Cities and Towns*. First Annual Report, Aalbourg, Denmark, 24–27 June 1994. Commission of the European Communities, Directorate XI, XI/307/94-EN.

Faucheux, S. & O'Conner, M. (1998) Introduction. In: *Valuation for Sustainable Development* (eds S. Faucheux & M. O'Conner). Edward Elgar, Cheltenham.

Faucheux, S., Pearce, D. & Proops, J. (1996) Introduction. In: *Models of Sustainable Development* (eds S. Faucheux, D. Pearce & J. Proops). Edward Elgar, Cheltenham.

Ferry, D.J., Brandon, P.S. & Ferry, J.D. (1999) *Cost Planning of Buildings*, 7th edn. Blackwell Publishing Ltd, Oxford.

Finco, A. & Nijkamp, P. (2001) Pathways to urban sustainability. *Journal of Environmental Policy & Planning*, **3**, 289–302.

Fleming, A., Lee, A. & Kagioglou, M. (2009) *Generic Disaster Management and Reconstruction Process Protocol, Consultative Guide*. RICS/University of Salford, Salford.

Folke, C., Carpenter, S., Elmqvist, T., Gunderson, L., Holling, C.S. & Walker, B. (2002) Resilience and sustainable development: Building adaptive capacity in a world of transformations. *Ambio*, **31**(5), 437–440. Published by Allen Press on behalf of the Royal Swedish Academy of Sciences.

Forrester, J. (1969) *Urban Dynamics*. Productivity Press, Portland, OR.

Forte, C. & De Rossi, B. (1996) *Principi di economicia ed estimo*. Etas Libri, Milan.

Foxon, T.J., Leach, M., Butler, D., *et al.* (1999) Useful indicators of urban sustainability: Some methodological issues. *Local Environment*, **4**(2), 137–149.

Francescato, G. (1991) Housing quality: Technical and non-technical aspects. In: *Management, Quality and Economics in Buildings* (eds A. Bezelga & P. Brandon), pp. 602–609. E & FN Spon, London.

G8 University Summit (2009) Torino Declaration on Education and Research for Sustainable and Responsible Development (Turin Declaration). http://www.g8university.com/contenuti/file/G8US%202009_FD_VER%203.0_2009%2005%2019_ultima-firmata.pdf (accessed December 2009).

GBS (2001) *I principi di redazione del bilancio sociale*, May 2001.

Gilkinson, N., Sharp, C., Curwell, S. & Cooper, R. (2002) SMART: Sustainable Material Advice and Resourcing Tool for the construction sector. In: *First Scottish Conference for Postgraduate Research of the Built and Natural Environment*, Glasgow Caledonian University, Scotland, p. 176.

Glasson, J., Therival, R. & Chadwick, A. (1994) *Environmental Impact Assessment*. University College, London.

Gordon, A. (1974) The economics of the 3 Ls concept. *Chartered Surveyor B & QS Quarterly*, RICS, Winter 1974.

Gore, A. (2006) *An Inconvenient Truth: The Planetary Emergency of Global Warming and What We Can Do about It*. Rodale, New York.

Graedel, T.E. (1998) *Streamlined Life-cycle Assessment*. Prentice Hall, New Jersey.

Green Building Challenge (1998) *An International Conference on the Performance Assessment of Buildings*, 26–28 October 1998, Vancouver, Canada.

Griffioen, S. (1995) The relevance of Dooyeweerd's 'Theory of Social Institutions'. In: *Christian Philosophy at the Close of the Twentieth Century* (eds S. Griffioen & B.M. Balk), pp. 139–158. Uitgeverij, Kampen.

Guy, S. & Marvin, S. (1997) Splintering networks: Cities and technical networks in 1990s Britain. *Urban Studies*, **34**(2), 191–216.

Haberl, H., Fischer-Kowalski, M., Krausmann, F., Weisz, H. & Winiwarter, V. (2004) Progress towards sustainability? What the conceptual framework of material and energy flow accounting (MEFA) can offer. *Land Use Policy*, **21**, 199–213.

Habitat (2001) *Cities in a Globalizing World: Global Report on Human Settlements*. Earthscan, London.

Hametner, M. & Steurer, R. (2007) Objectives and indicators of sustainable development in Europe: A comparative analysis of European coherence. *ESDN Quarterly Report*. December. http://www.sd-network.eu/?k=quarterly%20 reports&report_id=7

Hamilton, A., Mitchell, G. & Yli-Karjanmaa, S. (2002) The BEQUEST toolkit: A decision support system for urban sustainability. *Building Research & Information*, **30**(2), 109–115.

Hardi, P. & Zdan, T. (1997) *Assessing Sustainable Development*. International Institute for Sustainable Development, Winnipeg.

Hart, H. (1984) *Understanding our World*. University Press of America, Lanham, MD.

Hart, M. (1999) *Guide to Sustainable Community Indicators*, 2nd edn. Hart Environmental Data, North Andover, MA.

Hinloopen, E., Nijkamp, P. & Rietveld, P. (1983) Quantitative discrete multiple criteria choice models in regional planning. *Regional Science and Urban Economics*, **13**, 77–102.

Hinna, L. (ed.) (2002) *Il Bilancio Sociale*. Il Sole 24 Ore, Milan.

Horner, R.M.W. (2004) *Assessment of Sustainability Tools. Building Research Establishment*, Glasgow, pp. 1–46. Report number 15961. http://download. sue-mot.org/envtooleval.pdf (accessed 26 July 2009)

IntelCities – Intelligent Cities project (No: IST 2002-507860) EU VI Framework, Information Society Technologies. http://www.intelcitiesproject.com (accessed 12 October 2007).

IntelCities – Intelligent Cities project (No: IST 2002-507860) EU VI Framework, Information Society Technologies. http://www.intelcitiesproject.com

Intelcity (2003) – Towards Intelligent Sustainable Cities Roadmap (No: IST 2001-37373) EU V Framework, Information Society Technologies. http:// www.scri.salford.ac.uk/intelcity/ (accessed 12 January 2009).

IUCN (1980) *World Conservation Strategy: Living Resources Conservation for Sustainable Development*. International Union for Conservation of Nature, Section 1.2, Gland, Switzerland.

Jackson, T. (1996) *Material Concerns: Pollution, Profit and Quality of Life*. Routledge, London.

Jackson, T. (2009) *Prosperity without Growth: Economics for a Finite Planet.* Earthscan, London.

Jacobs, J. (1992) *The Death and Life of Great American Cities.* Random House Inc., New York (1st edn, 1961, Vintage Books).

Kahnemann, D. & Tversky, A. (1984) Choices, values and frames. *American Psychologist,* **39**(4), 341–350.

Kaib, W. (1994) Urban marketing as a third way between centrally planned economy and market economy. In: *Urban Marketing in Europe* (eds G. Ave & F. Corsico), pp. 877–881. Torino Incontra Edizioni, Turin.

Kalsbeek, L. (1975) *Contours of a Christian Philosophy.* Wedge Publishing Company, Toronto.

Kazmierczak, A., Curwell, S.R. & Turner, J.C. (2007) Assessment methods and tools for regeneration of large urban distressed areas. In: *Proceedings of the International Conference on Whole Life Urban Sustainability and its Assessment,* Glasgow,27–29June2007.http://download.sue-mot.org/Conference-2007/ Papers /Kazmierczak. pdf for further details (accessed 24 July 2009).

Khakee, A. (1998) The communicative turn in planning and evaluation. In: *Evaluation in Planning* (eds N. Lichfield, A. Barbanente, D. Borri, A. Khakee & A. Prat), pp. 97–111. Kluwer Academic Publishers, Dordrecht.

Kieffer, S.W., Barton, P., Palmer, A.R., Reitan, P.H. & Zen, E. (2003) Mega-scale events: Natural disasters and human behavior. *Geological Society of America, 2003 Seattle Annual Meeting,* Seattle, WA, 2–5 November 2003, Abstracts with Programs: 432.

Klinckenberg, F. & Sunikka, M. (2007) *Better Buildings through Energy Efficiency: A Roadmap for Europe.* Eurima, Brussels.

Kohler, N. (2002) The relevance of BEQUEST: An observer's perspective. *Building Research & Information,* **30**(2), 130–138.

Kohler, N. (2003) Presentation: Cycles of transformation for the city and its culture. In: *Intelcity Workshop,* Siena (under the auspices of the University of Salford).

Koster, A. (1994) Urban marketing – A new approach for town planning and a chance for reactivation of sites in old-industrial regions. In: *Urban Marketing in Europe* (eds G. Ave & F. Corsico), pp. 662–667. Torino Incontra Edizioni, Turin.

Lancaster, K.J. (1966) A new approach to consumer theory. *Journal of Political Economy,* **84**, 132–157.

Leadership in Energy and Environmental Design (LEED) (1998) *Green Buildings Rating System.* US Green Buildings Council, San Francisco, CA.

Le Moigne, J.L. (1994) *La théorie du systeme général.* PUF, Paris.

Lichfield, N. (1996) *Community Impact Evaluation.* UCL Press, London.

Lichfield, N. (1999) Analisi dello stakeholder nella valutazione di un progetto. *Sviluppo economico,* **3**(2–3), 169–189.

Lichfield, N. & Prat, A. (1998) Linking ex-ante and ex-post evaluation in British town planning. In: *Evaluation in Planning: Facing the Challenge of Complexity* (eds N. Lichfield, A. Barbanente, D. Borri, A. Kakee & A. Prat), pp. 283–298. Kluwer Academic Publishers, Dordrecht.

Lichfield, N., Kettle, P. & Whitbread, M. (1975) *Evaluation in the Planning Process.* Pergamon Press Ltd, Oxford.

Lichfield, N., Barbanente, A., Borri, D., Kakee, A. & Prat, A. (eds) (1998) *Evaluation in Planning: Facing the Challenge of Complexity.* Kluwer Academic Publishers, Dordrecht.

Lombardi, P. (1997) Decision making problems concerning urban regeneration plans. *Engineering Construction and Architectural Management*, **4**(2), 127–142.

Lombardi, P. (1998a) Managing sustainability in urban planning evaluation. In: *Proceedings of the CIB World Congress, Symposium D: Managing Sustainability – Endurance Through Change* (ed. P. Brandon), Gavle, Sweden, 7–12 June 1998, pp. 2041–2050.

Lombardi, P. (1998b) Sustainability indicators in urban planning evaluation. In: *Evaluation in Planning* (eds N. Lichfield, A. Barbanente, D. Borri, A. Kakee & A. Prat), pp. 177–192. Kluwer Academic Publishers, Dordrecht.

Lombardi, P. (1999) Agenda 21 e monitoraggio dello sviluppo urbano sostenibile. In: *Analisi e valutazione di progetti e programmi di sostenibilità urbana* (ed. P. Lombardi). *Urbanistica* (112), June, 104–110 (English version 115–116).

Lombardi, P. (2000) A framework for understanding sustainability in the cultural built environment. In: *Cities and Sustainability. Sustaining our Cultural Heritage* (eds P.S. Brandon, P. Lombardi & P. Srinath), IV, pp. 1–25. Conference Proceedings, Vishva Lekha Sarvodaya, Sri Lanka.

Lombardi, P. (2001) Responsibilities toward the coming generation forming a new creed. *Urban Design Studies*, **7**, 89–102.

Lombardi, P. (2007) The analytic hierarchy process. In: *Sustainable Urban Development: The Environmental Assessment Methods*, Vol. 2 (eds M. Deakin, G. Mitchell, P. Nijkamp & R. Vreeker), pp. 209–222. Routledge, Oxon.

Lombardi, P. (2008). REGEN assessment of the Porta Nuova District's Central Railway Station. In: *Sustainable Urban Development: The Toolkit for Assessment*, Vol. 3 (eds R. Vreeker, M. Deakin & S. Curwell). Routledge, Oxon.

Lombardi, P. (2009) Evaluation of sustainable urban redevelopment scenarios. *Proceedings of the Institution of Civil Engineers: Urban Design and Planning*, **162**, 179–186.

Lombardi, P. & Basden, A. (1997) Environmental sustainability and information systems. *Systems Practice*, **10**(4), 473–489.

Lombardi, P. & Brandon, P.S. (1997) Towards a multimodal framework for evaluating the built environment quality in sustainability planning. In: *Evaluation of the Built Environment for Sustainability* (P.S. Brandon, P. Lombardi & V. Bentivegna). Chapman & Hall, London.

Lombardi, P. & Brandon, P.S. (1999) BEQUEST: Building Environmental Quality Evaluation For Sustainability Through Time Network. *Information Sheet 3*, Spring 1999. http://research.scpm.salford.ac.uk/bqextra

Lombardi, P. & Brandon, P.S. (2002) Sustainability in the built environment: A new holistic taxonomy of aspects for decision making. *Environmental Technology & Management International Journal*, **2**(1–2), 22–37.

Lombardi, P. & Brandon, P. (2007) The multimodal system approach to sustainability planning evaluation. In: *Sustainable Urban Development: The Environmental Assessment Methods*, Vol. 2 (eds M. Deakin, G. Mitchell, P. Nijkamp & R. Vreeker), pp. 47–66. Routledge, Oxon. ISBN: 978-0-415-32217-1.

Lombardi, P. & Cooper, I. (2007a) eDomus vs eAgora: The Italian case and implications for the EU 2010 strategy. In: *Expanding the Knowledge Economy: Issues, Applications*, Vol. 1 (Case Studies) (eds P. Cunningham & M. Cunningham), pp. 344–351. IOS Press, Amsterdam.

Lombardi, P. & Cooper, I. (2007b) Progress toward sustainable development in a knowledge society in Italy and EU. In: *Proceedings of the International*

Conference on Whole Life Urban Sustainability and its Assessment (eds M. Horner, C. Hardcastle, A. Price & J. Bebbington), Glasgow, 27–29 June 2007.

Lombardi, P. & Cooper, I. (2009) The challenge of the eAgora metrics: The social construction of meaningful measurements. *International Journal of Sustainable Development,* **12**, 2/3/3, 210–222.

Lombardi, P. & Curwell, S. (2002) Il progetto BEQUEST: metodologia e quadro di riferimento. *Urbanistica,* **118**, 23–27.

Lombardi, P. & Curwell, S. (2005) A scenarios' evaluation of the European intelligent city of the future. In: *Bridging the Gaps in Smart and Sustainable Development* (eds J. Yang, P.S. Brandon & A.C. Sidwell). *Proceedings of the SASBE Conference,* Blackwell Science, Oxford.

Lombardi, P. & Marella, G. (1997) A multi-modal evaluation of sustainable urban regeneration: A case-study related to ex-industrial areas. In: *Second International Conference on Buildings and the Environment,* CIB-CSTB, Vol. 2, Paris, 9–12 June 1997, pp. 271–279.

Lombardi, P. & Nijkamp, P. (2000) A new geography of hope and despair for the periphery: An illustration of the Border Temple Model. In: *Launching Greek Geography on the Eastern EU Border,* Vol. 1 (ed. L. Leontidou), pp. 275–306. Department of Geography, University of the Aegean, Lesbos.

Lombardi, P. & Stanghellini, S. (2008) Assessment methods underlying the planning and development of Modena city's CSR. In: *Sustainable Urban Development: The Toolkit for Assessment,* Vol. 3 (eds R. Vreeker, M. Deakin & S. Curwell). Routledge, Oxon, UK. ISBN: 978-0-415-32219-5.

Lombardi, P. & Zorzi, F. (1993) Comparison between aggregated techniques for assessing the effects of decision-making processes in the environmental field. In: *Economic Evaluation and the Built Environment,* Vol. 4 (eds A. Manso, A. Bezega & D. Picken), pp. 126–138. Laboratorio Nacional de Engenheria Civil, Lisbon.

Lombardi, P., Cooper, I., Paskaleva, K. & Deakin, M. (2009) The challenge of designing user-centric e-Services: European dimensions. In: *Strategies for Local E-Government Adoption and Implementation: Comparative Studies* (ed. C. Reddick), pp. 460–477. IGI Global Books, Hershey, PA.

Lombardi, P., Huovila, P. & Sunikka-Blank, M. (2010) The potential of e-participation in sustainable development evaluation – Evidence from case studies. In: *Politics, Democracy and E-Government* (ed. C.G. Reddick), pp. 1–16. IGI Global Books, Hershey, PA.

Lovelock, J. (2009) *The Vanishing Face of Gaia: A Final Warning.* Penguin Press, London.

LUDA – Large Urban Distressed Areas. EU V Framework. http://www.luda-project.net/

Lundin, M. & Morrison, G.M. (2002) A life cycle assessment based procedure for development of environmental sustainability indicators for urban water systems. *Urban Water,* **4**, 145–152.

Marvin, S. & Guy, S. (1997) Infrastructure provision, development process and the co-production of environmental value. *Urban Studies,* **34**(12), 2023–2036.

Matsuo, T. (2006) The role of indicators in policy design and best practices in Japan. In: *Proceedings of SLT/CERT Workshop on Energy-Efficiency in Buildings,* Paris, 27–28 November 2006.

Mawhinney, M. (2002) *Sustainable Development. Understanding the Green Debates.* Blackwell Publishing Ltd, Oxford.

May, A., Mitchell, G. & Kupiszewska, D. (1997) The development of the Leeds quantifiable city model. In: *Evaluation of the Built Environment for Sustainability* (eds P. Brandon, P. Lombardi & V. Bentivegna). E & FN Spon, London.

Mazzola, F. & Maggioni, M.A. (eds) (2001) *Crescita regionale ed urbana nel mercato globale. Modelli, politiche, processi di valutazione.* Angeli, Milan.

Meadows, D. (1999) Indicators and information systems for sustainable development. In: *The Earthscan Reader in Sustainable Cities* (ed D. Satterthwaite), pp. 364–393. Earthscan, London.

Mitchell, G. (1996) Problems and fundamentals of sustainable development indicators. *Sustainable Development*, **4**(1), 1–11.

Mitchell, G. (1999) A geographical perspective on the development of sustainable urban regions. In: *Geographical Perspectives on Sustainable Development.* Earthscan, London.

Mitchell, G., May, A. & McDonald, A. (1995) PICABUE: A methodological framework for the development of indicators of sustainable development. *International Journal of Sustainable Development & World Ecology*, **2**, 104–123.

Mjwara, P. (2008) Introduction. In: *Exploring Sustainability Science: A Southern African Perspective* (eds M. Burns & A. Weaver). Sun Press, Stellenbosch, South Africa.

Munda, G. (2005) Multiple criteria decision analysis and sustainable development. In: *Multiple Criteria Decision Analysis* (eds J. Figueira, S. Greco & M. Ehrgott), pp. 953–987. Springer, New York.

Nath, V., Heans, L. & Devuyst, D. (eds) (1996) *Sustainable Development.* VUB Press, Brussels.

Newman, P.W.G. (1999) Sustainability and cities: Extending the metabolism model. *Landscape and Urban Planning*, **44**, 219–226.

Nijkamp, P. (ed.) (1991) *Urban Sustainability.* Gower, Aldershot.

Nijkamp, P. (2007) The role of evaluation in supporting a human sustainable development: A cosmonomic perspective. In: *Sustainable Urban Development: The Environmental Assessment Methods*, Vol. 2 (eds M. Deakin, G. Mitchell, P. Nijkamp & R. Vreeker), pp. 94–109. Routledge, London.

Nijkamp, P. & Pepping, G. (1998) A meta-analytic evaluation of sustainable city initiatives. *Urban Studies*, 35(9), 1481–1500.

O'Conner, M. (1998) Ecological-economic sustainability. In: *Valuation for Sustainable Development* (eds S. Faucheux & M. O'Conner). Edward Elgar, Cheltenham.

Odum, M.T. & Odum, E.C. (1980) *Energy Basis for Man and Nature.* McGraw Hill Inc., New York.

OECD (1994) *Report on Environmental Indicators.* Organisation for Economic Cooperation and Development, Paris.

OECD (2003a) *Composite Indicators of Country Performance: A Critical Assessment.* DST/IND(2003)5, Organisation for Economic Cooperation and Development, Paris.

OECD (2003b) *Environment Indicators. Development, Measurement and Use.* Organisation for Economic Cooperation and Development, Paris.

OECD (2008). *Key Environmental Indicators.* Organisation for Economic Cooperation and Development, Paris.

Pearce, D. (2005) Do we understand sustainable development?. *Building Research & Information*, 33(5), 481–483.

Pearce, D. & Markandya, A. (1989) *Environmental Policy Benefits: Monetary Valuation*. OECD, Paris.

Pearce, D. & Turner, R. (1990) *Economics of Natural Resources and the Environment*. Harvester Wheatsheaf, Hemel Hempstead.

Pearce, D. & Warford, J. (1993) *World Without End: Economic, Environment and Sustainable Development*. Oxford University Press, Oxford.

Porter, G. (2000) Quoted in Mawhinney, M. (2002) *Sustainable Development. Understanding the Green Debates*. Blackwell Publishing, Oxford.

Powell, J., Pearce, D. & Craighill, A. (1997) Approaches to valuation in LCA impact assessment. *International Journal of Life Cycle Assessment*, **2**(1), 11–15.

Prior, J. (ed.) (1993) *Building Research Establishment Environment Assessment Method, BREEAM, Version 1/93, New Offices*. Building Research Establishment Report, 2nd edn.

Pugh, C. (1996) Sustainability and sustainable cities. In: *Sustainability, the Environment and Urbanisation* (ed. C. Pugh). Earthscan Publications Ltd, London.

Pugliese, T. & Spaziante, A. (eds) (2003) *Pianificazione strategica per le città: riflessioni dalle pratiche*. Franco Angeli, Milan.

de Raadt, J.D.R. (1991) Cybernetic approach to information systems and organization learning. *Kybernetes*, **20**, 29–48.

de Raadt, J.D.R. (1994) Expanding the horizon of information systems design. *System Research*, **2**(3), 185–199.

de Raadt, J.D.R. (1997) A sketch for human operational research in a technological society. *System Practice*, **10**(4), 421–442.

Rees, W. (1992) Ecological footprints and appropriated carrying capacity: What urban economics leaves out. *Environment and Urbanisation*, **4**(2), 121–130.

Rees, M. (2004) *Our Final Century: Will the Human Race Survive the Twenty-first Century?* Arrow Books Ltd, London.

Rees, W.E. & Wackernagel, M. (1996) Urban ecological footprints: Why cities cannot be sustainable – and why they are key to sustainability. *Environmental Impact Assessment Review*, **16**, 223–248.

Reitan, P. (2005) Sustainability science – And what's needed beyond science. *Sustainability: Science, Practice & Policy* **1**(1), 77–80. http://ejournal.nbii.org/archives/vol1iss1/communityessay.reitan.html (accessed December 2009).

Rittel, H. & Webber, M. (1973) Dilemmas in a general theory of planning. *Policy Sciences*, **4**, 155–169, Elsevier Scientific Publishing Company Inc., Amsterdam. (Reprinted in Cross, N. (ed.) (1984) *Developments in Design Methodology*, John Wiley & Sons, Chichester, pp. 135–144.)

Robert, K.-H. (2002) *The Natural Step Story: Seeding a Quiet Revolution*. New Society Publishers, Gabriola Island, Canada.

Rosen, S. (1974) Hedonic prices and implicit market: Product differentiation in pure competition. *Journal of Political Economy*, **82**, 34–55.

Roy, B. (1985) *Mèthodologie, multicritére d'aide á la dècision*. Economica, Paris.

Rydin, Y. (1992) Environmental impacts and the property market. In: *Sustainable Development and Urban Form* (ed. M. Breheny). Earthscan Publications Ltd, London.

Saaty, T.L. (1980) *The Analytic Hierarchy Process for Decision in a Complex World*. McGraw-Hill, New York.

Schendler, A. & Udall, R. (2005) *Leed is Broken…Let's Fix It*. Snowmass Skiing, Aspen, CO. Community Office for Resource Efficiency. http://www.

aspensnowmass.com/environment/images/LEEDisBroken.pdf (accessed 27 February 2008).

Selman, P. (1996) *Local Sustainability*. Paul Chapman, London.

Selman, P. (2000) *Environmental Planning*. Sage, London.

Senge, P. (1990) *The Fifth Discipline*. Doubleday Publishers, New York.

SPARTACUS – System for Planning and Research in Towns and Cities for Urban Sustainability. Final Report. Submitted for approval to DG XII in October, 1998. The Executive Summary appears illustrated at www.ltcon.fi/spartacus

Stahel, W. (1996) The service economy: Wealth without resource consumption? In: *Clean Technology: The Idea and Practice*, Royal Society Discussion Meeting, 29–30 May 1996, London.

Stanner, D. & Bourdeau, P. (eds) (1995) The urban environment. In: *Europe's Environment: The Dobris Assessment*, pp. 261–296. European Environment Agency, Copenhagen.

Sunikka, M. (2006) *Policies for Improving Energy Efficiency if the European Housing Stock*. IOS Press, Amsterdam.

Suzuki, H., Dastur, A., Moffatt, S. & Yabuki, N. (2009) *Eco2 Cities. Ecological Cities as Economic Cities*. The International Bank for Reconstruction and Development/The World Bank, Washington, DC.

Sveiby, K.-E. (2004) *The Intangible Assets Monitor*. http://www.hanken.fi/staff/sveiby/blog/files/CVacadSveiby.pdf

Sveilby, K.E. & Armstrong, C. (2004) Learn to measure to learn! In: *Opening Key Note Address IC Congress*, Helsinki, 2 September 2004. http://www.hanken.fi/staff/sveiby/blog/files/CVacadSveiby.pdf

Therivel, R. (1998) Strategic environmental assessment of development plans in Great Britain. *Environmental Impact Assessment Review*, **18**(1), 39–57.

Therivel, R. (2004) *Sustainable Urban Environment – Metrics, Models and Toolkits: Analysis of Sustainability/Social Tools*. Oxford, North Hinksey Lane. http://download.sue-mot.org/soctooleval.pdf

Therivel, R., Wilson, E., Thompson, S., Heaney, D. & Pritchard, D. (1992) *Strategic Environmental Assessment*. Earthscan, London.

Tian, L. (2005) Some key issues about building environmental performance assessment system. In: *Proceedings of the 2005 World Sustainable Building Conference* (SB05Tokyo), Tokyo, 27–29 September 2005.

Toffler, A. (1985) *Future Shock*. Pan, London.

UNCED – United Nations Conference on Environment and Development (1992) *Earth Summit 92* (*Agenda 21*). Regency Press, London.

UNCSD – United Nations Conference on Sustainable Development (1996) *CSD Working List of Indicators*. United Nations Division for Sustainable Development. http://www.un.org/esa/sustdev/worklist.htm

UNEP Book. http://www.unep.fr/pc/sbc/documents/Buildings_and_climate_change.pdf

United Nations (2001) Report on the state of the indicators of sustainable development. *9th Session of the UN Commission on Sustainable Development*, New York, 16–17 April 2001.

United Nations (2007) *Indicators of Sustainable Development: Guidelines and Methodologies*. United Nations Publications, New York. http://www.un.org/esa/sustdev/natlinfo/indicators/guidelines.pdf

Vandevyvere, H. (2009) De beoordeling van duurzame wijken. *Ruimte*, **1**(1), 28–35.

Vandevyvere, H. & Neuckermans, H. (2009) Strategies for urban sustainability in Flanders. In: *From Problem to Promise: Building Smartly in a Changing Climate, Proceedings of the 3rd CIB International Conference on Smart and Sustainable Built Environments (SASBE 2009)* (eds M. Verhoeven & M. Fremouw), Delft, 15–19 June 2009, p. 99. ISBN: 978-90-5269-372-9.

Van Kooten, C. & Bulte, E. (2000) *The Economics of Nature*. Blackwell, Oxford.

Voogd, H. (1983) *Multi-Criteria Evaluation for Urban and Regional Planning*. Pion, London.

Voogd, H. (1995) Environmental management of social dilemmas. *European Spatial Research and Policy*, **2**, 5–16.

Vreeker, R., Deakin, M. & Curwell, S. (eds) (2008) *Sustainable Urban Development. The Toolkit for Assessment*. Routledge, Oxon.

Wackernagel, M. & Rees, W. (1995) *Our Ecological Footprint*. New Society Publishers, Philadelphia, PA.

Wackernagel, M., Mcintosh, J., Rees, W. & Woollard, R. (1993) *How Big is Our Ecological Footprint? A Handbook for Estimating a Community's Appropriated Carrying Capacity*. Taskforce on Planning Healthy and Sustainable Communities, University of British Columbia, Vancouver.

WCED (Brundtland Commission) (1987) *Our Common Future*. United Nations, New York.

Wood, C. (1995) *The Environmental Assessment of Plans, Programmes and Policies: A Comparative Review*. EIA Centre, Planning and Landscape Department, University of Manchester, Manchester.

Zeppetella, A. (1997) Environmental assessment in land use planning: A rhetorical approach. In: *Evaluation of the Built Environment for Sustainability* (eds P. Brandon, P.L. Lombardi & V. Bentivegna), pp. 344–362. E & FN Spon, London.

Websites

hqe2r.cstb.fr/
http://atlas.nrcan.gc.ca/site/english/maps/peopleandsociety/QOL/quality_of_life_model.jpg/image_view
http://crisp.cstb.fr
http://ec.europa.eu/environment/eia/eia-support.htm;
http://ec.europa.eu/information_society/eeurope/i2010/index_en.htm
http://esl.jrc.it/envind/index.htm
http://europa.eu.int/comm/eurostat
http://hutchinson@snw.org.uk
http://iisd.ca/measure/compendium.asp
http://iiSustainable Development.ca/measure/faqs.htm
http://iucn.org/info_and_news/press/wbon.html
http://lnx.ylda.org/sito/article.php3?id_article=234
http://research.scpm.salford.ac.uk/bqtoolkit/
http://research.scpm.salford.ac.uk/bqtoolkit/;
http://southeast.sustainability-checklist.co.uk/
http://urbanobservatory.org/indicators
http://upetd.up.ac.za/thesis/available/etd-02162007-151426/unrestricted/19thesbat.pdf

http://www.aggregain.org.uk/sustainability/sustainability_tools_and_
    approaches/index.html

http://www.wbcsd.org/templates/TemplateWBCSD5/layout.asp?Click
    Menu=special&type=p&MenuId=MTUxNQ

http://www.basden.demon.co.uk/Dooy/summary.html

http://www.bfrl.nist.gov/oae/bees.html

http://www.bioregional.com/programme_projects/ecohous_prog/bedzed/
    bedzed_hpg.htm

http://www.bre.co.uk/

http://www.cambridge.gov.uk/ccm/content/policy-and-projects/sustainable-
    developmentguidelines.

http://www.ciesin.columbia.edu/indicators

http://www.ciesin.columbia.edu/indicators/ESI/

http://www.ciesin.columbia.edu/indicators/ESI/;

http://www.co.pierce.wa.us/services/family/benchmrk/gol.htm

http://www.edilone.it/attualita/index.php?page=details&id=1730

http://www.eea.eu.int

http://www.elsevier.com/locate/eiar

http://www.environment.detr.gov.uk/epsim/indics/

http://www.eucen.org/BeFlex/CaseStudies/UK_SalfordUPBEAT.pdf

http://www.foe.co.uk/campaigns/sustainable_development/progress

http://www.fsv.edu/~cpm/safe/safelis.html

http://www.hanken.fi/staff/sveiby/blog/files/CVacadSvei by.pdf

http://www.hanken.fi/staff/sveiby/blog/files/CVacadSveiby.pdf

http://www.iaia.org/Non_Members/Activity_Resources/Key_Citations/
    environm.doc

http://www.ibec.or.jp/CASBEE/english/index.htm

http://www.iisbe.org/index.html

http://www.iiSustainable Development1.ca/measure/bellagio1htm

http://www.inforegio.org/urban/audit/index.html

http://www.johannesburgsummit.org

http://www.kolumbus.fi/stoivan/Köln.htm

http://www.luda-europe.net/hb5/evaluation.php

http://www.meap.co.uk/meap/MEPLAN.htm

http://www.miniambiente.it

http://www.neweconomics.org

http://www.ocse.org/env/indicators/index.htm

http://www.oecd.org/statistics/

http://www.olywa.net/roundtable

http://www.panda.org/livingplanet/lpr00/

http://www.pebbu.nl/resources/allreports/

http://www.planum.net/topics/main/m-hab-documents-bbr.htm

http://www.progress.org/progsum/progsum.html

http://www.research.scpm.salford.ac.uk.bqextra

http://www.rprogress.org/programs/sustainability/ef/

http://www.rprogress.org/projects/gpi/

http://www.rsc.salford.ac.uk/bqextra/toolkit

http://www.scci.salford.ac.uk/intelcity

http://www.scn.org/sustainable/susthome.html

http://www.sd-network.eu/?k=quarterly%20reports&report_id=7

http://www.smartcommunities.ncat.org/landuse/tools.shtml
http://www.sue-mot.org.uk/
http://www.survery.ac.uk/CES/ee.htm
http://www.SustainabilityA-Test.net;
http://www.Sustainable Development-commission.gov.uk
http://www.theatlantic.com/atlantic/election/connection/ecbig/gdp.htm
http://www.un.org/Depts/unsustainable Development/
http://www.un.org/esa/sustdev/indi6.htm
http://www.un.org/esa/sustdev/iSustainable Development.htm
http://www.un.org/esa/sustdev/worklist.htm
http://www.unchs.org/gua/gui/guide.html
http://www.unchs.org/org/guo/gui/guide.html
http://www.unchs.org/programmes/guo
http://www.undp.org/hdr2001/
http://www.unep.ch/earthw/indstat.htm
http://www.unhabitat.org/programmes/guo/guo_guide.asp
http://www.unicef.org/pon98
http://www.vtt.fi/cic/eco/eng_prop.htm
http://www.vtt.fi/yki/yki6/master/master.htm
http://www.weforum.org/pdf/Gcr/EPMTGR/Contents.pdf
http://www.worldpaper.com/2001/jan01/ISI/2001%20Information%
    20Society%20Ranking.html
http://www.worldwatch.org/pubs/sow/sow98
http://www.worldwatch.org/pubs/us/us98
http://www1.oecd.org/publications /e-book/4201131e.pdf
http://www2.upc.es/ciec/

Bibliography

Adams, D. (1994) *Urban Planning and the Development Process*. UCL Press, London.

Albers, L. & Nijkamp, P. (1989) Multidimensional analysis for plan or project evaluation: How to fit the right method to the right problem. In: *Evaluation Methods for Urban and Regional Planning*, Vol. 6 (ed. A. Barbanente), pp. 29–46. IRIS-CNR, Bari.

Allwinkle, S. & Speed, C. (1997) Sustainability and the built environment: Tourism impacts. In: *Evaluation of the Built Environment for Sustainability* (eds P.S. Brandon, P.L. Lombardi & V. Bentivegna). E & FN Spon, London.

Alwaer, H., Sibley, M. & Lewis, J. (2008a) Factors and priorities for assessing sustainability of regional shopping centres in the UK. *Architectural Science Review*, **51**(4), 391–402.

Alwaer, H., Sibley, M. & Lewis, J. (2008b) Different stakeholder perceptions of sustainability assessment. *Architectural Science Review*, **51**(1), 47–58.

Arrow, K.J. & Fisher, A.C. (1974) Environmental preservation, uncertainty and irreversibility. *Quarterly Journal of Economics*, **88**, 312–319.

Arrow, K.J. & Raynard, H. (1986) *Social Choice and Multicriterion Decision Making*. MIT, Boston, MA.

Ave, G. & Corsico, F. (eds) (1994) *Urban Marketing in Europe*. Torino Incontra Edizioni, Turin.

Banister, D. & Burton, K. (1993) *Transport, the Environment and Sustainable Development*. E & FN Spon, London.

Barbanente, A. (ed.) (1992) *Evaluation Methods for Urban and Regional Planning*, Vol. 6. IRIS-CNR, Bari.

Barbier, E.B. (ed.) (1993) *Economics and Ecology*. Chapman & Hall, London.

Barret, P. (1993) *Profitable Practice Management*. E & FN Spon, London.

Evaluating Sustainable Development in the Built Environment, Second Edition
By Peter S. Brandon and Patrizia Lombardi   © 2011 Peter S. Brandon and Patrizia Lombardi

Barret, P. & Holling, J. (1991) *The Future Direction of Quality Management for the Construction Professions in the UK*. Department of Surveying, University of Salford, Salford.

Barton, H. & Bruder, N. (1995) *A Guide to Local Environmental Auditing*. Earthscan, London.

Baumol, W.J. & Oates, W.E. (1988) *The Theory of Environmental Policy*. Cambridge University Press, Cambridge.

Becker, J. (2004) Making sustainable development evaluations work. *Sustainable Development*, **12**, 200–211.

Beerepoot, M. & Sunikka, M. (2005) The role of the EC energy certificate in improving sustainability of the housing stock. *Environment and Planning B: Planning and Design*, **32**(1), 21–31.

Bentivegna, V., Mondini, G., Nati Poltri, F. & Pii, R. (1994) Complex evaluation methods: An operative synthesis on multicriteria techniques. In: *Proceedings of the 4th International Conference on Engineering Management*, Melbourne, Australia, April, pp. 1–18.

BEQUEST – Building Environment Quality Evaluation for Sustainability through Time Network (1999) *Report 1998–99*, EC Environment and Climate Research Programme, Theme 4: *Human Dimensions and Environmental Change*. Directorate D – RTD Actions: Environment – E.U. DG12.

Bettini, V. (1996) *Elementi di ecologia umana*. Einaudi, Turin.

Betty, M. (1976) *Urban Modelling*. Cambridge University Press, Cambridge.

Betty, M. (1995) Planning support systems and the new logic of computation. *Regional Development Dialogue*, **16**(1), 1–17.

Betty, M. (1998) Evaluation in the digital age. In: *Evaluation in Planning* (eds N. Lichfield, A. Barbanente, D. Borri, A. Khakee & A. Prat), pp. 251–274. Kluwer Academic Publishers, Dordrecht.

Betty, M. & Densham, P. (1996) Decision support, G.I.S. and urban planning. *Sistema Terra*, **1**(1), 72–76.

Bezelga, A. & Brandon, P.S. (eds) (1991) *Management, Quality and Economics in Buildings*. E & FN Spon, London.

Bezzi, C. & Palumbo, M. (eds) (1998) *Strategic di valutazione*. Gramma, Perugina.

Bichard, E. & Cooper, C.L. (2008) *Positively Responsible*. Elsevier, Oxford.

Birtles, T. (1997) Environmental impact evaluation of buildings and cities for sustainability. In: *Evaluation of the Built Environment for Sustainability* (eds P.S. Brandon, P.L. Lombardi & V. Bentivegna), pp. 211–223. E & FN Spon, London.

Bishop, R.C. (1982) Option value: An exposition and extension. *Land Economics*, **1**, 1–15.

Bishop, R.C. & Heberlein, T.A. (1979) Measuring values of extra-market goods: Are indirect measures biased? *American Journal of Agricultural Economics*, **12**, 926–932.

Boardman, A., Greenberg, A., Vining, A. & Weimer, D. (1996) *Cost-Benefit Analysis: Concepts and Practice*. Prentice-Hall, Upper Saddle River, NJ.

Bobbio, L. (1996) *La democrazia non abita a Gordio*. Angeli, Milan.

Bocchi, M. & Ceruti, M. (eds) (1994) *La sflda delta complessita*. Feltrinelli, Milan.

Bonnes, M. (ed.) (1993) Perception and evaluation of urban environment quality. In: *Proceedings of the MAB-UNESCO International Symposium*, Edigraf, Rome, 28–30 November.

Bonnes, M. & Bonaiuto, M. (1993) Users' perceptions and experts' evaluations of the quality of urban environment: Some comparative results from the MAB-ROME project. In: *Perception and Evaluation of Urban Environment Quality* (ed. M. Bonnes), pp. 179–193. *Proceedings of the MAB-UNESCO International Symposium*, Edigraf, Rome, 28–30 November 1991.

Boulding, K. (1956) General system theory: The skeleton of science. *Management Science*, **2**, 197–214.

Brandon, P.S. (1993) *Intelligence and Integration: Agenda for the Next Decade*. Department of Surveying, University of Salford, Salford.

Brandon, P.S. & Betts, M. (eds) (1995) *Integrated Construction Information*. E & FN Spon, London.

Brandon, P.S. & Lombardi, P. (1995) L'approccio multimodal per la valutazione della qualità dell'ambiente costruito nella pianificazione sostenibile. *Genio Rurale*, **12**, 57–63.

Brandon, P.S. & Lombardi, P. (2001) Structuring the problem of urban sustainability for holistic decision making. In: *Proceedings of the First International Virtual Congress on Ecology and the City*, Departament de Construccions Arquitectoniques, UPC, Barcelona, March 2001.

Brandon, P.S. & Powell, J.A. (eds) (1984) *Quality and Profit in Building Design*. E & FN Spon, London.

Brandon, P.S., Basden, A., Hamilton, I. & Stockley, J. (1988) *Expert Systems: Strategic Planning of Construction Projects*. The Royal Institution of Chartered Surveyors, London.

Brandon, P.S., Lombardi, P. & Srinath, P. (eds) (2000) *Cities and Sustainability: Sustaining our Cultural Heritage*. Conference Proceedings, Vishva Lekha Sarvodaya, Sri Lanka.

Bravi, M. (1998) Metodo del prezzo edenico. In: *La valutazione economica del patrimonio culturale* (ed. G. Sirchia). Carocci, Milan.

Bravi, M. & Lombardi, P. (1994) *Techniche di valutazione. Linguaggi e organizzazione de DATE-BASE*. Celid, Turin.

Breheny, M.J. & Rookwood, R. (1993) Planning the sustainable city region. In: *Planning for a Sustainable Environment* (ed. A. Blowers). Earthscan Publications Ltd, London.

Breheny, M.J., Gent, T. & Lock, D. (1993) *Alternative Development Patterns: New Settlements*. HMSO, London.

Bresso, M. (1982) *Pensiero economico e ambiente*. Loescher, Turin.

Bruinsma, F.R., Nijkamp, P. & Vreeker, R. (2002a) A comparative industrial profile analysis of urban regions in Western Europe: An application of rough set classification. *Tijdschrift Economische en Sociale Geografie*, **93** (4), 454–463.

Bruinsma, F.R., Nijkamp, P. & Vreeker, R. (2002b) Urban regions in an international competitive force field: A cross-national comparative study on planning of industrial sites. In: *Urban Regions: Governing Interacting Economic, Housing, and Transport Systems* (eds J. van Dijk, P. Elhorst, J. Oosterhaven & E. Wever). Nederlandse Geografische Studies, Utrecht.

Cadman, H. & Payne, G. (eds) (1990) *The Living City*. Routledge, London.

Camagni, R. (ed.) (1996) *Economia e pianificazione delta città sostenibile*. Il Mulino, Milan.

Camp, R.C. (1989) *Benchmarking: The Search for Industry Best Practices that Lead to Superior Performance*. ASQC Quality Press, Milwaukee, WI.

Cap Gemini (2004) *Online Availability of Public Services: How is Europe Progressing.* Cap Gemini Ernst & Young, London. http://www.capgemini.com/news/2003/0206egov.shtml (accessed 28 April 2009).

Castells, M. (1996) The rise of the network society. In: *The Information Age: Economy, Society and Culture,* Vol. I. Blackwell, Oxford.

CEC – Commission of the European Communities (1993) *Towards Sustainability.* Office for Official Publications of the European Communities, Luxembourg.

CEC (2000) Communication from the Commission to the Council, the European Parliament, the Economic and Social Committee and the Committee of the Regions. *Social Policy Agenda.* 28 June 2000. COM (2000) 379 final, Commission of the European Community, Brussels.

CEC (2002) *eEurope 2005: An Information Society for All.* COM (2002) 263, Commission for the European Community, Brussels.

CEC (2004) *eEurope 2005 Action Plan: An Update. eEurope Advisory Group.* COM (2004) 380, Commission for the European Community, Brussels.

Cecchini, A. & Fulici, F. (1994) *La valutazione di impatto urbano.* Angeli, Milan.

Checkland, P.B. (1981) *System Thinking, System Practice.* John Wiley, New York.

Checkland, P.B., Forbes, P. & Martin, S. (1990) Techniques in soft systems practice. Part 3: Monitoring and control in conceptual models and in evaluation studies. *Journal of Applied System Analysis,* **17**, 29–37.

Clark, B.D. (1995) Improving public participation in environmental impact assessment. *Built Environment,* **20**(4), 294–307.

Clark, D. (1997) Hedonic values of noxious activity: A comparison of US worker responses by race and ethnicity. In: *Evaluation of the Built Environment for Sustainability* (eds P.S. Brandon, P.L. Lombardi & V. Bentivegna), pp. 382–398. E & FN Spon, London.

Clawson, M. & Knetsch, J.L. (1966) *The Economics of Outdoor Recreation.* John Hopkins University Press, Baltimore, MD.

Clementi, A., Dematteis, G. & Palermo, P.C. (eds) (1996) *Le forme del territorio italiano.* Laterza, Rome.

Clough, D.J. (1984) *Decisions in Public and Private Sectors: Theories, Practices and Processes.* Prentice-Hall, Englewood Cliffs, NJ.

Coccossis, H. & Nijkamp, P. (1995) *Planning for Our Cultural Heritage.* Avebury, Hants.

Colantonio, A. & Dixon, T. (2009) *Measuring Socially Sustainable Urban Regeneration in Europe.* Oxford Institute for Sustainable Development (OISD), Oxford Brookes University, Oxford. Obtained through the Internet: http://www.brookes.ac.uk/schools/be/oisd/sustainable_communities/resources/Social_Sustainability_and_Urban_Regeneration_report.pdf

Cole, R. (1997) Prioritising environmental criteria in building design. In: *Evaluation of the Built Environment for Sustainability* (eds P.S. Brandon, P. Lombardi & V. Bentivegna). E & FN Spon, London.

Cole, R.J., Rousseau, D. & Theaker, I.T. (1993) *Building Environmental Performance Assessment Criteria Version 1: Office Buildings.* The BEPAC Foundation, Vancouver.

Cole, R.J., Campbell, E., Dixon, C. & Vrignon, J. (eds) (1995) Linking and prioritising environmental criteria. In: *Proceedings of the International Workshop CIB TG-8,* Toronto, 15–16 November.

Commissione delle Comunità Europee (1994) *Orientamenti per l'UE in materia di indicatori ambientali e di contabilità verde nazionale.* COM(94) 670, Brussels.

Commissione Europea (2001) Direttiva 2001/42/CE del Parlamento Europeo e del Consiglio concernente la valutazione degli effeti di determinanti piani eprogrammi sull'ambiente, Luxemburgh. http://europa.eu.int/comm./environment/eia/full-legal-text/0142_it.pdf (accessed 27 June 2001).

Construction Industry Board (1997) *Constructing Success: Code of Practice for Clients of the Construction Industry.* Telford, London.

Cook, T.M. & Russell, R.A. (1989) *Introduction to Management Science.* Prentice-Hall, Englewood Cliffs, NJ.

Cooper, R.G. (1990) Stage-gate system: A new tool for managing new products. *Business Horizons*, **33**(3), 44–54.

Cooper, R.G. (1994) Third-generation new product processes. *Journal of Product Innovation Management*, **11**, 3–14.

Cooper, I. (2000) Inadequate grounds for a 'design-led' approach to urban design. *Building Research & Information*, **28**(3), 212–219.

Cooper, R.G., Kagioglou, M., Aouad, G., Hinks, J., Sexton, M. & Sheath, D. (1998) The development of a generic design and construction process. In: *European Conference, Product Data Technology (PDT) Days*, Building Research Establishment, Watford, March 1998.

Cooper, I., Hamilton, A. & Bentivegna, V. (2005) Sustainable urban development: Networked communities, virtual communities and the production of knowledge. In: *Sustainable Urban Development: The Framework, Protocols and Environmental Assessment Methods*, Vol. 1 (eds S. Curwell, M. Deakin & M. Symes), pp. 211–231. Routledge, London.

Corsi, P. (2006) Towards 2020: The eGovernment Research Trajectory, Intelligent Cities, *International Research Conference*, Siena, Italy. http://www.intelcitiesproject.com/wcmsite/jsps/index.jsp?type=page&lg=en&classId=5057&cid=5321&cidName=NEWS.

Cox, E. (1999) *The Fuzzy Systems Handbook*, 2nd edn. Academic Press, New York.

Cruickshank, H. & Fenner, R.A. (2007) The evolving role of engineers: Towards sustainable development of the built environment. *Journal of International Development*, **19**, 111–121.

Cummings, R.G., Brookshire, D.S. & Schulze, W.D. (1986) *Valuing Environmental Goods: An Assessment of the Contingent Valuation Method.* Rowman & Allanheld, Totowa, NJ.

Curti, F. & Gibelli, M.C. (eds) (1996) *Pianificazione strategica e gestione dello sviluppo urbano.* Alinea, Firenze.

Dalkey, N.C. (1967) *Delphi.* Rand Corporation, New York.

Daly, H.E. (1990) Towards some operational principles of sustainable development. *Ecological Economics*, **2**(1), 87–102.

Dasgupta, P. & Pearce, D.W. (1972) *Cost-Benefit Analysis: Theory and Practice.* Barnes & Noble, London.

Dasgupta, P.S., Sen, A. & Marglin, S.A. (1972) *Guidelines for Project Evaluation.* United Nations Industrial Development Organisation, Vienna.

Davies, L. & Ledington, P. (1991) *Information in Action. Soft Systems Methodology.* Macmillan Education Ltd, Hong Kong.

Davoudi, S. (1997) Economic development and environmental gloss: A new structure plan for Lancashire. In: *Evaluation of the Built Environment for Sustainability* (eds P.L. Brandon, P. Lombardi & V. Bentivenga). E & FN Spon, London.

Deakin, M. (2000a) Developing sustainable communities in Edinburgh's South East Wedge. *Journal of Property Management*, **4**(2), 72–78.

Deakin, M. (2000b) Modelling the development of sustainable communities in Edinburgh's South East Wedge. *Property Management,* **4**(2), 72–88.

Deakin, M. (2005) Evaluating sustainability: Is a philosophical framework enough?. *Building Research & Information,* **33**(5), 476–480.

Deakin, M., Huovila, P., Rao, S., Sunikka, M. & Vreeker, R. (2002c) The assessment of sustainable urban development. *Building Research & Information,* **30**(2), 95–108.

Dente, B. (1989) *Politiche pubbliche e pubblica amministrazione.* Maggioli, Rimini.

Department of the Environment (1993) *Environmental Appraisal of Development Plan: A Good Practice Guide.* HMSO, London.

Directive 2001/42/CE: Commissione Europea, Direttiva 2001/42/CE del Parlamento Europeo e del Consiglio concernente la valutazione degli effeti di determinati piani e programmi sull'ambiente, Luxembourg. http://europa.er.int/comm/environment/eia/fulllegal-text.0142_it.pdf (accessed 17 June 2001).

Directive 85/337/EEC and amendment 97/11/EC.

Dixon, J., Carpenter, R. & Fallon, L. (1986) *Economic Analysis of the Environmental Impacts of Development Projects.* Earthscan, London.

Dixon, J.A., Fallon, S.L., Carpenter, R.A. & Sherman, P.B. (1994) *Economic Analysis of Environmental Impacts.* Earthscan Publications Ltd, London.

Du Plessis, C. (2006) Thinking about the day after tomorrow. New perspectives on sustainable building. In: *Rethinking Sustainable Construction 2006 Conference,* Sarasota, FL, 19–22 September 2006.

Du Plessis, C. & Holm, D. (1999) The process of sustainable development in the design and construction of the built environment. *Open House International,* **24**(2), 64–72.

Dupuit, J. (1844) De la misure de l'utilité des travaux publics. *Annales des ponts et chaussées,* (2), 332–375.

Edwards, S. & Bennett, P. (2003) Construction products and life-cycle thinking. *UNEP Industry and Environment* (joint edition combining Sustainable Building & Construction), **26**(2–3), 57–62.

EPA Pollution Prevention Information Clearinghouse: call +1 (202) 260-1023 ore-mail ppic@epamail.epa.gov

Eriksson, D. (1997) Postmodernity and system science: An evaluation of J.L. Le Moigne's contribution to the management of the present civilization. *System Practice,* **10**(4), 395–408.

European Commission (1993) *Toward Sustainability (The Fifth EC Environmental Action Programme).* Commission of the European Community, CEC.

European Commission (1994) *Europe 2000+ Cooperation for European Territorial Development.* Office of Publications of the European Commission, Luxembourg, Brussels.

European Commission (1997) European spatial development perspective. First official draft paper presented to the *Informal Meeting of Ministers Responsible for Spatial Planning of the Member States of the European Union,* Noordwijk, 9–10 June 1997. Englewood Cliffs, NJ.

European Commission (1998) European spatial development perspective. Complete draft paper presented to the *Meeting of Ministers Responsible for Spatial Planning of the Member States of the European Union,* Glasgow, 8 June 1998. Office for the Official Publications of the European Commission, Luxembourg and Brussels.

European Commission (2002) *Visions and Roadmaps for Sustainable Development in a Networked Knowledge Society*. Office for the Official Publications of the European Commission, Luxemburgh and Brussels.

European Commission Regional Policy and Cohesion (1997) *The EU Compendium of Spatial Planning System and Policies*. Office for the Official Publications of the European Commission, Luxembourg and Brussels.

European Environment Agency Task Force (1995) *Europe's Environment: The Dobris Assessment*. Earthscan, Copenhagen.

European Union, EU (1997) The Göteborg resolution. In: *Third Environment Conference of Regional Ministers and Political Leaders*, Göteborg, Sweden, 18–20 June 1997.

Eurostat (2005) *Measuring Progress towards a More Sustainable Europe. Sustainable Development Indicators for the European Union*. Office for Official Publications of the European Communities, Luxembourg.

Evans, J.R. & Olson, D.L. (1998) *Introduction to Simulation and Risk Analysis*. Prentice-Hall, Englewood Cliffs, NJ.

Fenner, R.A. & Ryce, T. (2008) A comparative analysis of two building rating systems. Part 1 (Evaluation). *Proceedings of the Institution of Civil Engineers, Engineering Sustainability*, **161**(ES1), 55–63.

Figueira, J., Greco, S. & Ehrgott, M. (eds) (2005) *Multiple Criteria Decision Analysis*. Springer, New York.

Finnigan, J. (2002) Complexity: A core issue for sustainable development. *Sustainability Network Update* No 12E, July 2002. CSIRO, Glen Osmond, Australia.

Finsterbusch, K., Llewellyn, L.G. & Wolf, C.P. (eds) (1983) *Social Impact Assessment Methods*. Sage Publications, London.

Fischer, M.M., Scholten, H.J. & Unwin, D. (eds) (1996) *Spatial Analytical Perspectives on G.I.S.* Taylor & Francis, London.

Fishburn, P.C. (1970) *Utility Theory for Decision Making*. Wiley, New York.

Fishburn, P.C. (1982) *The Foundation of Expected Utility*. Reidel Publishing Co., Dordrecht.

Fisher, F. & Forester, J. (eds) (1993) *The Argumentative Turn in Policy Analysis and Planning*. Duke University Press, Durham, NC.

Flanagan, R. & Norman, G. (1993) *Risk Management and Construction*. Blackwell Science, Oxford.

Fleming, A., Lee, A., Aouad, G. & Cooper, R.G. (2000) The development of a process mapping methodology for the Process Protocol Level 2. In: *Third European Conference on Product and Process Modelling in the Building and Related Industries*, Lisbon, Portugal.

Florio, M. (1991) *La valutazione degli investimenti pubblici*. Il Mulino, Bologna.

Forrester, J. (1996) Argument, power and passion in planning practice. In: *Explorations in Planning Theory* (eds S.J. Mandelbaum, L. Mazza & R.W. Burchell), pp. 241–262. Urban Policy Research Center, Rudgers State University, New Brunswick, NJ.

Frederick, K.D. & Rosenberg, N.J. (1994) *Assessing the Impacts of Climate Change in Natural Resource Systems*. Kluwer Academic Publishers, Dordrecht.

Friend, D. & Friend, J. (1991) *STRAD, The Strategic Adviser*. Stradsoft Ltd, Sheffield Science Park.

Friend, J.K. & Jessop, W.N. (1969) *Local Government and Strategic Choice*. Tavistock Publications, London.

Fusco Girard, L. (1987) *Risorse architettoniche e culturali.* Angeli, Milan.

Fusco Girard, L. & Nijkamp, P. (1997) *Le valutazioni per lo sviluppo sostenibile della città e del territorio.* Angeli, Milan.

Garrod, G. & Willis, K. (1991) *The Hedonic Price Method and the Valuation of Countryside.* Countryside Change Working Paper, 14, University of Newcastle Upon Tyne, Newcastle Upon Tyne.

van Geenhuizen, M., Banister, D. & Nijkamp, P. (1995) Adoption of new transport technology: A quick scan approach. *Project Appraisal*, **10**(4), 267–275.

Giaoutzi, M. & Nijkamp, P. (1993) *Decision Support Model for Regional Sustainable Development.* Avebury, Aldershot.

Glasser, H. (1998) On the evaluation of wicked problems: Guidelines for integrating qualitative and quantitative factors in environmental policy analysis. In: *Evaluation in Planning* (eds N. Lichfield, A. Barbanente, D. Borri, A. Khakee & A. Prat), pp. 229–250. Kluwer Academic Publishers, Dordrecht.

Grace, K. & Ding, C. (2008) Sustainable construction—The role of environmental assessment tools. *Australia Journal of Environmental Management*, **86**(3), 451–464.

Graham, A. & Bergvall, B. (1994) Performance indicators in soft systems methodology. In: *Proceedings of the 17th IRIS Conference on Information Systems Research*, Oslo, 6–9 August, pp. 890–910.

Graham, S. & Marvin, S. (1996) *Telecommunications and the City.* Routledge, London.

Gramlich, E. (1990) *Guide to Benefit-Cost Analysis.* Prentice-Hall, London.

Gray, J. & Tippett, H. (1993) Building quality assessment: A prerequisite to economic analysis. In: *Economic Evaluation and the Built Environment*, Vol. 4 (eds A. Manso, A. Bezelga & D. Picken), pp. 79–89. Laboratorio Nacional de Engenheria Civil, Lisbon.

Griffioen, S. & Balk, B.M. (eds) (1995) *Christian Philosophy at the Close of the Twentieth Century.* Uitgeverij, Kampen.

Griffioen, S. & Mouw, J. (1983) *Pluralism and Horizons.* Eerdmans Publishing Company, Grand Rapids, MI.

Grillenzoni, M., Ragazzoni, G., Bazzani, G. & Canavari, M. (1997) Land planning and resource evaluation for public investments. In: *Evaluation of the Built Environment for Sustainability* (eds P. Brandon, P. Lombardi & V. Bentivegna). E & FN Spon, London.

Guba, E.G. & Loncoln, Y.S. (1989) *Fourth Generation Evaluation.* Sage, London.

Haines, Y.Y. & Changkong, V. (eds) (1985) *Decision Making with Multiple Objectives.* Springer, Berlin.

Hall, P. (1994) *Cities of Tomorrow.* Blackwell, Oxford.

Hall, P. & Pfeiffer, U. (2000) *Urban Future 21.* E & FN Spon, London.

Ham, C. & Hill, M. (1986) *Introduzione all'analisi delle politiche pubbliche.* Il Mulino, Bologna.

Hammer, M. & Champy, J. (1993) *Re-engineering the Corporation.* Nicholas Brealey, London.

Hargreaves, H.S., Hillis, M., Lyons, B., Sugden, R. & Weale, A. (1992) *The Theory of Choice. A Critical Guide.* Blackwell Publishers, Oxford.

Hart, M. (2002) A better view of sustainable community. December 2004. http://www.sustainablemeasures.com/Sustainability/ABetterView.html

Heijungs, R. & Guinée, J.B. (1992) *Environmental Life Cycle Assessment Method of Products.* Centre of Environmental Science, Leiden.

Helsinki Metropolitan Area Council (1998) Pääkaupunkiseudun liikenne-järjestelmän strategisen tason ympäristövaikutusten arviointi (The Strategic

Environmental Assessment of the Helsinki Metropolitan Area Transport). *Plan Revision B* 1998:4.

Hotelling, H. (1949) *The Economics of Public Recreation*. US Department of the Interior, National Park Service, Washington, DC.

IntelCities – Intelligent Cities project (No: IST 2002-507860) EU VI Framework, Information Society Technologies. http://www.intelcitiesproject.com (accessed 12 October 2007).

INU (1998) La nuova legge urbanistica. Indirizzi per la riforma del processo di pianificazione della città e del territorio. *Urbanistica Informazioni*, **157**.

IPPC (Intergovernmental Panel on Climate Change) (2007a) *Climate Change 2007: Climate Change Impacts, Adaptation and Vulnerability. Summary for Policy Makers*. IPPC Secretariat, Geneva.

IPPC (Intergovernmental Panel on Climate Change) (2007b) *Climate Change 2007: The Physical Science Basis. Summary for Policy Makers*. IPPC Secretariat, Geneva.

ISO (2000) *Life Cycle Assessment – Principles and Guidelines*. ISO CD 14 0402. International Standard Organization, Geneva.

ITU (1999) *Challenges to the Network: Internet for Development*. International Telecommunication Union, Geneva. http://www.itu.org

Jackson, P. (1990) *Introduction to Expert Systems*. Addison-Wesley, New York.

Janssen, R. (1991) *Multiple Decision Support for Environmental Problems*. Kluwer Academic Publishers, Dordrecht.

Janssen, R. (1992) *Multiobjective Decision Support for Environmental Management*. Kluwer Academic Publishers, Dordrecht.

Johansson, P.O. (1993) *Cost-Benefit Analysis of Environmental Change*. Cambridge University Press, Cambridge.

Johnes, P., Vaughan, N., Cooke, P. & Sutcliffe, A. (1997) An energy and environmental prediction model for cities. In: *Evaluation of the Built Environment for Sustainability* (eds P. Brandon, P. Lombardi & V. Bentivegna). E & FN Spon, London.

Jowsey, E. & Kellett, J. (1996) Sustainability and methodologies of environmental assessment for cities. In: *Sustainability, the Environment and Urbanisation* (ed. C. Pugh). Earthscan Publications Ltd, London.

Kagioglou, M., Cooper, R., Aouad, G., Hinks, J., Sexton, M. & Sheath, D. (1998) *Final Report: Generic Design and Construction Process Protocol*. University of Salford, Salford.

Kagioglou, M., Cooper, R. & Aouad, G. (1999) Re-engineering the UK construction industry: The process protocol. *Second International Conference on Construction Process Re-Engineering* (CPR-99), Sydney, Australia, 12–13 July 1999.

Kallberg, V.-P. & Toivanen, S. (1997) *Framework for Assessing the Effects of Speed*. MASTER Working Paper (report 1.2.3).

Kallberg, V-P. & Toivanen, S. (1998) *Framework for Assessing the Impacts of Speed in Road Transport*. MASTER Deliverable 8 (report 1.2.4).

Kant, I. (1988) *Critique of Pure Reason*. J.M. Dent & Sons Ltd, London.

Keeney, R.L. & Raiffa, H. (1976) *Decisions with Multiple Objectives, Preferences and Value Tradeoffs*. John Wiley & Sons, New York.

Khakee, A. (1997) Evaluation and planning process: Methodological dimension. In: *Evaluation of the Built Environment for Sustainability* (eds P. Brandon, P.L. Lombardi & V. Bentivegna), pp. 327–343. E & FN Spon, London.

Klir, G.J. & Yuan, B. (1995) *Fuzzy Sets and Fuzzy Systems*. Prentice-Hall, Englewood Cliffs, NJ.

Kotler, P. (1986) Marketing management. In: *Analisi, pianificazione e controllo.* ISEDI, Turin.

Kozlowski, J. & Hill, J. (1993) *Towards Planning for Sustainable Development: A Guide for the Ultimate Threshold Method.* Avebury, Aldershot.

Krutilla, J.V. (1967) Conservation reconsidered. *American Economic Review,* **62**(4), 777–795.

Krutilla, J.V. & Eckstein, O. (1958) *Multiple Purpose River Development.* John Hopkins University Press, Baltimore, MD.

Krutilla, J.V. & Fisher, A.C. (1975) *The Economics of Natural Environments: Studies in the Valuation of Commodities and Amenity Resources.* John Hopkins University Press, Baltimore, MD.

Kuhn, T.S. (1970) *The Structure of Scientific Revolutions.* University of Chicago Press, Chicago, IL.

Kuik, O. & Verbraggen, H. (eds) *In Search of Indicators of Sustainable Development.* Kluwer Academic Publishers, Dordrecht.

Lahti, P., Kangasoja, J. & Huovila, P. (2006) Electronic and mobile participation in city planning and management. In: *Experiences from INTELCITIES – An Integrated Project of the 6th Framework Programme of the European Union: Cases Helsinki, Tampere, Garðabær, Frankfurt,* City of Helsinki Urban Facts, Helsinki, March 2006.

Lancashire County Council (1994) *Report 19: Environmental Appraisal of the 1991–2006 Lancashire Structure Plan,* December. Lancashire County Council Environmental Policy Unit, Preston.

Le Moigne, J.L. (1990) *La modération des systèmes complex.* Dunod, Paris.

Lichfield, N. (1988) *Economics in Urban Conservation.* Cambridge University Press, Cambridge.

Lichfield, N., Hendon, M., Njikamp, P., Realfonso, A. & Rostirolla, P. (1990) *Cost-Benefit Analysis in the Conservation of Built Cultural Heritage.* Ministero dei Beni Culturali, Rome.

Lindblom, C. (1965) *The Intelligence of Democracy.* Free Press, New York.

Lindblom, C.E. & Cohen, D. (1979) *Usable Knowledge.* Yale University Press, New Haven (CT) and London.

Linstone, H.A. & Turoff, M. (eds) (1976) *The Delphi Method: Techniques and Applications.* Addison-Wesley, Reading, MA.

Locket, A.G. & Islei, G. (eds) (1988) *Improving Decision Making in Organisations.* Springer, Berlin.

Lynch, K. (1960) *The Image of the City.* The Technology Press & Harvard University Press, Cambridge, MA.

Mak, J.P., Anink, D.A.F., Kortman, J.G.M., Lindeijer, E. & van Ewijk, H. (1996a) *Eco-Quantum, Final Report: Design of a Calculation Method to Determine the Environmental Load of a Building in a Quantitative Way* (in Dutch). Gouda, The Netherlands.

Mak, J.P., Anink, D.A.F., Kortman, J.G.M. & van Ewijk, H. (1996b) *Eco-Quantum 2, Final Report: Sensitivity Analysis* (in Dutch). Gouda, The Netherlands.

Mak, J., Anink, D. & Knapen, M. (1997) Eco-Quantum, development of LCA based tools for buildings. In: *Proceedings of 2nd International CIB Conference: Task Group 8 – Buildings and the Environment,* Paris, 9–12 June 1997.

Mandelbrot, B. (1983) *The Fractal Geometry of Nature.* W.H. Freeman, New York.

Marglin, S. (1967) *Public Investment Criteria: Benefit-Cost Analysis for Planned Economic Growth.* MIT Press, Cambridge.

Markandya, A. & Richardson, J. (eds) (1992) *Environmental Economics*. Earthscan, London.

Marshall, A. (1920) *Principles of Economics*. Macmillan, London.

Massam, B. (1988) Multi-criteria decision making (MCDM) techniques in planning. *Progress in Planning*, **30**(1), 1–84.

Maturana, H. & Varela, F. (1980) *Autopoiesis and Cognition*. D. Reidel, Dordrecht.

Maturana, H. & Varela, F. (1987) *The Tree of Knowledge*. Shambhala, Boston, MA.

Meadows, H. (1972) *The Limits to Growth*. Universe Books, New York.

Mega, V. (1996) Our city, our future: Towards sustainable development in European cities. *Environment and Urbanisation*, **8**(1), 133–154.

Meijer, F., Itard, L. & Sunikka-Blank, M. (2009) Comparing European residential building stocks: Performance, renovation and policy opportunities. *Building Research & Information*, **35**(5), 543–556.

Merkhofer, M.W. (1987) *Decision Science and Social Risk Management*. D. Reidel Publishing Co., Boston, MA.

Merret, S. (1995) Planning in the age of sustainability. *Scandinavia Housing & Planning Research*, **12**, 5–16.

Miltin, D. & Satterthwaite, D. (1996) Sustainable development and cities. In: *Sustainability, the Environment and Urbanisation* (ed. C. Pugh). Earthscan Publications Ltd, London.

Misham, E.J. (1964) *Welfare Economics: Five Introductory Essays*. Random House, New York.

Mitchell, G. (2000) Indicators as tools to guide progress on the sustainable development pathway. In: *Sustaining Human Settlements: Economy, Environment, Equity and Health* (ed. R. Lawrence). Urban International Press, London.

Mitchell, G. (2001) Forecasting urban futures: A systems analytical perspective on the development of sustainable cities and urban regions. In: *Geographical Perspectives on Sustainable Development* (eds M. Purvis & A. Grainger). Earthscan, London.

Mitchell, R.C. & Carson, R.T. (1989) *Using Surveys to Value Public Goods: The Contingent Valuation Method*. Resources for the Future, Washington, DC.

Moffat, S. & Campbell, E. (1998) *Vision, Tools and Targets. Environmentally Sustainable Development Guidelines for Southeast False Creek*. The Sheltair Group-Inc., Vancouver. Submitted to Central Area Planning, City of Vancouver, 18 April 1998.

Moffat, S. & Kohler, N. (2008) Conceptualizing the built environment as a social ecological system. *Building Research & Information*, **36**(3), 248–268.

Montemurro, F. (2003) Il bilancio parla chiaro al cittadino. *Il Sole 24 Ore*, 27/01/03.

Morris, P. & Therivel, R. (eds) (1995) *Methods of Environmental Impact Assessment*. UCL Press, London.

Musgrave, R.A. (1995) *Finanza pubblica, equità, democrazia*. Il Mulino, Bologna.

Nannariello, G. (2000) *Environmental Management and Sustainable Development*, EUR 19721 EN. European Commission, Joint Research Centre (Hrsg.), Ispra.

Nasar, J.L. (1990) The evaluative image of the city. *Journal of the American Planning Association*, **56**, 41–53.

Nattrass, B. & Altomare, M. (1999) *The Natural Step for Business: Wealth, Ecology and the Evolutionary Corporation*. New Society Publishers, Gabriola Island, Canada.

Nattrass, B. & Altomare, M. (2002) *Dancing with the Tiger: Learning Sustainability Step by Natural Step.* New Society Publishers, Gabriola Island, Canada.

Neary, S.J., Symes, M.S. & Brown, F.E. (eds) (1994) The urban experience: A people–environment perspective. In: *Proceedings of the 13th Conference of the International Association for People–Environment Studies*, Manchester, 13–15 July 1994. E & FN Spon, London.

Neskey (NEw partnerships for Sustainable development in the Knowledge EconomY) Roadmap (2003). www.vernaallee.com/value_networks/Neskey_Exec_Summary.pdf (accessed 22 April 2009).

Nijkamp, P. (2003) Il ruolo della valutazione a supporto di uno sviluppo umano sostenibile: una prospettiva cosmonomica. In: *L'uomo e la città* (eds L. Fusco Girard, B. Forte, M. Cerreta, P. De Toro & F. Forte), pp. 455–470. F. Angeli, Milan.

Nijkamp, P. (2006) Review of the book "Evaluating sustainable development in the built environment" by P.S. Brandon, P. Lombardi. *Environment and Planning C: Government and Policy*, **24**, 473–474.

Nijkamp, P. & Perrels, A. (1994) *Sustainable Cities in Europe: A Comparative Analysis of Urban Energy and Environmental Policies.* Earthscan, London.

Nijkamp, P. & Sponk, J. (1991) *Multiple Criteria Analysis: Operational Methods.* Gower, Aldershot.

Nijkamp, P., Rietveld, P. & Voogd, H. (1990) *Multicriteria Evaluation in Physical Planning.* Elsevier, Amsterdam.

Norgaard, R. & Howarth, R. (1991) Sustainability and discounting the future. In: *Ecological Economics* (ed. R. Costanza). Columbia University Press, New York.

Nuti, F. (1987) *Analisi costi e benefici.* Il Mulino, Bologna.

OECD (1997) *Better Understanding Our Cities. The Role of Urban Indicators.* Head of Publications Service, Organisation for Economic Cooperation and Development, Paris.

OECD (2001) *Citizens as Partners: Information, Consultation and Public Participation in Policymaking.* Organisation for Economic Cooperation and Development, Paris.

OECD (2005) *Policy Brief: Public Sector Modernisation: Open Government.* Organisation for Economic Cooperation and Development, Paris.

Ombuen, S., Ricci, M. & Segalini, O. (2000) *I programmi complessi.* Il Sole 24 Ore, Milan.

Ostrom, E. (1990) *Governing the Commons.* Cambridge University Press, Cambridge.

Ott, W.R. (1978) *Environmental Indexes: Theory and Practice.* Ann Arbor Science, Ann Arbor, MI.

Palermo, P.C. (1992) Modelli di valutazione e forme di razionalità. In: *Interpretazioni dell'analisi urbanistica* (ed. P.C. Palermo). Franco Angeli, Milano.

Palmer, J., Cooper, I. & van der Vost, R. (1997) Mapping out fuzzy buzzwords – Who sits where on sustainability and sustainable development. *Sustainable Development*, **5**(2), 87–93.

Palmquist, R.B. (1991) Hedonic methods. In: *Measuring the Demand of Environmental Quality* (eds J. Brandon & C. Kolstad). North Holland, Amsterdam.

Pearce, D. (1983) *Cost Benefit Analysis.* Macmillan, London.

Pearce, D. & Nash, C.A. (1981) *The Social Appraisal of Project: A Text in Cost-Benefit Analysis*. Macmillan, London.

Pearce, D., Markandya, A. & Barbier, E.B. (1989) *Blueprint for a Green Economy*. Earthscan Publications Ltd, London.

Pearce, D.W., Atkinson, G. & Mourato, S. (2006) *Cost-Benefit Analysis and the Environment. Recent Developments*. OECD, Paris.

van Pelt, M.J.F. (1994) *Ecological Sustainability and Project Appraisal*. Averbury, Aldershot.

Pettersen, T.D. (1999) *Økoprofil for Næringsbygg (Ecoprofile for Office Buildings)*. Norwegian Building Research Institute, Oslo, January (reference document).

Plattner, G.K., Stocker, T., Midgley, P. & Tignor, M. (eds) (2009) *IPCC Expert Meeting on the Science of Alternative Metrics. Meeting Report, Intergovernmental Panel on Climate Change*, UNEP, Oslo, Norway, May 2009. http://www.ipcc.ch/

Polanyi, M. (1967) *The Tacit Dimension*. Routledge & Kegan Paul, London.

Porter, A.L. (1980) *A Guidebook for Technology Assessment and Impact Analysis*. North Holland, New York.

Pratchett, L. (1999) New technologies and the modernization of local government: An analysis of biases and constraints. *Public Administration*, **7**(4), 731–750.

Pré Consultants B.V. (1997) *The New SimaPro 4 for Windows*. Amersfoort, The Netherlands.

Prigogine, I. & Stenger, I. (1984) *Order Out of Chaos*. Bantam, New York.

Prizzon, F. (1994) *Gli investimenti immobiliari*. Celid, Turin.

Repetto, R. (ed.) (1985) *The Global Possible*. Yale University Press, New Haven, CT.

Repetto, R., McGrath, W., Wells, M., Beer, C. & Rossini, F. (1989) *Wasting Assets: Natural Resources in the National Income Accounts*. World Resources Institute, Washington, DC.

Report from the Commission to the Council of 20 September 2002, Analysis of the "open list" of environment-related headline indicators COM(2002) 524 final, 25–28 October 2005, University of Stirling. ISBN: 1-85769-218-7.

Rietveld, P. (1979) Multiple objective decision methods and regional planning. In: *Studies in Regional Science and Urban Economics*, North-Holland, New York.

Rodgers, R. (1999) *Towards an Urban Renaissance*. E & FN Spon, London.

Roscelli, R. (ed.) (1990) *Misurare nell'incertezza*. Celid, Turin.

Rowe, D. (1991) Delphi – A re-evaluation of research and theory. *Technological Forecasting and Social Change*, **39**, 235–251.

Roy, B. & Bouyssou, D. (1993) *Aide multicritère à la dècision: mèthods et cas*. Economica, Paris.

Ruddock, L. (1992) *Economics for Construction and Property*. Edward Arnold, London.

Ruddock, L. (ed.) (1999) Information support for building economics. In: *Proceedings of the CIB-W55 Building Economics International Workshop*, Salford, 1–5 September1999, CIB Publication 210.

Saaty, T.L. (1995) *Decision Making for Leaders*, Vol. II, AHP Series. RWS Publications, Pittsburgh, PA.

Saaty. T.L. (1996) *Decision Making with Dependence and Feedback. The Analytic Network Process*. RWS Publications, Pittsburgh, PA.

Saaty, T.L. & Vargas, L.G. (1982) *The Logic of Priorities, Applications in Business, Energy, Health, Transportation.* Kluwer-Nijhoff, The Hague.

Saaty, T.L. & Vargas, L.G. (1984) Inconsistency and rank preservation. *Journal of Mathematical Psychology,* **28**, 205–214.

Scettri, M. (2000) La valutazione tassonomica. In: *Valutazione 2000. Esperinze e riflessioni* (ed. M. Palumbo), pp. 430–438, Franco Angeli, Milano.

Schultz, J. (1996) What has sustainability to do with ethics? In: *Sustainable Development* (eds V. Nath, L. Heans & D. Devuyst), pp. 137–157. VUB Press, Brussels.

Selman, P. (1995) Local sustainability. *Town Planning Research,* **66**(3), 287–302.

Simon, H.A. (1947) *Administrative Behaviour.* The Macmillan Co., New York.

Simon, H.A. (1982) *Models of Bounded Rationality,* Vol. 2. MIT Press, Cambridge, MA.

Simonotti, M. (1997) *La stima immobiliare.* Utet, Turin.

Sirchia, G. (1997) The economic valuation of cultural heritage. In: *Evaluation of the Built Environment for Sustainability* (eds P.S. Brandon, P. Lombardi & V. Bentivegna), pp. 426–434. E & FN Spon, London.

Sirchia, G. (1998) *La valutazione economica del patrimonio culturale.* Carocci, Milan.

Skitmore, M. (1989) *Contract Bidding in Construction.* Longman Group Ltd, Hong Kong.

Smith, V.K. (1974) *Technical Change, Relative Prices, and Environmental Resource Evaluation.* John Hopkins University Press, Baltimore, MD.

Spendolini, M.J. (1992) *The Benchmarking Book.* American Management Association, New York.

Stanghellini, S. (ed.) (1995) La valutazione del piano: le istanze, gli approcci. *Urbanistica* **105**, 48–89.

Stanghellini, S. (ed.) (1996) *Valutazione e processo di piano,* INU (7). Allinea, Florence.

Stanghellini, S. & Mambelli, T. (2001) Evaluation of strategic programs for the local sustainable development: A case study. In: *Proceedings of the 7th Joint Conference on Food, Agriculture and the Environment.* Kluwer Academic Press, Dordrecht.

Stanghellini, S. & Stellin, G. (1996) Politiche di Riqualificazione delle Aree Metropolitane: domanda di valutazione e contributo delle discipline economico-estimative. In: *Proceedings of the XXVI CeSET Seminar,* Milan, 17–18 October 1996, pp. 34–52.

Stellin, G. & Rosato, P. (1998) *La valutazione economica dell'ambiente.* CLUP, Turin.

Stone, P.A. (1989) *Development and Planning Economy.* E & FN Spon, London.

Stoner, J.A. F. & Wanke, C. (1986) *Management.* Prentice-Hall, Englewood Cliffs, NJ.

Strauss, D.F.M. (1984) An analysis of the structure of analysis. *Philosophia Reformata,* **49**, 35–56.

Strauss, D.F.M. (1995) The significance of Dooyeweerd's philosophy for the modern natural sciences. In: *Christian Philosophy at the Close of the Twentieth Century* (eds S. Griffioen & B. Balk), pp.127–138. Uitgeverij, Kampen.

Strijbos, S. (1997) Wisdom, ethics, and information technology: Some philosophical reflections. *System Practice,* **10**(4), 443–457.

SWEHOL (1996) Managing our technological society. In: *Proceedings of the Second Working Conference,* Priorij Emmaus, Maarssen, 15–19 April 1996.

Therivel, R. & Partidario, M.R. (1996) (eds) *The Practice of Strategic Environmental Assessment*. Earthscan, London.

Thompson, P. (1991) The client role in project management. *Project Management*, 9(2), 90–92.

Triplett, J. (2004) *Handbook on Hedonic Indexes and Quality Adjustments in Price Indexes: Special Application to Information Technology Products*. DSTI/DOC(2004)9, OECD Publications, Paris. http://www.oecd.org/dataoecd/37/31/33789552.pdf

Turner, R.K. (ed.) (1988) *Sustainable Environmental Management: Principles and Practice*. Westview Press, Boulder, CO.

UNCHS – United Nations Centre for Human Settlement (1996) *The Indicators Programme: Monitoring Human Settlements for the Global Plan of Action*. Paper at *United Nations Conference on Human Settlement (Habitat II)*, Istanbul, June 1996.

UNCHS – United Nations Centre for Human Settlement (2001a) *The State of the World's Cities Report*, New York, 6–8 June 2001. http://www/unchs.org/istambul+5/statereport.htm

UNCHS – United Nations Centre for Human Settlement (HABITAT) (2001b) *Cities in a Globalizing World: Global Report on Human Settlement*. Earthscan Publications, London. www.un.org/ga/istambul+5/globalreport

UNCSD (2001) *Indicators of Sustainable Development: Guidelines and Methodologies*. United Nations Conference on Sustainable Development, New York.

UNDP (2004) *The Human Development Report*. United Nations Development Programme.

UNESCO (2002) *Measuring and Monitoring the Information and Knowledge Societies: A Statistical Challenge*. United Nations Educational, Scientific and Cultural Organisation. www.uis.unesco.org

United Nations (1995) Work programme of indicators of sustainable development of the Commission on Sustainable Development. *Paper by United Nations Department for Policy Coordinator and Sustainable Development*.

United Nations (2008) *The Millennium Development Goals Report – 2008*. United Nations, New York.

United Nations (2009) *The Millennium Development Goals, Report 2009*, United Nations Department of Economic and Social Affairs (DESA), July 2009, New York. http://www.un.org/millenniumgoals/pdf/MDG_Report_2009_ENG.pdf

Vale, B. & Vale, R. (1993) Building the sustainable environment. In: *Planning for a Sustainable Environment* (ed. A. Blowers). Earthscan Publications Ltd, London.

Viviani, M. (2002) Il bilancio sociale in ambiente pubblico. In: *Il Bilancio Sociale* (ed. L. Hinna). Il Sole 24 Ore, Milan.

Voogd, H. (1998) The communicative ideology and ex ante planning evaluation. In: *Evaluation in Planning* (eds N. Lichfield, A. Barbanente, D. Borri, A. Khakee & A. Prat), pp. 113–126. Kluwer Academic Publishers, Dordrecht.

Wakely, P. & You, N. (2001) *Implementing the Habitat Agenda: In Search of Urban Sustainability*. Development Planning Unit, University College, London.

Walras, L. (1954) *Elements of Pure Economics* (trans. W. Jaffe). American Economic Association and Royal Economic Society, London.

Warner, M.L. & Preston, E.H. (1984) *Review of Environmental Impact Assessment Methodologies*. US Environmental Protection Agency, Washington, DC.

Waters, B. (1995) Christian theological resources for environmental ethics. *Biodiversity and Conservation*, **4**, 849–856.

Wegener, M. (1994) Operational urban model: State of the art. *Journal of the American Planning Association*, **60**(1), 17–29.

William, P., Anderson, P. & Kanaroglou, E. (1996) Urban form, energy and the environment: A review of issues, evidence and policy. *Urban Studies*, **33**(1), 7–35.

Willis, K., Beale, N., Calder, N. & Freer, D. (1993) *Paying for Heritage: What Price Durham Cathedral?* Countryside Change Unit Working Paper 43, London.

Winfield, M. & Basden, A. (1996) An ontologically based method for knowledge elicitation. In: *Managing the Technological Society: The Next Century's Challenge to O.R. SWOT: Proceedings of the International Conference of the Swedish Operations Research Society*, 1–3 October 1996, University of Lulea, Sweden, pp. 72–93.

Winpenny, J.T. (1991) *Values for the Environment*. HMSO, London.

Witte, J. (ed.) (1985) *Herman Dooyeweerd: A Christian Theory of Social Institutions*. The Herman Dooyeweerd Foundation, Canada.

Zavadskas, E., Peldschus, F. & Kaklauskas, A. (1994) *Multiple Criteria Evaluation of Projects in Construction*. Vilniaus Technikos Universitetas, Russia.

Zeleny, M. (1994) In search of cognitive equilibrium: Beauty, quality and harmony. *Journal of Multi-Criteria Decision Analysis*, **3**, 3–13.

Zeppetella, A. (1995) *Retorica per l'ambiente*. Angeli, Milan.

Zeppetella, A., Bresso, M. & Gamba, G. (1992) *Valutazione ambientale e processi decisionali*. La Nuova Italia Scientifica, Rome.

Index

Note: page numbers in *italics* refer to figures or tables

Evaluating Sustainable Development in the Built Environment, Second Edition
By Peter S. Brandon and Patrizia Lombardi © 2011 Peter S. Brandon and Patrizia Lombardi